PM 102

According to the Olde Curmudgeon

PM 102

According to the Olde Curmudgeon

An Introduction to the
Basic Concepts of
Modern Project Management

Francis M. Webster Jr.

Project Management Institute

Library of Congress Cataloging-in-Publication Data

Webster, Francis Marion.
    PM 102, according to the Olde Curmudgeon : an introduction to the basic concepts
of modern project management / Francis M. Webster, Jr.
        p.   cm.
    Includes bibliographical references and index.
    ISBN: 1-880410-78-8
    1. Project management.   I. Title.

T56.8 .W42 2002
658.4'04 – – dc21   2002069976

ISBN: 1-880410-78-8

Published by: Project Management Institute, Inc.
              Four Campus Boulevard
              Newtown Square, Pennsylvania 19073-3299 USA
              Phone: +610-356-4600 or Visit our website: www.pmi.org
              E-mail: pmihq@pmi.org

10   9   8   7   6   5   4   3   2   1

Dedication

To my wife of now almost fifty years, who continued to stick with me through both *PM 101* and *PM 102*. Also to our children, all professionals in their own fields now, who have put up with my discussions of MPM over the years and are, in varying degrees, practicing MPM today.

Contents

Figures   ix

Tables   x

Foreword   xi

Preface   xiii

Acknowledgements   xiv

Chapter X—Estimating   1
    Characteristics of an Activity   5
    Essential Variables of an Activity   6
    A Conceptual Model of an Activity   10
    Summary   21

Chapter XI—Basic Calculations for Scheduling: The Critical Path Method (CPM)   25
    The Basic Calculations   27
    Ways to Reduce Project Duration   40
    Summary   44

Chapter XII—Resource Management   49
    Introduction   49
    A Taxonomy of Resources   50
    Managing Managerial Resources   59
    Managing Human Resources   68
    Managing Financial Resources   77
    Managing Physical Resources   80
    Managing Intangibles   94
    Summary   96
    Appendix XII.A—Mars Pathfinder Project   98
    Appendix XII.B—Mars Pathfinder Project   101

Chapter XIII—Project Scheduling   103
    Introduction   103
    What is Scheduling?   105
    Objectives of Scheduling   106
    Types of Scheduling   108
    Considerations in Scheduling   120
    Summary   138
    Appendix XIII.A—Computer Scheduling of Resources   141
    Appendix XIII.B—Mars Pathfinder Project   155
    Appendix XIII.C—Mars Pathfinder Project   157

Chapter XIV—Time/Cost Tradeoff in Scheduling   159
 Introduction   159
 History   160
 The Basic Concepts of CPPS   161
 Factors Affecting the Opportunity Cost   170
 Factors Affecting the Activity's Costs   170
 Some Extensions   174
 Summary   174

Chapter XV—Cost Management   177
 Scope Cost Management   178
 Design Cost Control   180
 Schedule Cost Management   181
 Subcontract Cost Management   182
 Materials Cost Management   183
 Labor Cost Management   188
 Equipment Cost Management   196
 Change Cost Control   199
 Overall Cost Management   202
 Cost Systems   212
 Summary   212
 Appendix XV.A—Mars Pathfinder Project   214

Chapter XVI—Quality in Projects   215
 Four Aspects of Quality   217
 Achieving Quality   232
 Who Benefits from QM?   234
 Appendix XVI.A—Mars Pathfinder Project   237

Chapter XVII—Uncertainty and Risk Management   239
 Understanding Uncertainty and Risk   241
 Project Risk Management   250
 A Taxonomy of Risks   254
 Uncertainty   261
 Summary   268
 Appendix XVII.A—Program Evaluation and Review Technique (PERT)   272
 Appendix XVII.B—Monte Carlo PERT   277
 Appendix XVII.C—Decision Theory   281
 Appendix XVII.D—Mars Pathfinder Project   283

Chapter XVIII—Reporting & Control   285
 Who Can You Really Manage?   286
 Managing the Manageable   287
 System Design   310
 Management Style   315
 Managing Your Management   318
 Summary   320
 Appendix XVIII.A—Mars Pathfinder Project   321
 Appendix XVIII.B—Mars Pathfinder Project   322

Chapter XIX—An Epilogue   325

References   327

Index   329

Figures

Figure X.1 Cost as a Dependent Variable 7

Figure X.2 A Conceptual Model of an Activity 11

Figure XI.1d Slack 28

Figure XI.1c The Latest Start and Finish Times 28

Figure XI.1b The Earliest Start and Finish Times 28

Figure XI.1a The AOA PND 28

Figure XI.2 The AON PND 34

Figure XI.3a A More Complex Project 36

Figure XI.3b The Critical Path on a More Complex Project 39

Figure XIII.1 A Project for Scheduling 109

Figure XIII.2 A Typical Resource Profile 110

Figure XIII.3 Early Schedule Resource Profile 111

Figure XIII.4 Late Schedule Resource Profile 113

Figure XIII.5 Leveled Resource Requirements—Time Constrained 114

Figure XIII.6 Resource-Constrained Schedule 116

Sam's Resource Analysis

Figure XIII.A.1 Activity Rank 143

Figure XIII.A.2 Availability List 144

Figure XIII.A.3 Lower Envelope 146

Figure XIII.A.4 Upper Envelope 147

Figure XIII.A.5 Combined Upper and Lower Envelopes with Average Resource Requirements 148

Figure XIII.A.6 Logic for a Time-Constrained Resource Requirement 150

Figure XIII.A.7 Logic for a Resource-Constrained Schedule 152

Figure XIV.1 Activity Cost Data for a Simple Project 162

Figure XIV.2 Cost Curves for a Simple Project 163

Figure XIV.3 Least Cost Curve for a Simple Project 164

Figure XIV.4 Cost Data for a More Realistic Project 165

Figure XIV.5 Cost Curves for a More Complex Project 166

Figure XIV.6 Least Cost Curve for a More Complex Project 167

Figure XIV.7 Cost Curve of a Typical Activity 171

Figure XV.1 Cost versus Volume 197

Figure XV.2 Cost versus Time 198

Figure XV.3 Budgeted Cost of Work Scheduled 206

Figure XV.4 BCWS versus BCWP 207

Figure XV.5 BCWS versus BCWP versus ACWP 208

Figure XVI.1 The Rework Cycle 231

Figure XVII.A.1 Example Project for Illustrating PERT and Monte Carlo PERT 275

Figure XVIII.1 The Progressive Elaboration of a Project 291

Tables

Table X.2   Cost Estimating   3
Table X.1   Activity Duration Estimating   3
Table XI.1c   Tabular Calculations for an AOA PND—Early Times   31
Table XI.1b   Tabular Calculations for an AOA PND—The Data   31
Table XI.1a   Tabular Calculations for an AOA PND—The Activities   31
Table XI.d   Tabular Calculations for an AOA PND—Late Times   32
Table XI.1f   Tabular Calculations for an AOA PND—Negative Slack   33
Table XI.1e   Tabular Calculations for an AOA PND—Slack   33
Table XI.2c   Tabular Calculations of an AON PND—Late Times and Slack   35
Table XI.2b   Tabular Calculations for an AON PND—Early Times   35
Table XI.2a   Tabular Calculations for an AON PND—The Data   35
Table XI.3a   Calculations of a More Complex PND—Early Times   37
Table XI.3b   Calculations of a More Complex PND—Late Times and Slack   38
Table XII.1   Taxonomy of Resources   51
Table XIII.1   Some Concepts of Critical Chain   117
Table XIII.2   Probability That at Least One Activity Will be Late for Varying Numbers of Predecessors of a Merge Node   136
Table XIV.1   Crashing a More Complex Project   166
Table XIV.2   Crash Alternatives with Two Critical Paths   168
Table XV.1   Product Breakdown Structure of Physical Features   179
Table XV.2   Product Design Characteristics (Abbreviated from PM 101, Chapter VII)   180
Table XV.3   Analysis of Variances   209
Table XVII.1   States of Knowledge of an Event   241
Table XVII.A.1   PERT Calculations   276
Table XVII.B.1   Random Samples from the Duration Estimates   278
Table XVII.B.2   Results of Simplified Monte Carlo Simulation   279

Foreword

Note from the Olde Curmudgeon: Differing from standard
publishing practice, this Foreword has been written by three
individuals because of their different and essential perspectives on
project management: Dave Cleland, the strategic and conceptual;
Hans Thamhain, the technology research and consulting; and Les
Prudhomme, the practitioner.

In *PM 101*, Fran Webster presented an introduction to the basic concepts of
modern project management. In his next book, *PM 102*, he continues to offer
excellent guidance on how to deal with many of the quantitative aspects of
managing projects. He provides clear explanations on such topics as estimating,
resource management, scheduling, and cost management, as well as uncertainty
and risk management, to name a few. His presentation of quality in projects
provides a clear philosophy for practicing project managers to use in their
working world. He saves the best for last, as shown in chapter XVIII, Reporting
and Control.

Taken together, *PM 101* and *102* provide a marvelous portable pair of
books that provide the project manager insight into the details of how to
manage projects. Practicing project managers will want to have these compact
books available as a source for the latest insights on how to attain project performance objectives within cost and schedule standards. The material is clearly
presented from a user's perspective. It gives project managers, engineers, and
other professionals ready-to-use advice on how to manage the details in the
techniques and processes so necessary to attain project purposes.

This book can be used most effectively by practicing project managers. In
addition, those individuals who are undertaking training or education initiatives
in project management will find this book contributes to the enhancement of
individual knowledge and skills in the exciting field of project management.

David Cleland, Professor Emeritus,
Department of Industrial Engineering, University of Pittsburgh

PM 102 According to the Olde Curmudgeon presents a very effective extension of Francis Webster's earlier book, *PM 101*. Webster takes a refreshing and different approach to project management, discussing the processes, tools, and techniques in a clear, application-oriented style, well illustrated, emphasizing real-world situations, challenges, benefits, and limitations. Filled with anecdotes of contemporary project management practice, the book tells the reader how to get into the proper frame of mind for becoming an effective project leader who gets results in today's challenging business environment. The new book also integrates *A Guide to the Project Management Body of Knowledge (PMBOK® Guide)* Standards well. *PM 102* should be appealing to both professional practitioners and newcomers to project management.

Hans J. Thamhain, Ph.D., PMP, Bentley College

In his first book on project management, *PM 101*, Dr. Fran Webster, writing as the Olde Curmudgeon, presented an introduction to project management in a light-hearted and very readable manner. The book dealt very effectively with the concepts of project management, the processes involved in a project, and the essential skills required of an effective project manager. Sprinkled liberally throughout the book were snippets of expert advice from the experienced and wizened Olde Curmudgeon. This publication was just right for the beginning project manager in need of a primer, as well as for the "old-timer" needing a refresher on the human side of project management. In his epilogue of *PM 101*, Dr. Webster promised a sequel. Well, here it is!

PM 102 starts where *PM 101* left off. Generally following the knowledge areas of the Project Management Institute's (PMI®) *A Guide to the Project Management Body of Knowledge (PMBOK® Guide)*, the Olde Curmudgeon dives into the details of the work processes required for effectively managed projects.

So what's new? Hundreds of books have been written on these topics. Textbooks abound on project management processes such as cost, schedule, quality, risk, and human resource management. Several aspects set this book apart from others. Most notable are the author's approach to teaching complex and interrelated topics in the context of a story and his way of relating process theory and project interrelationships to a simple project scenario. His interjection of personal observations and tidbits of wisdom from real-life experiences adds credibility and a personal touch. The author not only advocates the KISS (Keep It Simple, Stupid) concept as a project management tool, he incorporates it in his writing style. As a result, he has made *PM 102* both engaging and entertaining to read and instructional as well. This book serves as both a textbook on project management and as a reference guide on concepts and individual work processes. *PM 102* is destined to become a part of every project manager's reference library.

Les Prudhomme, PMP, Associate Director, Construction Industry Institute

Preface

This book is the completion of the set of chapters started in *PM 101*. Sam (for Samuel or Samantha, whichever you choose) has continued to demonstrate the concepts discussed in the chapters. The preface for *PM 101* is largely applicable to *PM 102*.

During the interim between writing the chapters and actual publication, there have been revisions to *A Guide to the Project Management Body of Knowledge (PMBOK® Guide)* that are not incorporated in *PM 102*. This is inevitable as, from the beginning, the *PMBOK® Guide* was conceived as a dynamic document. Project managers and contributors to the language of project management, as well as readers of *PM 101* and *PM 102*, are advised to keep current on revision to the *PMBOK® Guide*.

The Olde Curmudgeon (OC), and Sam, hope you find reading these two books a worthwhile experience and that it helps you to become a better project manager. Friendly debate of the ideas presented here is welcomed. Send any such comments, as well as anecdotes of interesting and peculiar things that you have witnessed on projects, to fmwebster@aol.com.

Acknowledgements

The Olde Curmudgeon (OC) accepts responsibility and apologizes for any shortcoming in this book. Most evident is that he has not worked on projects in the newer virtual team or even in the modern real-time computer environment. Thus, anyone operating in these environments should consider how to adapt the concepts contained herein, which should be considered advanced study and can be assisted by the many good articles that have appeared in Project Management Institute (PMI®) publications and by attending local, national, and international meetings.

It would be impossible to give either specific citations for all the information contained in this book or to recognize all those who contributed to the Olde Curmudgeon's *education* over the years. The articles and books cited are for the benefit of the reader, to delve further into these fine sources.

Special thanks are given to Dave Cleland, Hans Thamhain, and Les Prudhomme for taking the time to read the manuscript and make suggestions. Thanks also to Bud Baker for his encouraging comments on Chapter XVIII, Reporting and Control.

Appreciation is expressed to PMI for permission to use material contained in *A Guide to the Project Management Body of Knowledge (PMBOK® Guide)* and other publications, such as the *Mars Pathfinder Project* submitted for the PMI 1998 Project of the Year by the Jet Propulsion Laboratory. Paraphrased excerpts from this document appear in the appendices at the end of some of the chapters.

Chapter X

Estimating

Sam realized early on the urgency of this project. It must be completed before the river floods and so they will have time to plant crops in the spring. Analysis of the history of the family clearly indicates that the later the project is completed the larger the job, as all the species multiplied. Thus, Sam worried about how long it would take to perform the project.

When Sam asked one of the elders how long the project would take, the elder, not being a person of many words, replied, "That depends!" Sam finally coaxed out of the elder that it depends on what resources will be used, how many of these resources, how much work has to be done, and a host of other variables.

Sam decided the first step was to estimate the resources and time required for each activity. Sam quickly realized that there was something else to learn about projects.

Everybody has made estimates of time, resources, and costs. It is inescapable in modern life. We estimate the time it will take to fix a meal, to perform chores around the house, and to travel to work or on a vacation. We estimate the resources required to give a party or to move into a new facility (whether it be a residence, office, or manufacturing building). We estimate the costs to remodel a room or build a cabin. And yet most people probably have not thought carefully about what it is they are doing when making these estimates.

Two popular methods employed for estimating are WAG and SWAG. One difference between these is the oft-repeated admonition to make a WAG estimate, double it, and then redouble it. Clearly these often lead to errors in estimating and unfavorable performance on projects. What are the relevant variables affecting an activity's estimates?

The *PMBOK® Guide* on Estimating

In the Glossary of *A Guide to the Project Management Body of Knowledge (PMBOK® Guide)* is the following entry:

> **Estimate.** An assessment of the likely quantitative result. Usually applied to project costs and durations and should always include some indication of accuracy (e.g., ± x percent). Usually used with a modifier (e.g., preliminary, conceptual, feasibility). Some application areas have specific modifiers that imply particular accuracy ranges (e.g., order-of-magnitude estimate, budget estimate, and definitive estimate in engineering and construction projects). (Project Management Institute 2000)

The *PMBOK® Guide* identifies seven inputs for activity duration estimating and eight inputs for cost estimating (Project Management Institute 2000). The modeling of these processes is presented in Tables X.1 and X.2.

These models are appropriate for the *PMBOK® Guide* but do not really provide insight into the problems of estimating activities in a project.

Estimates Made by Whom?

Who makes the estimates makes a difference!

2

Inputs
1. Activity List
2. Constraints
3. Assumptions
4. Resource Requirements
5. Resource Capabilities
6. Historical Information
7. Identified Risks

Tools and Techniques
1. Expert Judgment
2. Analogous Estimating
3. Quantitatively-Based Durations
4. Reserve Time (Contingency)

Outputs
1. Activity Duration Estimates
2. Basis of Estimate
3. Activity List Updates

TABLE X.1
Activity Duration Estimating

Inputs
1. Work Breakdown Structure
2. Resource Requirements
3. Resource Rates
4. Activity Duration Estimates
5. Estimating Publications
6. Historical Information
7. Chart of Accounts
8. Risks

Tools and Techniques
1. Analogous Estimating
2. Parametric Modeling
3. Bottom-Up Estimating
4. Computerized Tools
5. Other Cost Estimating Methods

Outputs
1. Cost Estimates
2. Supporting Detail
3. Cost Management Plan

TABLE X.2
Cost Estimating

One approach is to have the individual responsible for the activity make the estimate. This is often necessary if the activity is truly unique. It is generally appropriate if that individual is to "buy in" to the estimate. One of the often-used excuses for failing to complete an activity in the estimated time is, "I didn't say I could do it in that duration!" To eliminate that as an excuse, it is desirable to seek "buy in." If the individual makes the estimate, even though it may be negotiated, there is more commitment to meet it.

Another approach is to have professional estimators do the estimating. They will more likely have data from past experience or from industry standards to support their estimates. This approach is often used in the construction industries.

Either of these approaches can be augmented by computerized estimating tools. They tend to add objectivity to the estimates, as well as speed up the process. Most of us are familiar with the procedures used in automotive repair facilities where there are standard times for various procedures. When these are used, they also become a bogey for the mechanic, as well as a predetermined cost for the customer.

All of these approaches have problems. The first approach is often biased by the estimator's perception of the likely punishment if the estimate is exceeded. This often leads to inflated estimates. The real problem is that in such an environment the activities are seldom completed, or reported completed, in less than the estimated time. This leads to projects requiring an excessively long time to complete, resulting in more costly and noncompetitive proposals.

The second approach may not accurately reflect how the activity is going to be performed. This can be overcome by allowing yourself sufficient time to plan the project in detail and communicate adequately with the estimator(s). The estimator should factor in the characteristics of the performing organization based on experience and judgment.

More recently, advocates of the Critical Chain approach to project management have proposed obtaining estimates of the variability in performing an activity. This permits the expression of the longest time it may take but uses the more ambitious expected value of the duration as the basis for scheduling the project. The difference between the pessimistic and expected times is then allowed for in a buffer at the end of a "critical chain." Based on this, it is expected that some activities will exceed their estimated duration. An integral part of the concept is the "relay-race" mentality that encourages reporting completion as soon as the activity is completed and the immediate start of the following activity. This permits the capture of any time savings achieved and therefore a shortening of the duration of the project.

Also integral to Critical Chain is the elimination of multitasking (i.e., working on more than one activity at a time). Working on one activity at a time leads to greater efficiency and thus a shorter activity duration, resulting in less cost and earlier project completion.

Critical Chain seems like an advisable approach if the organization adopts the sophisticated view of uncertainty that is assumed in this approach. There are some questionable aspects of the Critical Chain model that should be modified to more accurately reflect the relevant underlying theory of the approach (Webster 2001). These include determining the measure of variability, the use of Monte Carlo PERT computational procedures, and the guidelines for managing the process through the buffers. All of these are relatively easy to correct.

CHARACTERISTICS OF AN ACTIVITY

Activities in a project vary in the degree to which they are understood. Some are very familiar and can be estimated quite accurately. Others are truly unique and defy accurate estimating. Most are somewhere in between. Unlike their counterparts in the repetitive manufacturing environment, many project activities are performed only once or a few times. There is no opportunity to apply time study techniques to determine an accurate estimate of the time required to perform the activity. Furthermore, synthesizing a time estimate using micropredetermined time standards is not cost effective. Thus, there is likely to be a greater difference between the estimates and actuals for project activities than for work performed repetitively. This can be frustrating to those more accustomed to the manufacturing environment.

Since this is an introductory discussion of estimating, it will be assumed that activities can be estimated with certainty. This will aid in understanding the concepts involved. In Chapter XVII, there will be an examination of uncertainty and how it can be considered both in estimating and in calculating project characteristics using the resulting probability distributions.

ESSENTIAL VARIABLES OF AN ACTIVITY

It has been customary in project management literature to focus on the three variables of an activity: time, quality, cost. An alternative paradigm, shown in Figure X.1, Cost as a Dependent Variable, may be more useful in understanding the problems of estimating and managing activities. This paradigm views cost as a dependent variable that is a function of time, resource application, and performance objectives (Webster 1979). Consider these variables one at a time, all other things being equal.

Performance Objectives

The whole purpose of a project is to achieve some outcome(s) as represented by technical and/or other objectives for the product(s) of the project, i.e., the deliverables. These objectives are allocated to various components of the product and transformed into objectives for the activities of the project. As the project progresses—that is, the activities are performed—the objectives are achieved to one degree or another.

There may also be objectives for the project itself, such as minimizing time, cost, risk, or rework.

During the design phase, the objectives are translated into specifications for each component of the product of the project. These specifications define the desired outcomes in operational terms as required by other participants on the project.

The difference between the planned and achieved objectives for the product of the project (i.e., deliverables) can be defined as quality in the sense of conformance to specifications. For purposes of this discussion, quality is:

$$\text{Quality} = \text{Achieved Outcome/Desired Outcome} \times 100$$

Thus, perfect quality is represented by 100 percent achievement of desired outcomes. Note that in this formulation, quality can exceed 100 percent but it may or may not provide anything of value to the client.

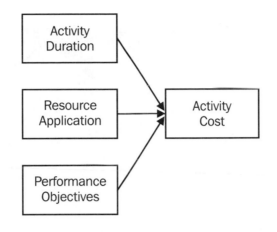

FIGURE X.1
Cost as a Dependent Variable

This ratio of quality typically drives all other aspects of the project. Ideally, an activity is completed when this ratio equals one. The objectives of a specific activity may prove to be more difficult to achieve than expected. Its objectives may have to be reduced and other activities' objectives raised, resulting in additional work.

To be consistent with current concepts of total quality management (TQM), the desired outcomes must be continually updated to reflect the best understanding of the client's needs and desires. Failure to update these desired outcomes will result in an imprecise definition of scope and, perforce, poor scope management. It will also lead to failure to fully satisfy the needs of the client, an outcome that can lead to all sorts of dysfunctional results, including legal claims in the short run and loss of future business in the long run.

Project costs typically increase exponentially with increasing technical objectives. For example, with existing technologies, a radio can be produced inexpensively that receives FM radio signals and produces a sound that is intelligible. As the desired excellence of sound is increased, the cost to produce the radio increases faster than the excellence of the sound. Thus, the higher the technical objectives for the product of the project, the higher the cost of the project. On the other hand, increasing the objectives for the project, such as minimizing rework or disputes, may actually reduce the costs of the project.

Time/Duration

All activities require some amount of time for their performance. In general, the time required is equal to the work content divided by the resource application rate. That is, an activity with a work content of forty labor hours with one person assigned should have a duration of forty hours. If a person is assigned to work half time on the activity the theoretical duration would be eighty hours. However, there are probably "make-ready" and "put-away" elements that have to be performed each time the activity is stopped. Typically this increases the total time required to perform the activity.

Theoretically, if two persons are assigned, the activity should have a duration of twenty hours. If it is a "team" activity, such as making a bed, it could take less than twenty hours. Sometimes it may take more time if the extra people cannot coordinate their efforts adequately.

The work content will be different depending on the technology or methodology that is used. For example, the activity might involve cutting some wooden boards. This could be performed by at least four technologies—a manual hand saw, an electric hand saw, a table saw, or a radial arm saw—with progressively less work content, as measured by labor hours. Each of these has a make-ready and put-away time as well as a performance time. The manual and electric saws both require measuring and marking (drawing the line along which to saw). The sawing time would typically be less for the electric saw. With the table and radial arm saws, only the measuring would be necessary, assuming a fence or guide is used. If the number of boards to cut is large, a jig can be used to eliminate the need for measuring. With the radial arm saw long pieces can be cut very quickly using a jig.

There are other costs (e.g., resources) that are relevant to consider in determining the appropriate methodology. If you are cutting several boards there are at least three methodologies—measure each piece and saw separately, cut several boards at a time, or make a fixture that guides the saw.

The technology and methodology must be stated explicitly for the work content estimate to be meaningful. Often the technology and methodology are stated in standard procedures describing how an activity of this type is to be performed. In general, the appropriate technology and methodology are determined by economic analysis. For the typical activity, given a specific combination of technology and methodology, the cost is a bowl-shaped function of the duration and the resource application rate.

There is an optimum. Attempting to perform the activity in less time may cost more than is implied by the ratio of time reduction. For example, if overtime is used to reduce the duration, the cost increases by at least the overtime premium. It may increase even more due to rework caused by errors produced due to haste. Similarly, stretching the activity duration will lead to less efficiency, resulting in higher costs. Working on the activity twenty-four hours per day (three crews) or increasing the crew size is a change in the resource application rate.

Resource Application Rates

For any specific activity there is a most appropriate type and amount of resource(s). For example, on a construction project there will likely be a mix of craft persons and laborers, each with different cost rates. Care must be exercised to ensure that each activity is performed by the appropriate resource to avoid paying premium rates for work that can be done by a less costly resource. For example, a skilled carpenter should not be used to shovel dirt if an unskilled laborer can do it. On the other hand, the skilled carpenter should not stand idle waiting for an unskilled laborer to become available to move the dirt.

The complication in assigning resources stems from the fact that the activity and the preferred resource often do not become available at the same time. The time at which the activity becomes available to work on is dependent upon the completion of its predecessor activities. The time at which the resource becomes available is dependent on the completion of other activities on which that resource is required. The activities may have no sequential relationship and their times of availability often do not coincide. Thus, tradeoffs must be made between assigning a less than optimum resource, allowing work on the activity to proceed, or delaying the start of an activity until the optimum resource is available. Computer routines for assigning resources can be helpful in resolving such conflicts, although few project scheduling software packages really consider the tradeoff between alternative resources.

While cost is a major criteria for project success, this model makes it clear that cost is not managed directly, but rather through managing the independent variables that affect the ultimate cost of the project.

A CONCEPTUAL MODEL OF AN ACTIVITY

Figure X.2, A Conceptual Model of an Activity, provides a more detailed model, including some suggestions as to the relationship between planned variables of the activity and the actual values of these variables. The model details the many facets involved in estimating, in order to make clear what must be considered. As a practical matter, most estimators probably do not explicitly consider all of these factors all of the time. Estimating practices and data implicitly consider many of these factors. It is important to understand the factors and how they relate to each other to ensure adequate consideration of all factors.

Project/Activity Objectives

The first step in estimating is to establish a clear understanding of the objectives for the project and each element of its work breakdown structure (WBS). Each activity should contribute to the ultimate achievement of one or more of those objectives. To the extent that an organization has routinized the performance of certain activities, this contribution can be implicit. To the extent that the activity is unique or varies substantially from normal practice, the objectives should be explicitly identified.

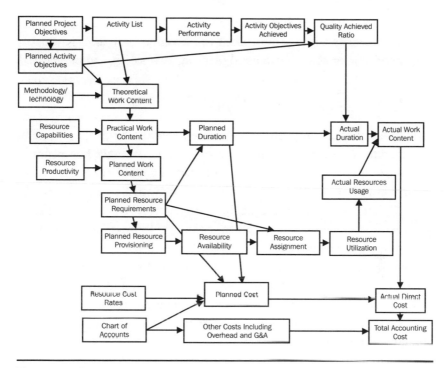

FIGURE X.2
A Conceptual Model of an Activity

An example of the need for explicitly identifying project objectives is the construction of a plant for producing a pharmaceutical for which there is expected to be a market for only five years. Because the facility cannot be used for another product after the original product becomes obsolete, it too should have a five-year design life. It follows then that the equipment should be designed for a shorter life than would be normal practice. If this objective is not related down to the specific design activities, designs could be chosen that were excessive for the application.

Similarly, a book publishing project should make explicit the desired life and quantity to be produced of the book so that the appropriate paper (regular or acid neutral) and printing technology can be selected.

Methodologies and Technologies

Methodologies and technologies for elements of the project must be specified to ensure the activities are estimated accordingly. For example, it is more efficient to lay a brick wall using elevator-type scaffolding than frame-type scaffolding, both in adjusting the scaffold to the appropriate work height and in actual bricklaying. The choice between these would be an important input in estimating the duration of the bricklaying activity.

Similarly, a choice between cast-in-place and precast concrete construction would impact the project network plan and the manner in which other activities are performed. In developing a computer program one choice might be between various compilers versus an automated coding system.

Theoretical Work Content

Given these decisions, it is reasonable to estimate the work content of an activity. Work content is expressed in measures such as labor hours, machine hours, or hours per thousand lines of code. As a standard procedure, it is probably best to estimate the work content based on the preferred resource for that activity on that project.

In general, it is best to assume the most economical approach. Later, after time calculations have been performed, analysis may suggest that an alternative resource should be used that could get the activity done in less labor hours albeit at an increase in cost. If the more expensive alternative is selected to start with, it is not likely that the opportunity to use the less expensive resource will be recognized. Sometimes it is necessary to use a less capable resource due to schedule conflicts for the preferred resource.

Resource Capabilities

The estimator must know the capabilities of the resources to be used on the project. This not only applies to the preferred resource, but also to the alternative resources that might be used to perform the activity. For example, while a 20-ton crane might be the best choice normally (having adequate capacity), there may be some constraints that would make it desirable to use a 100-ton crane (due to its reach). Similarly, it might normally be desirable to print a book on a web press but, due to low volume, a xerographic copier might be selected. Writing a module of computer code in C++ might best be done by a senior programmer but that person may be unavailable at the time the activity will have to be done. Skill and experience can make substantial differences in time to perform a task.

Practical Work Content

If an explicit resource assignment can be made at this time, it is feasible to consider the impact of that assignment in the determination of the practical work content. For example, if the computer program is to be written in C++, and the programmers who will be writing it are not experienced in C++, they will inevitably take longer than the more experienced persons. They will refer to the programming manual more often, try more alternative approaches, and make more errors.

Resource Productivity

There are many factors that determine resource productivity. They include personal, supervisory, logistical, and organizational factors.

Personal factors include individual and work group work ethic, physical condition and health, personal problems (family, financial, emotional, and so on), education, and experience. Many of these can be managed by careful employee selection.

Supervisory factors include leadership style, training and guidance provided, and emphasis on removing obstacles to productivity. Some supervisors use an intimidating leadership style. Except for the most needy, least skilled individuals, this type of leadership style is generally counterproductive in the long run. The organization is responsible for ensuring that the individual is adequately trained for the specific work of an activity. The supervisor is immediately responsible for ensuring that work is performed consistent with that training. Often an individual's productivity decreases due to obstacles beyond their control. The supervisor should be alert to such obstacles and remove them, or at least minimize their effect. You can affect supervisory behavior by clearly communicating expectations and behaving in a manner to demonstrate and reinforce those expectations.

Logistical factors start with a realistic schedule, i.e., one for which it is likely that necessary predecessor work is completed before an activity is scheduled to begin. The first prerequisite for on-time completion of an activity is starting the activity on time. The second prerequisite is ensuring that all necessary information, materials, tools, and equipment are available without delay. Not so obvious is that the work space is available and conducive to productivity. (Is there anyone who has not had an experience of being placed at a desk in a hallway or other less than desirable space? Productivity is certainly affected.) It means ensuring that all equipment is maintained properly to minimize the chances of down time when the equipment is needed. It also means scheduling maintenance crews and activities at times other than when the equipment/space is most needed. Nothing is more frustrating to the individual or work group than to need to use a piece of equipment only to find that it is unavailable due to scheduled maintenance (often for the convenience of maintenance personnel or, worse, for administrative convenience). You, as project manager, must ensure that adequate logistic support is in place to achieve these conditions.

Organizational factors affecting productivity include minimizing change, having realistic expectations, appreciating contributions, and creating a productive organizational climate. Some organizations try to proceed on a project before they have well-established objectives. This often leads to rework and all the costs associated with it. Perhaps the most inconspicuous cost of rework is its impact on an individual's attitudes. The first instance of rework will likely be done with reasonable enthusiasm. The second instance will reduce the enthusiasm. Further repetitions can destroy esprit and will likely lead to defection of project team members. You must be proactive in managing changing requirements that cause rework. When change is necessary, it must be justified to the individual worker(s) to minimize its negative impact on attitudes.

Related to the above is having realistic expectations. People need challenge to elicit outstanding performance. If the challenge exceeds their self-perceived capabilities to perform, their productivity will likely fall off. The degree of challenge can be increased if there are appropriate rewards. If extra work hours are required, the organization must compensate directly, either monetarily, as compensatory time, or with bonus vacations. It is important to recognize that others are affected by this increased work time, specifically the family of the individual. Failure to recognize this can create distracting influences that will degrade productivity. Otherwise, intrinsic rewards are often most effective such as celebrations, picnics, or the like, and including you doing something crazy like swimming across a pond in midwinter, if the objectives are met.

Finally, organization climate, as represented by values, beliefs, and behaviors, can measurably affect productivity. You can mitigate dysfunctional climate factors and can, within limits, add to positive climate characteristics through leadership style.

You are responsible for optimizing all these factors to the extent possible. The estimator must predict the success that will be achieved in all these efforts in order to develop reasonable estimates of the durations and costs of the activities required to successfully complete the project.

Planned Work Content

Separate from considerations of capability are considerations of productivity. People in a given organization are affected by administrative procedures, accepted practice and norms, expectations for excellence versus output, and a host of other impacts. For example, one organization may have extensive time reporting requirements that take time out of each day, while another requires minimal administrative time each day. Peer pressure may tend to limit the output generated per day. Thus, resources, and especially human resources, tend toward a normal productivity level. An estimator familiar with the organization will estimate in accordance with that productivity level. Thus, the actual work content would be lower in the organization with higher productivity.

Planned Resource Usage

Given the planned duration and the resource assignments, the planned resource usage can be determined and costs estimated. Planned resource usage is the resources assigned to the activity (the application rate) for the duration of the activity. This is the data that will be used later to analyze total resource requirements on the project. These are inputs to the determination of the planned cost of the project. When combined with the resource cost rates and the chart of accounts, the project budget is developed at the work package level. This is then rolled up through the WBS to obtain the planned total project cost.

Thus, project cost is clearly a dependent variable derived from the project plan (activity list), resource applications, and durations driven by the technological objectives.

Planned Duration

Consideration must be given to resource availability. In many organizations, a person is assigned to an activity full time. In other organizations, each person is assigned more than one activity at a time and expected to perform some work on each of them on a continual basis. For example, a person might be assigned to work afternoons on an activity. This will determine the planned duration for the activity. Beyond the obvious considerations of availability are the seemingly random perturbations that further reduce availability. People get ill, have emergencies, take vacation, go to school, attend meetings, have to respond to unexpected correspondence or write special reports, and occasionally take a long lunch, perhaps with the client.

A corollary to Murphy's Law says that these perturbations always occur at the least convenient times. Some consideration must be given for these perturbations or the organization will consistently complete activities, and therefore projects, late and over budget.

Resource Rates

The rates at which labor is charged to the project may be the actual costs per payroll calculations or it might be some sort of standard cost for different resource classifications. Nevertheless, the amount charged to the activity will include fringe benefits, and such, to reflect the total cost per time unit of that labor.

Chart of Accounts

The chart of accounts may have an impact on exactly how some items are charged. It may be worthwhile to request an accountant familiar with your project to trace through the steps of determining how typical items on your project are charged.

Planned Cost

The planned cost can now be determined based on the planned duration, resource application rates, and cost per unit of resource.

Planned Resource Provisioning

From the resource assignments and the anticipated durations, the planned overall resource requirements can be determined. This is most easily accomplished by computer since it requires processing a large amount of data and may have to be repeated several times to resolve conflicts. From this, it becomes clear what the demands are on the resources and whether the resources available can accomplish all their tasks in the time available. This will be clearer after reading the discussion of resource management and scheduling in Chapters XII and XIII. If the resource requirements exceed availability, tradeoffs will have to be made involving alternative resources, performing tasks at less than the most desirable times, working overtime, and splitting activities, resulting in increased time to perform the work.

Resource Availability/Assignment

The actual availability of specific resources when it is time to assign them to your project may differ from your plans. Internally, the resources you planned to have available may have been assigned to another, perhaps higher priority, project. Sometimes the person is not available due to illness or the like. You may be forced to accept a resource with lesser abilities, resulting in a longer duration and greater responsibility for you to ensure that the work product is as required. Or you may get a more skilled person who may complete the activity sooner but at a higher rate and certainly a different cost. Externally, the market may determine the availability of the resources, leading to the same results as above.

Resource Utilization

Once the resources have been allocated to perform an activity, it is important to utilize them effectively. Often this does not happen. In spite of the best efforts, materials or equipment do not arrive per schedule, material is not as specified, and equipment fails at inopportune times. If the supervisor/project manager is effective in reassigning individuals to other tasks, lost time can be avoided. If adverse weather prevents effective utilization on one task, the people can be switched to other tasks. Alternatively, action can be taken to minimize the impact of adverse weather by installing protective covering such as viscene. Actions can be taken to minimize organizational perturbations such as meetings, reporting requirements, and inefficient systems. A concern about conditions on the project that can lead to health and physical problems can help avoid degradation of productivity. Working too many hours, especially in adverse weather, can lead to illness, which negates all other efforts to achieve high productivity.

Actual Duration

The model presented in Figure X.2 includes the actual duration, actual resource usage, and actual cost. The actual duration is typically driven by the delta that determines quality on projects where quality is the primary driver. Some projects are most severely constrained by total project duration and others by total cost. In such cases, compromise is inevitable. It may be done by explicitly relaxing client requirements or by accepting less than perfect quality.

Activity Performance/Activity Objectives Achieved/Quality Achieved Ratio

The activity is performed with the assigned resource and may achieve the required objectives in more or less time than the planned duration. The determination of completion may be based on the quality-achieved ratio. If all requirements are met early, the activity should be reported completed early. If it is not completed in the planned duration, alternative actions should be considered. Among those might be to reallocate technical objectives among related activities in such a way as to achieve required system objectives quicker and at less additional cost.

Actual Resources Usage

Perhaps some would deem it pessimistic to even consider that some project participants might utilize resources for other than the intended objectives of the activity. It happens and sometimes with at least the implicit sanction of management. When offering a plant manager the opportunity to close activity accounts as soon as the activity was completed, he declined. He understood the system well and would rather get some windows replaced in his plant than return unused project funds to corporate. In the less pessimistic view, some supervisors may provide less guidance than necessary to ensure that the activity is performed in an effective and efficient manner. Sometimes the requirements are not clearly understood or the person performing the work adds to the requirements to fulfill their own objectives. Regardless of the motivation, you need to be aware of the problem and spend the time necessary to ensure that your activities are receiving the attention they require and no more.

Actual Work Content

The product of actual resource usage and actual duration gives the actual work content. The only reason to expect that it is equal to the planned work content is that an effort is being made to use up the time or budget. When this happens your project will likely come in late and over budget. It is inevitable that at least one activity will take longer than its planned duration and incur more costs than planned. If all the others are equal, the total project will be either late or over budget, or both.

Actual Direct Cost

From these factors, the direct cost of the activity and, therefore the project, are determined. These are the costs over which you have direct control. But there are more.

Other Costs Including Overhead and General Administration

Accounting will add something to these to arrive at total project cost. Your project may well receive charges to cover the costs of the president of the organization and all those others who do not directly generate revenue. They will add something for all the facilities used by the corporation that are not directly related to your project or some other project or operation. There are a host of such costs that may be charged to your project. Especially for external projects, there will be some amount added as profit on this project. Complaining about these will be to no avail, for they are determined by corporate policy that is not likely to be changed for the sake of your project.

Total Project Cost

The sum total of all these factors will determine the success of your project and thence the measure of your success as a project manager. Be aware of how they happen and prepare yourself in the planning stages of the project for this reality.

SUMMARY

The importance, yet inadequacy, of estimates has been recognized for some time. As a result, techniques have been developed to improve estimating. Use an approach that is justified by your project and the nature of the contract. You may dream of bidding low, getting the contract, and making it up on changes. It may not happen. For one thing, the cost of the changes may exceed what extra you may be able to charge the client. On internal projects, you are not likely to get any additional fees as a result of the changes—perhaps a pat on the back.

The previous conceptual model is one of many that could be portrayed. It assumes that technical performance objectives are the primary drivers of the project. It is also generic and may not correspond exactly to your organization. You should consider developing a similar model that reflects the exigencies of your organization and project, both for your benefit and as a tool to convey these implications to members of your project team.

PM Network® occasionally publishes a listing of computer software packages to aid in estimating software development projects. Several products exist for construction projects. Some of these can accept data for other types of projects. Thus, if the improvement of estimating is determined to be desirable, there are alternatives available.

> Sam proceeded to develop the estimates for each activity in the WBS by stating the technical objectives (TO), technology/methodology (T/M), resources required (Res), and duration of the activity (Dur). Sam carefully considered the productivity expected and the actual time available by the workers in addition to the problems of finding the necessary animals and grape vines.

RAFT

Design Concept

TO – develop a design that can transport at least 10 people or 4 large animals per trip; build a prototype and test design concept; use prototype to put a crew across river to build landing

T/M – use manual labor to gather materials; use stone axe to cut small trees to fabricate prototype; use existing wool yarn to make ropes; use existing thongs to bind prototype raft together

Res – Sam, 1 woodcutter, 1 wool spinner, swimmers for one hour on last day

Dur – 6 days

Detail Design

TO – develop complete fabrication and assembly drawings and instructions; develop materials and equipment lists; develop test criteria and procedures

T/M – make all drawings and lists on birch bark with burnt stick; measurements to be in hands, with Sam's right hand being the standard; tests to be performed using the best swimmers in the family

Res – Sam, 1 birch-peeler, 1 stick-burner

Dur – 12 days

GATHER MATERIALS

Logs

TO – find; cut to size; transport 3 major logs and 22 minor logs to fabrication site—all to be straight and free of protrusions

T/M – use manual labor and stone axe to cut trees; use bulls to pull logs

Res – 4 woodcutters, 4 stone axes, 2 bulls, 2 bull leaders, 100 hands of heavy-duty thongs

Dur – 30 days

Hides

TO – find, kill, and return to camp 10 large animals having hides suitable for making thongs

T/M – hunt with bows and arrows and kill with clubs; pull back to camp with bull

Res – 3 hunters, 3 bows and 30 arrows, 3 clubs, 1 bull, 1 bull leader

Dur – 60 days

Vines

TO – find 800 hands of vines strong enough to hold 5 persons hanging on them at one time; cut and return to camp

T/M – search for vines individually; cut with team of 5 using cutting stones

Res – 5 viners, 5 cutting stones

Dur – 6 days to find, 6 days to cut and return to camp

PREPARE MATERIALS

Logs

TO – trim major logs to shape; split minor logs

T/M – use cutting stones, wedges, and wooden mallets

Res – 2 master woodcutters, 2 log-splitters, 2 mallets, 4 wedges, 6 cutting stones, 10 wedges, 4 mallets (they wear out)

Dur – 36 days

Hides

TO – butcher and skin animals; cure hides; cut into thongs

T/M – use herbs to cure hides; use cutting stones to make thongs

Res – 1 butcher/hide-curer

Dur – 18 days

Vines

TO – trim vines; treat with fat (for flexibility); tie together with thongs

T/M – rub with fat from animals brought back

Res – 5 viners, 5 cutting stones, fat from 5 animals

Dur – 6 days

ASSEMBLE

Deck

TO – final trim of split logs; tie together with thongs; install tether post in middle; install cleats for steering

T/M – use cutting stones, wood mallet, and stone axe; tie together with thongs

Res – 2 master woodcutters, 2 laborers, 4 cutting stones, 3 wooden mallets, 2 stone axes

Dur – 18 days

Movement

TO – attach vines and steering thongs

T/M – bind all loops and connections with thongs

Res – 2 viners

Dur – 2 days

TEST

Deck

TO – ensure that unit floats level and holds together under shifting load

T/M – tie to tree and load with 15 people; move them around to test stability

Res – Sam, 2 master woodcutters, 14 miscellaneous people

Dur – 2 days (1 for test and 1 for adjustments)

Movement

TO – ensure that vines and steering system work and will take stress

T/M – have 15 people pull on raft; if grapevine doesn't break it will be okay

Res – Sam, 2 master woodcutters, 15 stout people for about an hour

Dur – 1 day

Final Test

TO – test steering system to ensure that it will take the raft across the river; test system with 10 and then 15 people on board

T/M – cross with just Sam and master woodcutters; cross with 10 people; cross with 15 people

Res – Sam, 2 master woodcutters, 13 best swimmers

Dur – 1 day

Having completed this chore, Sam was ready for a day of rest.

Chapter XI

Basic Calculations for Scheduling: The Critical Path Method (CPM)

Sam was pleased with gaining an even greater understanding of how the raft project will be performed. The next question was how soon can all these tasks be accomplished and moving things across the river be started. He was quite anxious to know when each task had to be started in order to avoid delaying the completion of the project. This would require a new way of calculating a project schedule.

RAFT	ID	DURATION
Design		(DAYS)
Concept	DC	6
Detail Design	DDD	12
Gather Materials		
Logs	GML	30
Hides	GMH	60
Vines	GMV	12
Prepare Materials		
Logs	MPL	36
Hides	MPH	18
Vines	MPV	6
Assemble		
Deck	AD	18
Movement	AM	2
Test		
Deck	TD	2
Movement	TM	1
Final Test	TFT	1

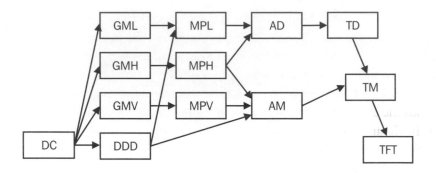

Many of the new techniques for planning and scheduling projects rely on a project network diagram (PND) as the common language. Most of these are critical path techniques (CPT) in which early and late start and completion times, slacks, and critical paths are determined.

The early start time indicates the earliest that an activity can be started. An activity cannot start until all its predecessors are completed. Therefore, an activity's early start time is determined by the finish time of the last of its predecessors. Thus if an activity has three predecessors that are expected to be completed by the end of 4, 3, and 8 days respectively, the activity cannot start until after the 8th day. *Its early start is the latest early finish of its predecessor's.*

The activity's earliest finish is simply its earliest start time plus its duration. Thus, if the activity requires 6 days, its early finish is the 14th day.

An activity's late start is determined by its late finish time. Thus, if the activity must be completed by the end of day 20 and it requires 5 days, it must be started by the end of day 15.

The activity's latest finish is determined by the late starts of any following activities. If the activity has 4 followers, having latest start times of 30, 26, 28, and 20 respectively, it must be completed no later than day 20. *Its latest finish is the earliest late start of its followers.* The latest completion time for any activity that has no followers is the required completion time for the project, i.e., the project is not completed until all activities of the project are completed.

The early start and finish times indicate the earliest the activity can be performed. The late start and finish times indicate the latest an activity can be performed. The earliest start and the latest completion times define the window in which an activity can be performed. This information is used by the scheduler to determine when the activity is scheduled to be performed.

Slack is the difference between the early start and late completion minus the duration of the activity. It is the difference between the time available and the time required for performing an activity. Positive slack is desirable because it provides flexibility in scheduling the activity. Negative slack indicates that the project, per the existing plan, cannot be completed by the desired completion date.

The critical path is the set of activities forming a contiguous path through the PND that requires the greatest amount of time to perform and therefore, determines the shortest duration within which the project can be completed, ceteris paribus.

In a nutshell, that is all there is to the simplest CPT, generally known as the Critical Path Method (CPM). In this chapter you will learn how to calculate each of these values and determine the critical path. After thoroughly understanding these concepts you will learn, in subsequent chapters, about variations and other calculations on the PND.

THE BASIC CALCULATIONS

One of the advantages of Activity-on-Arrow (AOA) notation is that it is easy to visualize the passage of time along the arrows. (Note: This is a *disadvantage* in the planning phase because it invites the planner to schedule before the planning is completed.) We will use AOA to illustrate the basic calculations for the simplest project plan from Chapter IX of *PM 101*, the trip from New York City to Los Angeles as shown in Figure XI.1a. The same calculations will then be done using the Activity-on-Node (AON) PND for this project plan.

Calculations on the PND

The calculations can be performed on the PND. While it is easy to comprehend and appears logical and convenient, it will soon become

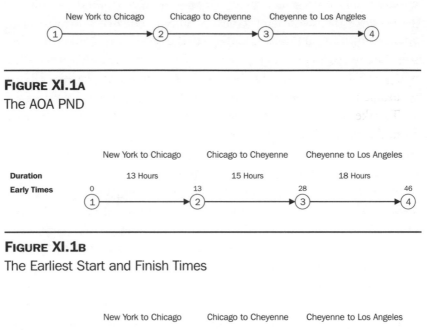

FIGURE XI.1A
The AOA PND

FIGURE XI.1B
The Earliest Start and Finish Times

FIGURE XI.1C
The Latest Start and Finish Times

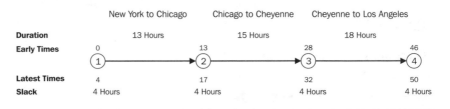

FIGURE XI.1D
Slack

apparent that it is not a very good practice. More than anything else, it puts a lot of information on the PND, much of which is likely to change if there are any changes to the PND or deviations from schedule in performing the project. Trying to recalculate on the PND will not only be tedious at best, but also prone to errors. Thus it would be necessary to draw a new PND, a very laborious task.

To take advantage of the ease of understanding we will first perform the calculations on the PND. First we must calculate the earliest times that each activity can be performed. It is easy to recognize that event 1 is a starting event, as it has no predecessor(s). Thus, we can assign a start time of 0 to it as the earliest start of the activity "New York to Chicago." Thirteen hours are required to drive this distance, i.e., perform this activity. Thus it can be finished at the end of 13 hours. Activity 2–3 can then start at time 13 and can be completed by time 28 and the project can be completed by time 46.

Suppose the project must be completed by 50 hours. Thus we must reach event 4 no later than time 50. Activity 3–4 requires 18 hours and so must start no later than time 32. Following this procedure we find that activity 1–2 must start no later than time 4.

From this we can also see that there are 4 days of difference between the early and late times. This is slack. Note that it is the same for each event and therefore for each activity. Thus, it is not true that each activity can be delayed by 4 days. Only 4 days can be "wasted" before the project becomes critical. When this happens, any further delay will cause the project to be late.

Tabular Calculations

There are several advantages to performing these calculations in a tabular format.

❑ Drawing a network diagram manually is labor intensive. Performing the calculations on the diagram could lead to redrawing it if either the plan or estimates for the activities are changed and recalculation is necessary.

❑ If the calculations are performed on the network, it will be tempting to try to recalculate without erasing all previous calculations. This often leads to errors.

❑ Using the list form of the activities aids in becoming accustomed to visualizing the network from the listing. It will enhance your ability to analyze computer reports that are presented in list format. This is important in considering possible changes to the plan or schedule before making changes to the PND.

❑ The computer requires that data be entered in list format so it can perform the calculations for you.

The first step is to convert the diagram into a list that will facilitate calculations. Therefore we list the activities in sequence as they occur in the PND as shown in Table XI.1a.

Now add the estimated durations to the list. (These have been obtained from the Rand McNally Tripmaker program discussed before. Those durations were in hours and minutes [12:59; 15:07; and 17:35] but have been rounded for ease of manual calculations.)

Note: In the discussions that follow, each step in the example is identified in both the discussion and the tables by a number in braces, e.g., {1}. This is intended to assist you in following the process as it might be presented in a classroom on a chalkboard.

Next, we calculate the early start and completion times. Without thinking about the PND, note that activity 1–2 has no predecessor, i.e., 1 does not appear in the follower side of the activity list. Therefore, we assign a start time of 0 to it, {1}. This should be interpreted as the end of the "zeroth" hour, which is the same as the beginning of the first hour.

It takes 13 hours to perform activity 1–2 so the earliest it can be completed is time 13, {2}. This should be interpreted as "at the end of the 13th hour."

Now consider activity 2–3. Its predecessor event is 2. Therefore this activity cannot start until after the completion of all activities whose follower events are 2. In this case there is only one such activity and it is completed at time 13. Assign 13 as the start time for activity 2–3, {3}. Activity 2–3 requires 15 hours to perform so it will be completed at time 28, {4}.

Activity Predecessor - Follower
1 - 2
2 - 3
3 - 4

TABLE XI.1A

Tabular Calculations for an AOA PND—The Activities

Activity Predecessor - Follower	Duration
1 - 2	13
2 - 3	15
3 - 4	18

TABLE XI.1B

Tabular Calculations for an AOA PND—The Data

Activity Predecessor - Follower	Duration	Early Start	Early Complete
1 - 2	13	0 {1}	13 {2}
2 - 3	15	13 {3}	28 {4}
3 - 4	18	28 {5}	46 {6}

TABLE XI.1C

Tabular Calculations for an AOA PND—Early Times

Following the same procedure, the earliest that activity 3–4 can start is time 28, {5}. Adding its duration to its start time indicates that the earliest it can be completed is time 46, {6}. Since this activity has no followers, i.e., event 4 is not shown as a predecessor event for any activity, it completes the project and thus, the earliest the project can be completed is time 46.

This completes the early calculations.

Activity	Duration	Early		Late	
Predecessor - Follower		Start	Complete	Start	Complete
1 - 2	13	0	13	4 {12}	17{11}
2 - 3	15	13	28	17 {10}	32 {9}
3 - 4	8	28	46	32 {8}	50 {7}

TABLE XI.D

Tabular Calculations for an AOA PND—Late Times

Now suppose that this trip has to be completed by a certain time, say 50 hours. When must each activity be performed such that the project completion time will be achieved? This can be determined by the late start and completion calculations. The first step is to assign the desired completion time to all activities that end the project. Using the same logic as above, activity 3–4 is determined to be an ending activity because there are no activities that start with 4. Give it a completion time of 50, {7}. Activity 3–4 has a duration of 18 hours so it must be started no later than time 32 or it will not be completed until after time 50, {8}.

Activity 2–3 must be completed before activity 3–4 can start. Therefore, activity 2–3 must be completed no later than its follower activity, time 32, {9}. It has a duration of 15 hours and so it must start no later than time 17, {10}. Following the same procedure, activity 1–2 must be completed no later than time 17, {11}, and must be started no later than time 4, {12}.

We need to interpret what these calculations mean. Consider activity 1–2. It can start at time 0, i.e., at the beginning of hour 1. It can be completed by time 13, i.e., the end of hour 13. Its start could be delayed by as much as 4 hours, i.e., time 4, in which case it would not be finished until time 17. Thus, these numbers, and especially the early start of 0 and the late completion of 17, define the window within which activity 1–2 can be performed.

Delaying activity 1–2 is not without cost, however. If it is delayed by 1 hour, it will not be competed until time 14. Thus, activity 2–3

Activity Predecessor - Follower	Duration	Early Start	Early Complete	Late Start	Late Complete	Slack
1 - 2	13	0	13	4	17	4 {13}
2 - 3	15	13	28	17	32	4 {14}
3 - 4	18	28	46	32	50	4 {15}

TABLE XI.1E

Tabular Calculations for an AOA PND—Slack

Activity Predecessor - Follower	Duration	Early Start	Early Complete	Late Start	Late Complete	Slack
1 - 2	13	0	13	- 6	7	- 6
2 - 3	15	13	28	7	22	- 6
3 - 4	18	28	46	22	40	- 6

TABLE XI.1F

Tabular Calculations for an AOA PND—Negative Slack

could not start until time 14, and so on. This can easily be seen by calculating "slack." Slack is the difference between the time available and the time required for performing an activity. For activity 1–2, the time available is 17 hours (17 – 0 = 17). It requires 13 hours; therefore the slack is 4 hours (17 – 13 = 4), {13}.

In a similar manner, we can see that the slack on activity 2–3 is 4, {14}, and the slack on activity 3–4 is 4, {15}. Note that slack *is not* additive, i.e., we do not have 12 hours of slack on the project. We have only 4 hours of slack on the project. If we use an hour of slack on activity 1–2, whether by starting late or by taking 14 hours to perform it, it is gone on the rest of the project. Thus, the slack on activities 2–3 and 3–4 would then be only 3. If we delay the start of activity until time 5, we would then have slack of -1 hour on the remaining activities, i.e., the project will be late.

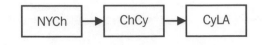

FIGURE XI.2
The AON PND

Another way in which we might incur negative slack is if the target completion date is too early. Thus, if the project had to be completed by time 40, the slack on all these activities would be -6 hours.

Negative slack at this stage is not serious. It is an indication that something must be done to reduce the time required to perform the project if it is to be completed by the target time of 40 hours. The alternative actions are discussed later in this chapter.

Earlier we mentioned the critical path. The critical path is the sequence of activities from the beginning to the completion of a project that requires the greatest amount of time to perform. Therefore, it determines the shortest time in which the project can be completed. In this simple project, that path is 1–2, 2–3, and 3–4. While it is obvious in this example, as the size and complexity of a project increases, the critical path will be less obvious, and sometimes completely unexpected.

The critical path is indicated by the set of activities that has the least positive (or most negative) slack. This set may contain more than one path through the network so it is important to analyze the set carefully, tracing the contiguous path or paths.

The significance of the critical path (as shown in Table XI.1f) is that, unless something is done to reduce the time required to perform this sequence of activities, the project will be late.

The concept of a critical path is also useful in analyzing portions of a project. For example, we might want to know what the critical path is between two milestones in the project. Thus, this "milestone" critical path would be the sequence of activities between these two milestones that take the longest time to complete.

We have now discussed the basic calculations using the AOA PND. It is important to understand how these same calculations are performed for a PND presented in the AON mode as shown in Figure XI.2.

Activity	Predecessor	Duration
NYCh	-	13
ChCy	NYCh	15
CyLA	ChCy	18

TABLE XI.2A

Tabular Calculations for an AON PND—The Data

			Early	
Activity	Predecessor	Duration	Start	Complete
NYCh	-	13	0 {1}	13 {2}
ChCy	NYCh	15	13 {3}	28 {4}
CyLA	ChCy	18	28 {5}	46 {6}

TABLE XI.2B

Tabular Calculations for an AON PND—Early Times

			Early		Late		
Activity	Predecessor	Duration	Start	Complete	Start	Complete	Slack
NYCh	-	13	0	13	4 {12}	17 {11}	4 {13}
ChCv	NYCh	15	13	28	17 [10]	32 [0]	4 {14}
Cyl A	ChCy	18	28	46	32 {8}	50 {7}	4 {15}

TABLE XI.2C

Tabular Calculations of an AON PND—Late Times and Slack

Again the first step is to prepare the data in a list format. That is presented in the first three columns. The only difference is that instead of using the endpoints of an activity, "i–j," to represent the logic, we use the names of the activities that are the predecessors of each activity. Thus, NYCh is a beginning activity, as it has no predecessors. Similarly, CyLA is an ending activity, as it is not shown as a predecessor for any other activity.

The early start and complete calculations are the same as before and the sequence is again shown by the numbers in braces.

Similarly, the late start and complete and slack calculations are the same as before. The interpretation is also the same.

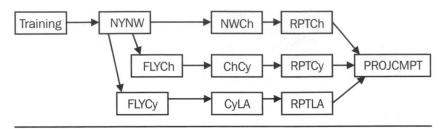

FIGURE XI.3A

A More Complex Project

Calculations of a More Complex PND

The next step in understanding the calculations is to perform them on a more complex project, namely that described in Figure IX.6 in Chapter IX of *PM 101*. As before, the first step is to convert the PND data to a list format. We have estimated times for each of the new activities. While going to Newark Airport is in the general direction to Chicago, it is still likely to take 13 hours to drive to Chicago. Note that in this project plan there are three followers of NYNW and three predecessors of PCMPT. These add to the complexity of the calculations.

Training has no predecessors, therefore it is a starting activity so it is assigned time 0, {1}, as the start time for the project. It has a duration of 1 hour so it cannot finish until time 1, {2}. NYNW is preceded by Training so it cannot start until time 1, {3}, and therefore, cannot finish until time 2, {4}. NYNW is the predecessor of three activities so its completion time of 2 is assigned to all three of them, {5}. The calculations proceed as before until we get to PCMPT. It has three predecessors. We post the completion time of these predecessors as PCMPT's start time in steps {17}, {19}, and {21}, each time crossing out all but the time that is latest. (In practice, we simply write these very small, select the latest, and write it in the space as the final result.) As a result we see that the earliest the project can be completed is time 27.

This shows that the project can be completed by time 27, or in 27 hours, a substantial improvement over the time 46, or 46 hours in the previous plan. Indeed, it is quite feasible to complete it in the target 40 hours.

Activity	Predecessor	Duration	Early Start	Early Complete
Training	-	1	0 {1}	1 {2}
NYNW	Training	1	1 {3}	2 {4}
NWCh	NYNW	13	2 {5}	15 {6}
FLYCh	NYNW	3	2 {5}	5 {8}
FLYCy	NYNW	6	2 {5}	8 {10}
ChCy	FLYCh	15	5 {9}	20{12}
CyLA	FLYCy	18	8 {11}	26{14}
RPTCh	NwCh	1	15 {7}	16{16}
RPTCy	ChCy	1	20{13}	21{18}
RPTLA	CyLA	1	26{15}	27{20}
PCMPT	RPTCh,	0	~~16~~{17}	
	RPTCy,		~~21~~{19}	
	RPTLA		27{21}	27{22}

TABLE XI.3A

Calculations of a More Complex PND—Early Times

Note that PCMPT does nothing more than summarize the three predecessors and is, therefore, not really necessary. The same information is provided by checking for the latest completion time of those three activities. That can be seen easier in Table XI.3b, where this superfluous activity has been eliminated.

We are now ready to perform the late start and complete calculations. As before, we start by assigning the target time 40 to all ending activities, i.e., those that are not shown as predecessors of any other activity. The calculations proceed as before, posting the activity late start times to the completion time of its predecessor as we go. In this backward calculation we use much the same approach as we did in the early calculations in dealing with the three activities having NYNW as their predecessors. Here we are looking for the earliest completion time and so we cross out the later ones as they are posted. To aid in recalling these decision rules for multiple predecessors and followers, remember that when calculating earliest, choose the latest; when calculating latest, choose the earliest. (Again these are generally written very small so we do not actually need additional lines for this information. Thus the extra lines are eliminated in Table XI.3b.)

			Early		Late		
Activity	**Predecessor**	**Duration**	**Start**	**Complete**	**Start**	**Complete**	**Slack**
Training	-	1	0	1	13 {42}	14 {41}	13
NYNW	Training	1	1	2	14 {40}	~~26~~ {39}	13
						~~24~~ {37}	
						15 {35}	
NWCh	NYNW	13	2	15	26 {38}	39 {29}	24
FLYCh	NYNW	3	2	5	21 {36}	24 {33}	19
FLYCy	NYNW	6	2	8	15 {34}	21 {31}	13
ChCy	FLYCh	15	5	20	24 {32}	39 {27}	19
CyLA	FLYCy	18	8	26	21 {30}	39 {25}	13
RPTCh	NWCh	1	15	16	39 {28}	40 {23}	24
RPTCy	ChCy	1	20	21	39 {26}	40 {23}	19
RPTLA	CyLA	1	26	27	39 {24}	40 {23}	13

TABLE XI.3B

Calculations of a More Complex PND—Late Times and Slack

This calculation shows that the latest the project can be started is time 13.

We are now ready to calculate slack. Training can start at time 0 and must be completed at time 14, i.e., this is the window in which it can be done. It requires one hour to perform, therefore it has 13 hours of slack. For this simple calculation, it can be seen that simply subtracting the early start from the late start times, or the early completion from the late completion times, is quicker and easier. Later, we will illustrate that this does not always hold true.

From this we see that the least slack is 13 hours and is on activities Training, NYNW, FLYCy, CyLA, and RPTLA, as shown in Figure XI.3b. Thus these five activities form the critical path. Delay of any of the activities on this path will delay the completion of the project beyond time 27. A delay of 3 hours on activity Training will reduce the slack on the remaining activities on this path to 10 hours.

Slack should be thought of as a resource and used carefully. On a project such as this it easy to imagine all sorts of delays that could happen including weather, road construction, and car trouble. If such

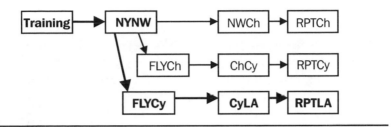

FIGURE XI.3B

The Critical Path on a More Complex Project

delays occur, they can be absorbed by the slack—up to a total of 13 hours—without jeopardizing the target completion time of 40. If the slack is used up in the beginning, there is no time contingency and the project will be late if there are further delays.

This concludes the discussion of the basic calculations of the critical path techniques done manually. There are reasons to know them well and there are reasons not to use them. The primary reason to know them well is the intuitive use of the data when it is presented in a computer report in this format. This intuitive feel can lead you to sense when something is not right in the plan, as well as to identify opportunities to improve performance on the project. It can also be useful for performing quick calculations when a computer is not available.

The reasons not to use it include:

❑ Time and labor costs, especially when compared to using a computer.
❑ Once the data is in a computer program, you can try different alternatives.
❑ The computer program allows you to indicate the work shift patterns, holidays, overtime allowed, and so on, plus putting the information into calendar date format.
❑ There are many other calculations that can be performed on a project plan that provide much greater value in using the data, such as scheduling the project and tracking performance against the schedule. These will be discussed in the following chapters.

WAYS TO REDUCE PROJECT DURATION

There are many ways to improve the performance on projects, as reflected in reducing the duration of the project. Several of these have a direct impact on the schedule. They are listed in a sequence that progresses from little cost or risk to higher cost and risk. Note that applying additional resources is number eleven in this list. They include:

1. *Managerial Attention and Involvement*—The impact of this is most notable in its absence. A project that is ignored by management will lose urgency to the point of being neglected by all involved. The interest of management will maintain the urgency, not only for the immediate project team, but also for those more indirectly involved. An occasional informed question will often be the catalyst to keep energy and attention focused. It will also keep management informed as to the need to remove any obstacles to the project before they have caused serious delays. Caution: Too much attention can be detrimental if it is interpreted as meddling or the like.

2. *Expediting*—This is basically taking whatever actions are appropriate to ensure that each activity is begun and completed on schedule. Responsibility for expediting can be delegated to a person for whom this is a major responsibility.

3. *Improved Methods*—They can range from simple to complex. At the simple end, a carpenter was cutting rafter ends and "bird's feet" notches. He was measuring all cuts separately and having another person hold the rafter while he cut it. A simple jig and a pattern were introduced to reduce the time substantially. On another project, intracompany mail was originally specified as the preferred means of communicating. When time reduction was deemed necessary, the method was changed to hand delivery. In another case, the method of testing a new automobile engine was changed resulting in the new engine being introduced a year earlier. On a construction project, a 120-ton precast concrete beam was called for. Originally it was to be cast off-site and transported in. Instead, it was cast at the foot of the columns on which it was to be installed. This change of methods permitted much more rapid progress on the rest of the building and earlier completion.

4. Reassign Resources—Various people possess different skills and degrees of skill. The person available to be assigned to an activity may not be the most skilled for that activity and thus may require longer to perform it than another person. Thus, simply reassigning people between activities to match their skills with the criticality of the activities can reduce the duration of the most critical activity.

5. Reallocate Resources—At certain times during a project there may be more resources allocated to a given activity than can be used effectively. Reallocating such resources from a noncritical activity to a critical activity can reduce the duration of the critical activity with no harm to project schedule on the noncritical activity.

6. Overlap Activities—Often a follower activity can be started before its predecessor is finished. This can often be used to make up time on a project schedule. Care must be exercised to ensure that no unexpected changes are introduced into the predecessor activity without the knowledge of the person(s) performing the successor activity. Thus, additional communication may be required.

7. Define the Activities in Greater Detail—By defining an activity in greater detail it is possible that some of the work can be performed by others, thus reducing the duration of the original activity. This requires the coordination of more people and possible loss of efficiency resulting in greater actual total work content.

8. Delete Certain Activities—An original project plan should be developed to perform the project at least cost and risk. The CPT-type software will highlight those activities on which time reduction is desirable. This is when actions should be taken that increase cost and/or risk. Note that the above seven actions have little impact on either cost or risk. When deleting activities it is likely that risk is increased. Often the activities that are deleted would have added to the quality assurance on the project. When this happens, there is an increased probability that an error will be introduced that will later require rework or worse.

9. Change the Technology Applied—Implicit in any approach to work is an assumption about the technology involved. The OC recently became very conscious of this when he introduced an electric planer into his woodworking efforts. There was an investment cost and a small usage cost (electricity and maintenance) but the reduction in time to process a piece of wood—as compared to sanding—was impressive. It also permitted greater accuracy in the process. In the previous example of substituting hand delivery for intracompany mail, today, email or groupware technology would be utilized. In building a masonry wall, the scaffolding might be changed from the classical modular type to an elevator type. In machining, a conventional tool might be replaced with a numerically controlled tool. Clearly, in all these there is an economic tradeoff but note that the savings due to reduction in time required to complete the project are a part of the economic decision. Note also that downgrading the technology of a component of the product of the project can also offer duration reductions, generally at some increase in risk and perhaps some degradation of the performance of the product of the project.

10. Subcontract or Buy—Sometimes project duration is dictated by a capacity limitation of a piece of equipment. A reduction in project duration can be achieved by subcontracting the activity or work package. Note that there is some loss of control over schedule but often a source can be found that can perform the work faster, better, and/or at less cost because of superior experience and/or facilities. Some additional liaison should be provided to ensure that the requirements are correctly understood and met.

11. Apply Additional Resources—While this has been an oft-used strategy for getting a project back on schedule, it ranks well down the list of preferred approaches. How often has the strategy, "Put everyone on overtime!" been used? Actually, additional resources can often lengthen the time required to perform a task, as more people must be coordinated, more tools supplied, and the probability of errors becomes greater. Nevertheless, selective application of additional resources can reduce the duration, but usually at some increase in cost. On the other hand, if inadequate resources were allocated to begin with, additional resources may actually reduce the cost as well as the duration.

12. Change Target Dates—Sometimes target dates are set arbitrarily. This is especially true for the early work on a project. It has been proven that a little more time for planning can reduce the cost, duration, and especially the rework required on a project. In one case, the delay of one month in issuing the bid package for a major construction contract resulted in an additional five million dollars of work being specified. It was estimated that if that work had been accomplished through contract add-ons and changes, it would have cost a twenty percent premium. Thus, the savings amounted to approximately one million dollars. Some times, there are portions of a project that are needed before other parts. For example, it may be advantageous to complete the office portion of a new manufacturing facility to allow occupancy by plant staff. Slipping the schedule on the less essential parts can often permit improvements in schedule for the more essential parts. Note that this requires the approval of the client.

13. Change the Scope of the Project—This is similar to changing target dates but more permanent. For example, while a new office facility or maintenance shop may have been included in the original project, the client may decide that they can continue to use an older facility or lease space. Deleting or delaying this work will permit the resources that would have been required otherwise to be used to speed delivery of the more essential parts of the project. In a software development project, it may be decided that, to meet tight schedules, some manual processing on exception transactions or accounts might substantially reduce the system development time. Clearly, another reason to adopt this strategy is to reduce the cost of the project.

14. Change the Person Responsible—Sometimes it is decided that the person responsible for the project, or some major aspect of it, just cannot get the job done. It may be due to inherent problems of the individual, such as human relations skills or an unexpected health problem, or it could be that the nature of the project has changed and the individual's capabilities no longer match the needs of the project. When this happens, even an experienced person will incur some delays in adapting to the project and in the project team adapting to the new person. Until both of these are accomplished, decisions will be delayed or of questionable quality. Rework may result and a series of perturbations will impact the project schedule for some time. If the need for change and the change itself are not accepted, it can create anxieties and other behavioral disturbances within the project team, some as severe as key personnel resigning.

15. Change the Management Information and Control System— This should generally be done with great reluctance as there is substantial lead-time in both installing the new system and getting the data translated and cleaned up. Even after these are accomplished there is typically a further delay in learning to use and trust the new system.

*16. Change the Organizational Structure—*This is a very severe action and should be only a last resort. New working relationships must be established. Old commitments within the organization must be renegotiated. Since these seldom happen instantaneously, it may take months for the organization to return to a stable equilibrium and efficient and effective operation.

Clearly, the decision to reduce the duration on a project is not simple. Probably the best strategy is the first one in the previous list, managerial attention. If this is present, the probability that a project will require drastic action will be less. The managerial attention must be used with caution, however, as it can be misconstrued and lead to unintended consequences. For example, if it is seen as meddling, it can harm team esprit. If it goes too far, the manager may become the de facto project manager as more and more the project team looks to the manager, instead of the project manager, to make decisions and provide direction.

SUMMARY

The calculations inherent in critical path scheduling are tedious, at best, when they are performed manually. They are ideal for computer application. However, understanding the manual calculations is an important skill that should be mastered by any manager with responsibility for projects. It is only through the intimate familiarity with the calculations and the use of the techniques in general that intuition is developed that will lead to recognition of problems and opportunities on projects.

An example of this was when the OC received a call from the management of a foundry, requesting his presence at a meeting some 500 miles away the next morning. The foundry was in the midst of a project to build a new cupola for producing casting quality iron. The supplier of the cupola had just informed the foundry that they would not be able to deliver the cupola until six months after the contracted date. The meeting was to seek a solution to this problem. We all arrived at the supplier's office and within a couple of hours, after pouring over the supplier's PND, the necessary questions had been asked to convince the supplier that they could indeed meet the original schedule date. This was done with no knowledge on the part of the OC of what was required to design and build a cupola. Without the intimate knowledge of the calculations and the intuitive feel for the planning logic, this successful troubleshooting would have been improbable.

All who may have any use of the output of CPT software are urged to invest the time necessary to gain this skill.

Sam was fascinated by the quick comprehension of these calculations. Sam had performed them mentally many times but was never sure of the accuracy of either the logic of the plan or of the calculations. After all, projects can get very complex quickly

More importantly, Sam knew that age-old question would soon be asked, "Are we about there yet?" It was bad enough to get that from a child, but getting it every day from a mother-in-law would be intolerable.

Sam was so pleased about these new skills that performing these calculations on the plan for the raft project became first priority. Sam reasoned that the rains could start as early as in 80 days so that was used as the late finish date.

Activity Description	ID	Predecessors	Duration (Days)	Early		Late		Slack
				Start	Finish	Start	Finish	
RAFT								
Design								
Design Concept	DC	-	6	0	6	-26	-20	-26
Detail Design	DDD	DC	12	6	18	10	22	4
Gather Materials								
Logs	GML	DC	30	6	36	-8	22	-14
Hides	GMH	DC	60	6	66	-20	40	-26
Vines	GMV	DC	12	6	18	58	70	52
Prepare Materials								
Logs	MPL	GML, DDD	36	36	72	22	58	-14
Hides	MPH	GMH	18	66	84	40	58	-26
Vines	MPV	GMV	6	18	24	70	76	52
Assemble								
Deck	AD	MPL, MPH	18	84	102	58	76	-26
Movement	AM	MPH, MPV, DDD	2	84	86	76	78	-8
Test								
Deck	TD	AD	2	102	104	76	78	-26
Movement	TM	TD, AM	1	104	105	78	79	-26
Final Test	TFT	TM	1	105	106	79	80	-26

Sam recognized that there was a problem. The critical path has 26 days of negative slack. Something had to be done. Most of the problem was with the hides, but getting the logs was also a problem. Cutting design time was not a desirable alternative as that could lead to rework later.

Getting the hides depended primarily on good fortune in finding the animals. Perhaps delaying the start of gathering vines for 30 days would let those people join the hunt and thereby help in finding animals sooner, say a reduction of 20 days, thus changing the 60 to 40. That still leaves 6 days of negative slack. Perhaps the preparation of the hides could start before all the animals are brought in. Sam considered starting tanning 9 days before the estimated completion of gathering the last hides.

Still there was the problem with the logs. Sam decided to overlap the gathering of the logs and their preparation by 20 days. While this would result in requiring a few more logs (because they could not be presorted before preparation), the extra time would be made up through the overlap. Thus, gathering logs was increased by 10 percent to 33 days.

Calculations with Overlap

Note: It is not the intention of this book to present all topics relevant to effectively use modern project management tools. The following is intended to illustrate briefly how the calculations of early and late start and finish times are modified when the overlap capabilities are used. The significant changes are highlighted by bold type. The durations of GML and GMH are changed and GMV starts at 36 per the above discussion. MPL now starts at 19, the finish of GML – 20. Similarly for MPH, starting 9 days before GMH finishes. Similarly, on the latest calculations, GMH must finish at 49, 9 days after MPH must start. GML must finish at 42, 20 days after MPL must start. Remember that the signs are reversed in the latest calculations.

Having considered all this, Sam was again in a quandary. Sam had not learned to perform the calculations when there were overlaps. Again, Sam returned to the Great Guru for help.

Activity Description	ID	Predecessors	Duration (Days)	Early		Late		Slack
				Start	Finish	Start	Finish	
RAFT								
Design								
Design Concept	DC	-	6	0	6	3	9	3
Detail Design	DDD	DC	12	6	18	10	22	4
Gather Materials								
Logs	GML	DC	~~30~~ 33	6	**39**	9	42	3
Hides	GMH	DC	~~60~~ 40	6	**46**	9	49	3
Vines	GMV	**DC(FS+30)**	12	~~6~~ 36	~~18~~ 48	58	70	**22**
Prepare Materials								
Logs	MPL	DDD, **GML(FS-20)**	36	~~36~~ 19	~~72~~ 55	22	58	3
Hides	**MPH**	**GMH(FS-9)**	18	~~46~~ 37	55	40	58	3
Vines	MPV	GMV	6	~~48~~ 48	~~36~~ 54	70	76	22
Assemble								
Deck	AD	MPL, MPH	18	55	73	58	76	3
Movement	AM	MPH, MPV, DDD	2	55	57	76	78	21
Test								
Deck	TD	AD	2	73	75	76	78	3
Movement	TM	TD, AM	1	75	76	78	79	3
Final Test	TFT	TM	1	76	77	79	80	3

Based on this plan and CPT calculations, Sam was satisfied that the project could be completed in time to take advantage of the increased flow of the river, but also be completed before flooding starts. Sam recognized that this schedule would require close supervision to ensure that no delays were encountered on the two critical paths.

Chapter XII

Resource Management

Sam knew that the plan was feasible technically and thought the resources were available. Not being sure that advantage had been taken of all the resources available, it was time to review what was available for this project. Sam decided to make a list of all the members of the family and what abilities each had and what constraint there might be on using them. Before doing this Sam thought it would be wise to visit the eldest member of the family to ask for help in thinking about this process. One of the general constraints was that some of the men and women had responsibilities for caring for the animals, preparing meals, and tending the children. It became apparent that knowing who would actually be available was very important.

INTRODUCTION

Effective and efficient use of resources must be the concern of every project manager. This starts at the earliest stages of project planning, manifest in the work breakdown structure's (WBS) strategic concept. This is best exemplified by the approach used on the Endicott Oil Field project (Flones 1987). They made some strategic decisions about where and by whom the work would be done, developed their WBS accordingly, and proceeded to complete the project in record time, in spite of severe local climate conditions. For example, the processing unit was fabricated and assembled on the Mississippi River and transported to Alaska on a barge.

At all levels it is important to ensure that all the resources are available when they are needed. Not only must the human resources be available, the materials, equipment, and supplies must be available at the place of use and ready to use.

In this chapter, we will explore the variety of resources that are brought to bear on a project and examine some of the principles for both effective and efficient use of each.

A TAXONOMY OF RESOURCES

First we need a taxonomy of relevant resources to understand where they fit into the scheme of a project. A taxonomy is presented in Table XII.1. At the first level under resources, the taxonomy divides into five classes—managerial, human, financial, physical, and intangible—and some of those into further subclasses. Perhaps the unique feature of this taxonomy is the recognition of a difference between those physical resources that are a part of the product of the project and those that are only a part of the project itself. That will be clarified later.

Managerial Resources

Simply put, the project manager's responsibility is to manage the project to successful completion. This implies bringing to bear any resources that can assist in accomplishing the project's objectives in an efficient, effective, and timely manner. Managerial resources are essential. It is tempting to consider only the managerial resources within the project team. Consideration should also be given to co-opting executives from both the performing and client organizations into the project, taking advantage of their status, power, and connections to accomplish tasks that may be very difficult for the project team to achieve.

All Resources
    Managerial
        Project Team
        Project Sponsor
        Executive
        Corporate Staffs
    Human
        Similar
        Unique
    Financial
        Project Costs
    Physical
        Part of the Product of the Project
            Equipment
            Materials
            Services
            Information
        Part of the Project
            Equipment
            Materials
            Services
            Information
    Intangible
        Ambient Conditions
        Space
        Time
        Information

TABLE XII.1
Taxonomy of Resources

Project Team

The project team is your most important resource. They need to work as a team, supporting each other's weak points and sharing your vision of the product of the project, as well as of the project itself. The selection of members of your team is important but sometimes you will have little choice in this. You do have the responsibility to meld them into a cohesive unit and to create the conditions that will motivate them to contribute their best efforts and energies.

Project Sponsor

Generally the most important executive resource is the project sponsor. Your sponsor may be your boss. This person must establish and maintain the project on a firm footing by selling its value to the organization, gaining support for its use of resources, and minimizing the impact of political interferences in the project's performance. The sponsor should establish the critical success factors and keep them in the consciousness of the project team. The sponsor should review the project plans, follow progress, solve problems as necessary, and always be sufficiently knowledgeable of its status to defend it from criticism in management meetings as well as with the various stakeholders.

Executives

While executive resources may be the most important of all resources, they are probably the most difficult resource for the project manager to manage. It is the rare project that can be undertaken and completed without the blessing, awareness, and involvement in some degree of the executives of the performing organization. Without this, the project is likely to founder for lack of resources and cooperation. With too much, the project is likely to get bogged down by slow decision-making, deteriorating morale of the project team, and the departure of key members.

Corporate Staffs

Many project managers may view corporate staffs more negatively than executives. Each staff has policies that must be followed and procedures that often seem like unnecessary "hoops" that must be jumped through. The procedures take time and project team resources to complete and thus, seemingly, have little to do with the "real work" of the project. There is a more enlightened view of these staffs; they may be very valuable resources. Let's consider just three.

Purchasing—Purchasing functions make significant contributions to corporate operations. If they did not they would soon disappear. They have contacts throughout industry and can often provide useful leverage in dealing with suppliers. On many projects purchased equipment, materials, and services represent a very significant portion of the total budget of the project. Thus, utilizing their services can save the project time, costs, and resources that might otherwise be required from project team members.

Personnel—The Personnel Department has a significant responsibility in most organizations. They are charged with recruiting competent personnel and keeping all personnel sufficiently happy in their employment so that the organization does not suffer appreciable labor problems. As a project manager you share those desires. Without competent personnel on your project it is not likely to be the success you desire. If there are labor problems on your project, you will experience less than the 100 percent effort you desire. Project managers often expect greater than 100 percent effort. To a very large extent, achieving greater than 100 percent effort is strictly a function of the project manager's leadership style and capabilities, but it cannot be achieved without competent and willing team members.

Legal—These are the people who will cross your "t's" and dot your "i's." However, in the process they are likely to recognize potential pitfalls and future problems because they are accustomed to reading legal documents. The OC was grateful for the review of a proffered contract. Not only did it bring peace of mind that they had "blessed" it, but it also provided assurance that, should future problems arise, the OC would not be out on that limb all alone.

Human Resources

It is the human resources available to the project that actually get the work done. Human resources get a lot of attention due to social, legal, physical, psychological, and other constraints on their usage. It is useful to consider two types of human resources: similar and unique. They have substantially different characteristics and require different considerations in scheduling and managing.

Similar

Similar human resources are typically craftspeople, as well as less skilled personnel. For example, most general carpenters possess the same skills. If one is not available today, another can perform the work.

Often they work in crews with members of the crew having similar capabilities. In general, an activity requiring similar resources can be completed in less time by adding additional units of the resource, either on the same shift or on additional shifts, or by overtime.

Unique

Unique resources are often professionals, highly educated with specific, often unique, skills or knowledge. It is not likely that one unit of such a resource can be substituted for another without some loss in efficiency or effectiveness.

Most people in most organizations are neither truly common nor unique. However, in the practicalities of scheduling, most fit into one of the two classes, similar or unique. Within a given organization, some otherwise similar resources are for all practical purposes unique. Thus, it is important to make this distinction in discussing scheduling of resources, and particularly human resources. Nevertheless, all humans are unique individuals and perform best if they are treated as such, recognizing their individual needs, motivations, and ambitions.

General Considerations

There are a number of general considerations that must be recognized to achieve high productivity from human resources. Those discussed in this chapter are: technologies and work methods, assigning appropriate resources, expediting resource availability, physical and physiological constraints, cultural and societal expectations, and reacting quickly to exogenous factors.

Financial Resources

Projects require financial resources, both in total and by period. Ideally the funds estimated to be required to perform the project would be made available. Realistically, you can expect competition from other projects and other needs for the available funds. Furthermore, it is normally the natural objective of the client to obtain the product of the project at the least cost, as it enhances the return on investment for the project. It seems to be a common assumption that the cost of the project has been overestimated and therefore that it can be performed at less cost if adequate pressure is applied. Thus, availability of total funds and funds by period is a realistic concern of a project manager.

Physical Resources

It would be the rare project that does not require some physical resources. Some projects are primarily involved in putting physical resources in place such as construction. Some are very equipment intensive while others require only the simplest equipment. Some require a lot of materials while others require very little. Physical resources may be constituent parts of the delivered product of the project, while others may simply be required to execute the project. Regardless, it is important for you to understand some basic concepts and principles associated with planning for and managing physical resources.

Part of the Product of the Project

Some physical resources become an integral part of the product of the project. These include equipment, materials, services, and information.

❑ *Equipment* that goes into the product of the construction project might include HVAC, electrical, plumbing, machine tools, conveyors (including elevators and escalators), desks and office machines, and so on. Equipment that goes into an aircraft includes propulsion, armament, communications, radar, seats, galley hardware, and the like. Equipment that goes into a new computer facility includes the computer, storage devices, communications hardware, climate control, hand trucks and dollies, and so on. For a surgery project there might be an artificial heart or the joint prosthetic. All of these items will remain in the product of the project.

❑ *Materials* that become an integral part of the product of a construction project include concrete, rebar, steel columns and beams, bricks and blocks, window and door units, roof decking and sealant, and fasteners. The aircraft project might include titanium sheets and prefabed parts, cable, wiring, tires, and so on. The computer project might include flooring components and cover, electric cable, HVAC ducts, and other such items. The surgical project might include sutures, cement (of course not the kind used in concrete), and blood, for example.

❑ *Services* include surveying, inspection, certification, and home health care. They are necessary components of the product of the project, but the results of their application are generally intangible with the exception of the paperwork that accompanies them and assures that they have been performed. Services to be provided to the product of the project can be categorized as commodity versus custom. Commodity services include such things as electricity, water, sewage, refuse disposal, and supply of process gases such as those used in welding. Custom services are provided on an ad hoc basis and are unique to the specific needs of the product of the project. An example of this might be continuing environmental monitoring by an independent agent.

❑ *Information* as an integral part of a project may not be so obvious. In the construction, aircraft, and computer projects it includes all the manuals (operating, service, safety, and so on) and warranties associated with the equipment, identification of all pipes, circuits, and equipment, and often training of operators. On the surgical project it includes instruction on what to do and not do to aid in the recovery and avoid recurrence of the need. Walking on crutches after hip replacement surgery is not an innate skill, especially going up and down stairs.

Part of the Project

Other physical resources do not become a part of the product of the project but are used in the process of executing the project.

❑ *Equipment* includes all sorts of items from very expensive units such as cranes and bulldozers in construction, to computers for testing code in a systems project, to laboratory devices in a drug development project. Again, it is easy to visualize some of the equipment used on a construction project such as cranes, bulldozers, field office trailers, welding machines, scaffolding, and so on. Hardware might include metal concrete forms, saw horses, and the like. On the aircraft project these would include dollies, forklifts, cranes, and all sorts of machine tools. Hardware might include jigs and fixtures, clamps, and such. The computer project might include nail guns, crimpers, electronic testing equipment, and so on. Surgical projects may use scalpels, heart-lung machines, gurneys, and beds.

❑ *Materials* include gravel used for temporary roads and storage areas, lumber for forms and safety barricades, and welding rods and viscene for protection from the weather. They are not really a part of the product of the project, but are required in the use of equipment and materials associated with the project. The temporary roads and storage area may well be abandoned upon completion of the project. Sometimes the areas must be restored to a pristine or other state upon completion of the project. Many of these are expendables such as fuel, lubricants, wiping clothes, and paper for reports and directions.

❑ *Services* include the work that is contracted to other organizations to perform. Services to the project can be categorized as commodity versus custom. Commodity services include such things as electricity, water, sewage, refuse disposal, and supply of process gases, such as those used in welding and maintenance of vehicles. Custom services are provided on an ad hoc basis and are unique to the specific needs of the product of the project. They include excavation, steel erection, roofing, and glazing on construction projects. They include independent testing of efficacy on a drug development project or the coding of programs on a system development project. They often also include ancillary services such as independent testing services for quality control, medical and legal services, and telecommunications services.

❑ *Information* includes client requirements and desires, specifications, standard methods and procedures, and schedule, cost, and quality data (both intended and actual). It often involves the transfer of knowledge and skills to the person who will perform the work, such as welders on a construction project or knowledge of a new language for computer programmers.

Intangibles

Intangibles are seldom thought of as resources that need to be managed. However, in ignoring them as a resource, we generally accept them as a risk factor. For example, starting construction of a major shoreline protection system just before hurricane season would be accepting a considerable risk that early work products would be at risk when they were most vulnerable. On the other hand, starting a major project in the far reaches of northern Canada in the summer would be a waste, as many such locales can only be reached during the winter when all the lakes and rivers are frozen over, forming natural highways. Thus, it is useful to consider these intangibles as resources that can be managed, at least to a degree.

Ambient Conditions

Ambient conditions include weather and the changes in climatic conditions over the seasons of a year. It also includes the zero gravity conditions of outer space. Normally weather is thought of as a risk factor. It can be thought of as a resource. The conditions extant in outer space are being researched to determine if it can affect the metallurgy, biology, or other outcomes of producing metals, crops, and other life forms.

Space

Space is discussed here as a matter of convenience. It could be space that will be an integral part of the project or it could be office or manufacturing space used by the project team. It is likely not given as explicit consideration as a resource as most of the other items discussed earlier.

Time

Time is an interesting anomaly. Most people consider time as a very explicit resource in scheduling work on a project. For example, overtime can be an expensive resource. However, time as represented by slack in the schedule is often ignored as a resource. Sometimes it is recognized but considered free. Like ignoring the weather, lack of favorable slack can lead to costly alternatives on the project.

Information

Information is generally thought of in terms of the two classes discussed previously under "Part of the Product of the Project" and "Part of the Project." There are other forms of information of which you must be aware. Political concerns of governmental bodies can forecast future obstacles and troubles. Likewise, community concerns can cause resistance to the project and its schedules. The project manager who becomes isolated from such concerns can easily be surprised. For example, a project involving interruption of traffic to businesses can result in protests that lead to requirements for temporary facilities that were not included in original plans. Not only do these temporary facilities add costs to the project but they can also lead to major delays in completing the project. Taking time to gain information of this type before a crisis develops can allow changes to the project that are much less deleterious and lead to much better relations with the relevant stakeholders.

MANAGING MANAGERIAL RESOURCES

It may have come as a surprise to think of executives and corporate staffs as resources available to the individual project. The OC has used these resources to his advantage. The trick in making effective use of them is to do so in such a way as to retain control of the project and its schedule. These people do not appreciate their advice being ignored or being put under too much schedule pressure. Thus, considerable tact is required in requesting assistance and in using it. This advice would serve the aspiring project manager well in most every aspect of managing a project.

Project Team

Of most immediate concern in staffing the project is the selection of the project management team (PMT). These are the people who will most directly affect the project outcome. It is your responsibility to choose the team members who can best meet the needs of the project. Sometimes these will be managerial needs and sometimes they will be technical needs. Seldom will the skills and knowledge of those assigned meet all the needs of the project. Some of the unmet needs can be supplemented in the selection of the next level of team members. As this proceeds, the WBS should be reviewed to ensure the best fit of the actual project team with the strategy for executing the project. Sometimes you will have little to say about who is on your team.

Then these people must be melded into a team that pursues the project's objectives without deviation or digression. In part this can be accomplished through the alignment process. On occasion it may be appropriate to counsel one or more members on their managerial or personal style to get it consistent with yours. Informal celebrations of specific accomplishments can be very effective in building esprit. One of the most effective ways to motivate the team members is to talk with each of them about their career hopes and ambitions. Often you will be able to provide opportunities to them that will enhance their objectives. When you can do this, it unleashes a degree of interest and energy that may surprise others who know the individual. Even the person approaching retirement has desires that can be enhanced in this manner.

Under-scheduling of the members of the project management team is hardly ever a problem. Occasionally the workflow on a project may result in some slack time for some individuals. For example, when a labor strike was called in the early stages of the construction of the Pontiac Silverdome, the project manager was told not to worry about the strike but go to the project office every day and plan and replan the project to get the best possible project plan. It paid off in a number of ways.

Overscheduling the members of the PMT is more likely. It is rare that the PMT member will have nothing they can do to improve the management of the project. It is far more likely that they will be constantly revising priorities between what tasks they must do, should do, and could do. Their "must do" task list is continually growing as new activities start and require attention during the process of the project. It is also being determined by meetings of the project team, meetings with those whose work they direct, and meetings with stakeholders. If the must do list grows too fast, two things may occur. Some of the tasks will get short shrift, resulting in less than adequate guidance to those dependent on those tasks. This can lead to poor performance, lower morale, and increased rework. You need to review the schedule to ensure that adequate guidance can be given to those activities requiring it.

Alternatively, the PMT member may put in extra hours on the project resulting in poorer performance overall, attitude/behavior problems (work and/or family related), and even health problems. You certainly should not become obsessed with these considerations but should also not be oblivious to them. If ignored completely, they can lead to unneeded problems on the project.

Behavior of all team members should be guided by knowledge and the practice of courtesy and good manners. While many project managers may deem the writings by Emily Post or Miss Manners to be totally irrelevant to their concerns, these guides may prove to be essential. For example, a project manager with poor table manners may never get invited to the executive dining room. The slovenly dresser may never be asked to substitute as speaker to an outside organization. Indeed, people with such habits would not likely ever be asked to be a project manager in many organizations.

Project Sponsor

How can you actually manage the relationship with the sponsor? First, it is not a simple task because the sponsor has some degree of authority over the project and often over the project manager. However, there are things that can be done to minimize dysfunctional behaviors. The most important task is to build the sponsor's faith in you as the project manager. That includes assuring the sponsor that you are capable and will manage the project effectively. This can be done through good planning, appropriate reporting of project progress, status, and future actions, honesty, attention to detail, dependability, and by avoiding behaviors not in the best interests of the organization and the project.

Good planning is inherent in good project management. Keeping the sponsor informed about relevant aspects of the project must be balanced with not requiring excessive time by the sponsor to comprehend the reports. Honesty is the foundation of trust but must always be used with tact. Attention to detail will ensure that you will seldom have to admit that you do not have the answer to a question. Dependability assures the sponsor that you will get the answer, if that is necessary, and that you will most likely have taken care of the problem before the question is raised. Avoiding dysfunctional behaviors means dressing, communicating, and behaving in the expected manner. The project manager is not free to be an eccentric individualist, at least not until after establishing an outstanding reputation for getting the job done. In short, every executive or manager wishes to avoid situations that could be embarrassing or otherwise harmful to their career.

Ask your sponsor for guidance as to what information is desired and in what format. Be forthright in sharing with your sponsor what you would like them to do to assist in achieving project success. Then design a system that is appropriate with special signals for critical information—critical as to time, importance, and privilege. Do not provide your sponsor with written information that could be harmful to your career. Too often it may be distributed to others before you can intervene.

The OC had an excellent relationship with one boss in this regard. The OC was manager of operations research for the corporation. We were not allowed to cross charge for our work for other units of the organization. The OC asked this boss to sit down with the client, after there was a firm proposal for a project, and "try to unsell the project." In part this was to obtain a commitment to provide resources to the project and in part it was to measure the commitment of the client to the success of the project. The approach proved to be quite effective.

A note to sponsors: Make it a habit of avowing that you learned of a problem as a result of your own probing. Do not put the project manager in the position of having complained about a problem to you.

Executives

Normally executives of the performing and client organizations are viewed as people whose desires must be met and whose egos must be coddled. This can lead to a passive view of these individuals as far as executing the project is concerned. The OC has found that a more active view of these individuals can be very useful in managing the project. Indeed, they may be the most important of all resources.

Managing executive resources is less obvious than the managing of physical and other human resources. It does need careful and deliberate consideration. There are executives in your organization who can be important to success on your project. One might be an executive you worked under prior to your current position. Another might be an executive who is especially interested in your project, although having no direct responsibility for it. For example, an advocate for greater use of computers in the organization in general may be an excellent ally in executive meetings in which your project may be discussed. An executive mentor may be useful to privately assess the attitude of all members of the executive committee and categorize them as either for, against, or neutral to your project, or even to you. Consider if there is anything that might encourage the neutral ones to be supporters, and, if the opportunity presents itself, consider doing something that may disarm those who are against you. Be sure you do the things necessary to maintain the good will of those who are supporters. Often your sponsor can accomplish these things better than you can yourself. It is wise to discuss your analysis and proposed actions with your sponsor to ensure its propriety and gain concurrence.

On some occasions an overzealous upper management or legislative body will allocate resources to a project faster than can be effectively absorbed by the PMT. In such cases, you should give some attention to other tasks that could be accomplished such as training or even inviting those least needed to take vacations while the opportunity is available.

Corporate Staffs

Corporate staffs are generally thought of as folks who write policies and procedures and then come to your operation to measure the degree to which you are following them. True, that is a part of their job. However, many of the people at corporate staff have had excellent training and experience that you can bring to bear on your project. This must be done adroitly and always with a clear understanding that you are asking for their advice and/or help without abrogating any of your responsibility as the project manager. This may be the most difficult part of seeking help from corporate staffs.

Adroitness includes never accusing the staff of failing in their job somehow. Rather, approach them from the point of view that you would like their assistance in overcoming an obstacle. This may be hands-on help or it may simply be granting a variance from a policy or procedure. Any time you seek staff assistance in this manner, and it is delivered, be sure to include it in the first appropriate report to executives and encourage your sponsor to comment on it at an appropriate executive meeting. It is probably well to document the commitment to help, regular progress reports, and upon completion, include a mention of the benefits received.

Purchasing

While it may not be the popular opinion, purchasing staff may be a best friend to your project. You and your team must exercise considerable restraint and caution to ensure that you do not negate the benefits available from effective purchasing practices as employed by the purchasing function. It is tempting to work directly with a vendor without the involvement of purchasing. While this may appear to be the only way to expedite the project, early involvement by purchasing can have substantial impact on the costs of the project as well as delivery, quality, and other problems in acquisition. You must actively manage the relationship between the project team and purchasing to ensure effective performance of this vital function. The purchasing activities should be incorporated into the project plan and the reporting system to ensure a high level of visibility of their performance. The best attitude is to view the purchasing function as one of the best protections you have to avoid costly and time-consuming mistakes.

The OC was a party to one of the most effective contributions to project success. This was a major plant construction project. The project reporting and control system discussed in Chapter XVIII was implemented. The activities that were the responsibility of corporate purchasing were all on one report with the responsible person being the vice president of purchasing. Since we identified all activities that were behind schedule, and printed them at the top of the report, we got his attention. He was very anxious to ensure that purchasing was not delaying the project.

There is a very important caveat on maintaining good relations with purchasing. Few things upset purchasing people more than fluctuations in schedule. Purchasers work hard to establish and maintain good working relationships with their suppliers. A part of this is establishing and adhering to schedule dates, especially those that are included in contractual terms. While it is important to include purchasing activities in the project plan and schedule, care must be taken to prevent the inevitable swings in the critical path technique (CPT) reports from annoying purchasing people. It is a fact of life that CPT systems are dynamic and a delay on one activity can impact all activities downstream from it. Thus, without special handling, the report received by the purchasing person can appear to be a constantly moving target. If that occurs, the purchasing person will start ignoring the reports and adhere to the contracted dates. Worse yet, the apparent delay in the need for a purchased item may be used to trade some more time on one item for earlier delivery of another item or other favor from the supplier. If this happens unbeknownst to the project team, and they work to get back on schedule, they may find that their efforts were fruitless due to the agreed-to delayed delivery of the needed item.

The solution to this dilemma is to introduce a system design feature that "absorbs" the usual perturbations to the CPT schedule and prevents them from being reflected in reports received by purchasing personnel. A special purchasing interface management report should be prepared to draw the attention of a key project team member who would screen the perturbations against agreed-to schedule targets and actual performance on purchased items to ensure that there is good reason to communicate any differences to purchasing.

Work with purchasing in a manner to get them to work with you and your project.

Personnel

More "good friends" can be found in the personnel staff. They can help you get the best people for your project. They can also help you avoid getting the wrong people on your project. You may need help in getting a job study done or a job description approved that will enable you to give a pay raise. Sometimes people in personnel have better "grapevines" about potential labor problems or assessments of performance of key individuals, including yourself. Having good relations with personnel staff may be the key in dealing with such problems.

One of the most important things personnel can do for you is to keep you from hiring someone who is likely to cause you problems later. They are experienced at screening resumes, interviewing, and contacting references to get you people with whom you can work.

Unfortunately, they are also responsible for ensuring the organization complies with all applicable laws, regulations, judicial decisions, and contracts. These often constrain what they can do for you and your project. On the other hand, they protect you and your project team from making unfortunate decisions that are contrary to these requirements and could cause you great grief.

Similarly, personnel is responsible for advising all executives and managers in the organization on the most effective allocation of the human resources available to the organization. This may lead them to recommend against your choices of the people you would like on your project team. The more importance they perceive of your project, the more likely they are to be persuaded that your choice is best for the overall organization.

Legal

It would be the rare project that could be undertaken without recognition of legal requirements and constraints. Even do-it-yourself projects around the home may be limited by zoning, building codes and permits, environmental requirements, and contracts for materials, services, and labor. For example, workmen's compensation provisions may limit who and how many you hire for the project.

Legal staff is responsible for protecting you and your team from making unwise decisions and defending you if you do. This does not mean that you should accept everything they say as the final word. Perhaps the best lesson learned in a business law course in college was to ask your lawyer for advice on consequences of alternative actions or decisions. You, as the project manager, are responsible for the decisions made on your project. You have the responsibility to assess the risk versus benefits of alternative decisions. In general, lawyers prefer alternatives that minimize the risk of legal liability and/or their risk of losing if they have to defend your actions or decisions in court. Such advice may not lead to the best business decision. After you have weighed the alternatives and make your decision you should take two more steps before implementing it. First, ask the lawyer to advise you on the best way to implement the decision. Second, inform your superior/sponsor of the circumstances, the alternatives, your decision, and how you intend to implement that decision. If you meet with resistance, perhaps you should reconsider the issue. This can lead to a very difficult decision if you are told something like "Okay, it's your decision, but you are on your own on it!"

Other Staffs

In general, the approach suggested for dealing with the above staffs should be followed in your relationship with other staffs. If you decide to make a decision, or take an action, that is different than the best advice you get, be sure to document the situation at least as thoroughly as you present it to your boss. If it does go sour, you may be required to defend the prudence of your decision or action in court, or at least to others in the organization.

It seems that one of the major motivations of staff executives is to brag about how their staff has contributed to corporate goals. Close behind this is a concern that their staff is performing effectively. For example, the OC was responsible for a purchasing department for a year. Many in the organization were critical of purchasing's performance. We simply started measuring the time between purchase request, purchase order, and delivery of the requested item(s). A monthly summary of that data proved that purchasing was doing a very adequate job on most items. On a few where they weren't, recognition of the problem led to improvements. The OC was pleased that, given that some people perceived a problem in purchasing, we had the opportunity to prove that the perceptions were not accurate in most cases and to receive recognition for the improved services of the purchasing department. Even the folks in purchasing were pleased as they sort of "got a monkey off their back" and could take pride that they were doing a good job.

The OC has always found value in following what he refers to as the "Wooden Nickel Theory." Essentially, it advises to do favors for those whose help you may need some day so that when you call on them, they will be favorably disposed toward you. For example, one of your best "friends" will be your boss's secretary. The biggest favor that person can do for you is to keep you out of your boss's office when your boss is having a bad day.

We have not mentioned consultants and other services to the project. In general, they are human resources and must be managed in much the same manner as other human resources. The major difference is that they are more independent than resources within the performing organization. To the extent that control is going to be exercised, its parameters must be established before and included in the contract. This may include naming the individual consultants who will perform the work to preclude them from moving on to other consulting contracts.

MANAGING HUMAN RESOURCES

Because projects are generally labor intensive, the management of human resources is an essential skill for the project manager. Furthermore, much of the work on projects is performed with minimal supervision and guidance, as compared to typical manufacturing situations.

It is useful to consider two types of human resources: similar and unique. The distinction between similar and unique resources is important to understand how they must be managed. It also makes a difference in scheduling. They have substantially different characteristics and require different considerations in scheduling and managing.

Similar

Craftspeople, as well as less skilled personnel, are typically similar human resources. To a large extent, management of these resources is governed by union contracts and local, state, and federal regulations. Even if they are not members of a union, union contracts define the expectations that must be met to avoid union organizing. Your personnel staff can be an invaluable resource for guidance on and negotiating grievances. Gain their cooperation early by seeking their advice before needing their assistance.

If there is sufficient reason, including the size and importance of the project, special arrangements can be made with the restrictive authority. For example, on a number of major construction contracts, special labor agreements for all trades on the project have been negotiated to meet the needs of the project. Clearly, this is not a form of relief that can be expected on every project.

Unique

Unique resources are often professionals, highly educated with specific, often unique, skills or knowledge. It is not likely that one unit of such a resource can be substituted for another without some loss in efficiency or effectiveness. For example, in considering a drafting room scheduling problem in an automobile company we learned that one draftsman or engineer could lay out a grill very well and fast, another was best at fenders, and another was best at doors. Assigning any of these to lay out another part resulted in longer duration to do the work and perhaps omission of certain considerations that were relevant.

An intriguing anecdote involved the development of a new approach to flying a jet fighter. It was purported that everyone concerned agreed that there was only one person who could solve this problem. He was brilliant in this area, but very reluctant to make commitments to do things on which he felt any degree of incompetence. It was decided that the only way to get him to agree to the challenge was to wine and dine him sufficiently to lessen his reluctance. It worked. While he was in a "relaxed" state of mind, he accepted the challenge, which he could not deny the next day. That is the purported story behind the on-screen display of essential information on fighter planes, a technology that may be used in automobiles soon, according to a recent news article. He was not only dissimilar, he was unique.

Not all unique resources require this kind of treatment. Most are quite reasonable and anxious to do their job well. Some do have enlarged egos and must be treated special to gain their enthusiastic participation on your project. One mark of a professional is high standards for their work. Professional engineers, for example, will not consent to releasing their work product until they are confident that it meets all the applicable requirements of the profession. There is good reason for this, as they can be held liable if they are found responsible for failure of the product of a project. Not only can it result in immediate damages, it can mean the end of a professional career.

General Considerations

There are other characteristics of human resources that apply to all. They include:
- Selection of technologies and methods to be applied
- Assigning appropriate resources to perform a specific activity
- Expediting resource availability
- Recognizing physical and physiological constraints
- Complying with societal and cultural expectations and constraints
- Reacting to external conditions.

Technologies and Methods

The conditions under which the work is to be done can determine the efficiency of the workers. An excellent reference for guidance in this area is the *Industrial Engineering Handbook* (Hobson 1992). It contains extensive information on work methods and product design for efficient production. While most of the articles are directed at repetitive operations in mass manufacturing, there are many lessons to be learned that apply on projects.

Remember that much of the work of projects can be performed in other modes using repetitive tasks. For example, in the process of building a house, the OC was asked by a carpenter to hold 2"×12"s while certain cuts were made. There were some fifty pieces to be cut the same way. After a very short delay, the carpenter was presented with a jig as well as a pattern and the remaining pieces were cut with less than half the labor cost. In the OC's experience, very few people, what ever their trade or profession, are familiar with the basic concepts of work design. Thus, you can have an impact on project cost by simply making project members conscious of better work methods. Depending on the size of the project, it may be worthwhile to have an industrial engineer assigned to the project, at least part time.

Assigning Appropriate Resources

Projects are characterized by a wide range and constantly changing mix of knowledge and skills. Each type of resource has characteristics that require different considerations in managing. These must be understood if the work of the project is to be scheduled in an effective and efficient manner. These two objectives not only imply accomplishing each activity using the most economical resource, but also coordinating the work across resources to minimize unnecessary costs.

Even within a specific similar resource group, there are differences in pay rates. The OC used this repeatedly in building a house. The OC and his lead subcontractor detailed the work ahead for the coming month. Each activity was coded as to the skills required. Thus, we both knew and agreed on that information and seldom had a high-priced carpenter shoveling dirt, for example. We knew when there was going to be dirt to be moved and ensured that we had adequate laborers or equipment to perform that work at the lowest cost. Had we not paid attention to that, such tasks would have cost at least double what they did. This becomes even more important the more differentiated the knowledge and skills.

Because of these differences between resources, one of the first principles of scheduling is to assign the most appropriate resources to perform a specific activity or element of an activity.

Expediting Resource Availability

We have previously discussed the "drafting room problem" and the likelihood of an activity being available to be worked on at the same time that the preferred resource is available to work on it. To some extent, you can influence this situation by expediting either the preceding activities or the completion of the work involving the resource. Before doing this, though, check to ensure that all other resources are available and ready to use.

Sometimes you may be forced into overtime just to get critical resources. This happened in constructing a plant that was critical to the client company, in a time period when the construction trades were fully occupied and would move from one job to another based on where they could get the greatest take-home pay—including overtime. Unfortunately, it was not long before productivity fell to the equivalent of an eight-hour shift with the workers getting paid for appreciable unproductive overtime.

Physical and Physiological Constraints

The most obvious reason to be concerned about such factors is the costs of injury on the job. There are costs of treatment, lost time, and compensation, not to mention possible large settlements as a result of court decisions. Recent experience with carpal tunnel syndrome makes it clear that stresses and strains can occur even on desk jobs.

The appreciation for the net time available given expected and unexpected demands upon the individual's time available for productive work is subtler. From time to time there are meetings in the parent organization that individuals are required to attend. Health and family problems may reduce time available. If this happens, depending upon the stage of the project and the anticipated duration of such perturbations, you should consider the temporary or permanent reallocation of responsibilities to minimize delays on the project.

Out of the above concerns there are two specific actions you should take. First, the meetings required of the PMT members should be managed to ensure that they are as productive as possible. This implies scheduling only those that are really necessary. It implies having agendas for the meetings, keeping to schedule, ensuring that all come prepared for the business at hand, and managing the meetings effectively. It also implies working with both the client and the performing organization to minimize meetings with them.

An area in which you, as the project manager, can have a direct impact on work efficiency is in determining the work periods. While there may be some outside forces determining what is feasible, you will typically have some discretion. Scheduling too much overtime may lead to increased costs. Studies have shown that the net output per day will increase for the first few weeks of overtime. Eventually, output per day deteriorates until it is equivalent to what was being achieved without overtime. Couple this with the possibility of an increase in the propensity to make errors and thus require rework, and continual overtime may be a lot less appealing. When overtime is called for, you would be well-advised to create a special sense of urgency and enthusiasm among those involved.

Human Engineering

It is useful to consider human resources in terms of "mechanical" capabilities and capacities. This is often referred to as "human engineering" or "Ergonomics." It has to do with such things as the physical dimensions of the human body, the capability to perform various tasks, the capacity to lift weight, and the ability to endure strains and stresses.

Work place design has long been a major area of practice of industrial engineering. Indeed, a good source of information is the *Industrial Engineering Handbook* (Hobson 1992). Knowledge of human physiology has been extended by research on both space flight and Olympic training. Much of that is applicable to work place design.

Human Needs

This tends to be more demanding on projects than any other mode of work. Human engineering focuses on the "mechanical" nature of humans. It is equally important to understand the psychological and social needs of humans. While many of these are common across all humans, some tend to vary across individuals for a variety of reasons. The wide range and constantly changing mix of resources requires an understanding and patience that is demanding.

Maslow identified a useful hierarchy of human needs. Maslow's model argues that there are five basic needs that motivate us: safety and security, physical (food and comfort), social, self-esteem, and self-actualization/fulfillment. These are hierarchical in nature and a lower-level need must be substantially filled before we are motivated by the next-higher need. Thus, we are willing to endure hunger if that is necessary for personal safety and security. If we are satisfied that we are safe and secure, we seek food and comfort. If we are reasonably comfortable and free from hunger we seek social interaction. Each need must be substantially sated for us to seek the next level need, except for the last. Self-actualization/fulfillment is different. In general, the more we get the more we want. It is like a familiar maxim, "success breeds success."

Self-actualizaton/fulfillment needs are especially relevant for the more knowledgeable and skilled professional persons. They are also potent for most craftspeople. There are relatively few people involved on projects whose safety and security, physical, and social needs are not being fulfilled today. Thus, the old "Bull of the Woods" management style is no longer applicable for the bulk of the labor force. The manager must be more skilled in motivating workers. This is especially true for project managers where the level of supervision of the worker is typically much less than in job shop and progressive line modes of work.

Prior to the Modern Quality Movement employers tended to view employees more as a "mechanical" resource, relying on the lower level Maslow needs to motivate. Workers recognized this as a "leave your brains at home" attitude on the part of management. The Modern Quality Movement argued, and demonstrated, that the human resource should be considered as a whole person, able to contribute far more than simple mechanical work. This not only required new attitudes on the part of managers but also new ways of managing to tap this greater contribution to the work place.

Society/Culture

Society places many expectations and constraints on the use of human resources. In addition to society at large, there are many societal units ranging from unions to professional societies that establish standards of behavior, expectations, and constraints. Indeed, the Project Management Institute (PMI®) has established standards in the form of ethics, certification, and the Project Management Body of Knowledge (PMBOK®). While these are not yet broadly accepted by society at large, it can be expected that over time, especially through judicial decisions, they will gain greater recognition and have a greater impact on the performance of project management.

Many legal requirements are imposed by governments. Other requirements are imposed by groups such as unions, while some may be imposed by an employment contract with a unique individual. Examples of such requirements include overtime compensation, work hours, and travel allowances. Sometimes quasi-legal requirements may be imposed by the performing or client organization. Sometimes, with adequate basis and preparation, an appeal to relax such requirements can be successful.

Political concerns of governmental bodies can forecast future obstacles and troubles. Likewise, community concerns can cause resistance to the project and its schedules. The project manager who becomes isolated from such concerns can easily be surprised. Remember our project involving interruption of traffic to businesses, which resulted in protests that lead to requirements for temporary facilities that were not included in original plans. Not only do these temporary facilities add costs to the project but they can also lead to major delays in completing the project. Taking time to gain information of this type before a crisis develops can allow changes to the project that are much less deleterious and lead to much better relations with the relevant stakeholders.

Many projects are international in scope involving diverse cultural backgrounds. Each culture has expectations and constraints. Religious practices differ widely around the world. Prayer time for Muslims is one example. These different practices can have a significant impact on project scheduling. In much of the world, work scheduling has been done based on Christian practices and holidays. This is no longer adequate on multicultural projects.

Psychological characteristics must be considered as well if the full utilization of human resources is to be achieved. Humans also have a need for social interaction that is essential to achieve cooperative relations as required on a project team.

You, as project manager, must be conscious of all these factors and avoid exceeding reasonable expectations and formal constraints, as well as encountering taboos. Failure to recognize these can cause, at the worst, an immediate work stoppage and, at best, dysfunctional relations between team members and groups. Failure to abide by these expectations and constraints will lead to negative attitudes toward the project and the performing organization.

Reacting to External Factors

How you react to external factors and conditions will have an impact on your project team. You may get "advice" from a variety of sources. Often the advice from two or more sources will be contradictory. Often it will conflict with decisions already made and directions already set. How you respond to this "help" will convey messages to your immediate project team and soon to all those working on the project. If you succumb to every bit of advice, you will soon have a reputation for being "wishy-washy." If you ignore all advice, you may expose yourself to severe criticism if the advice proves warranted. This puts a premium on seeking advice from those who really matter early in the project and then measuring later suggestions very carefully.

On the other hand, there will be many perturbations to your plan as you proceed through the project. You will have to assess each of them to determine what action to take and when. A frequent perturbation on outdoor work will be the weather. Maintaining an awareness of weather forecasts can alert you to the possibilities of unfavorable weather. Contingency plans can be prepared and decision criteria established so you are prepared to make quick and decisive decisions. This can aid you in preventing damage to work already done, scheduling work that could not proceed under adverse conditions, or incurring the costs of unproductive resources or even rework.

There will be times when the resources necessary to proceed with the day's work will not be available. This might be due to health, family, weather, accidents, or a host of other problems. Often this results in people doing nothing until given alternative directions. How quickly you deal with such perturbations will determine how much time is lost as a result, both in unproductive time and to delays on the project. By the same token, there will be opportunities from time to time that will permit acceleration of work scheduled for a later time, often accomplishing it with less work content. It is opportunities such as this that permit regaining of lost time and even getting ahead of schedule. The moral to this is really, don't be satisfied to stick strictly to schedule. Be aware of progress on the project and look for opportunities to improve on the schedule or plan.

MANAGING FINANCIAL RESOURCES

You can affect the scheduling of financial resources by making effective use of the cost capabilities of project management software. The basic concepts of earned value analysis permit a rather accurate projection of future cost flows. Accurately relating these to cash flows may require additional processing of this data. Even more importantly, the committing of costs and subsequent cash flow requires a deeper understanding of how the accounting is actually done in the performing organization. These concepts are discussed in Chapter XV, Cost Management.

Every organization has some limit on the funds available with which to undertake projects. Some organizations keep some reserve capacity to accept new projects. Others commit to near their limit. Some even over commit and have to abandon some projects in midstream. Existing projects may have their funds available reduced in future periods, reduced permanently, or canceled entirely. You should be aware of the potential for each of these scenarios. Occasionally, there may be a willingness to provide extra funds to permit accelerating the project. A good project management software capability, plus a well-planned project, should permit you to analyze alternatives and quickly adjust to the situation. Regardless of changes in funding the software should be able to recognize constraints on funds available and control authorization of work to remain within the limits imposed.

There are some concepts that you must understand, including the concept of a theoretical minimum cost for the project, the cost of funds employed on the project, and the motivations of the stake-holders with respect to funds.

Theoretical Minimum Cost

One concept, which is rather ethereal in nature, is that for any given project, there is some theoretical minimum cost within which the project can be performed. This minimum cost is determined solely by the requirements placed upon the project. Implied in this is the optimum duration for the project and the availability of resources that are most economically appropriate. While the exact value of this minimum may never be known, being conscious that it exists will guide you in making decisions about the project. The objective of the project manager is to perform the project as near to that minimum as possible, given the constraints and desires of the client. For example, if the client desires the completion of the project in less time than this theoretical minimum, it can be expected to result in increased costs. If the client limits the funds available by time period, this can result in increased costs. Regardless, you should strive to approach the theoretical minimum to the extent possible.

Total Project Cost

The cost of the project is the sum total of the costs of all the resources employed on the project. Often ignored is the cost of the funds employed. The cost of funds most relevant to the project manager is through the completion, i.e., acceptance by the client, of the project. Thus, for a twelve-month project with a cost of capital of 24 percent, $1,000 spent in the first month accrues a cost of capital of $243.37 by the end of the project. If that $1,000 could be delayed by one month it would save $24.38 by the end of the project, i.e., a two and one-half percent decrease in that cost. Projects of longer duration and more realistic dollar values increase these amounts substantially.

You also need to be aware that, for the client, the full cost of that extra project cost carries on through the end of the payback period for the project. Thus, that $24.37 could double if compounded through the end of a three-year payback period.

On the other hand, if the item is delayed to the maximum, and an unexpected further delay occurs, the project could be delayed or there could be very real extra costs to maintain the schedule. Thus, postponing the incurrence of costs cannot be taken without serious consideration of the risks. This is discussed in Chapter XVII, Uncertainty and Risk Management. It is the position of the OC that the project manager should be held accountable, in some manner, for the cost of funds employed.

Stakeholder Motivation

Success in managing the financial resources is very dependent upon the motivations of the stakeholders in the project. The client is often motivated to minimize the costs of the project as well as the chances that the product of the project will not work effectively. These are generally conflicting objectives. Those who perform the work are motivated to minimize their risk in performing the project. This can be manifest in schedule, budget, quality control, and the design/selection of components of the product of the project. The management of the performing organization may have bid the project to maximize the chances of winning the contract, sometimes with a bid that is unrealistic, with the expectation of savings in the performance of the project. You must be wary to prevent such motivations resulting in delivery of an unsatisfactory product.

Sometimes a project participant may attempt to add equipment or people to the organization to augment the capabilities of that participant at the expense of the project. You must be aware of the motivations of the various stakeholders in order to manage the financial resources effectively.

MANAGING PHYSICAL RESOURCES

It may not be obvious that there are different considerations in scheduling the physical resources on a project depending on whether they are a part of the product of the project or a part of the project. To draw attention to these differences and contrast them, we will consider the scheduling of physical resources for both aspects of the project at the same time.

Managing Equipment

Equipment that becomes an integral part of the product of the project is often characterized by long lead-times and considerable cost. Often it is fabricated specifically for the project at hand and it is not unusual for it to be custom designed. Thus, the scheduling of equipment involves many considerations. Even the method and timing of delivery are important considerations.

The more unusual the item, the greater the probability of very limited production facilities. Thus, it may be desirable to commit to a manufacturer well before final design is completed. By so doing, the availability of the manufacturer's capacity is assured. For example, it happened that two automotive companies were each building new ferrous casting plants. One of them placed their order for critical equipment about a month before the other. The nature of the equipment was such that the first plant tied up the facilities of the supplier for several months, thus delaying the second plant in receiving their equipment. This did not result in a comparable delay because the project plan was modified to minimize the impact. Nevertheless, there was a delay and some extra costs. The down side of this is that the cost may be higher. Being second to order means you may find a supplier that is not so "hungry." In some cases it may be desirable to make an early commitment to ensure the productive capacity of the supplier is available, even though the designs may be incomplete. When compared to being late getting a product to market, the additional cost to the project of this commitment may be trivial as compared to total costs of a delay.

Some items of equipment are so large that they determine construction sequence. For example, the compressors for the air conditioning system may be so large and heavy that they are required to be in place prior to erecting structural steel and certainly closing in of the compressor room. The space required to erect a tall fractionating column may preclude installing other facilities and pipe lanes until the column is in place. Thus, shear size and mass can dictate schedule.

The other side of the coin is that such equipment is often a major part of the project cost. For cost of capital reasons, as well as the necessity to protect such investments from vandalism and the weather, it is desirable to schedule such items as late as possible. One solution to this is to develop novel ways of solving such problems. Many companies have used off-site fabrication of processing modules. This avoids congestion at the site, permits work to be done under more favorable conditions (for example, under roof) thus leading to economies, and permits other work to proceed so that start up can proceed soon after delivery of the modules. The epitome of this was on the Endicott Oil Field project where the major processing unit was fabricated on a barge on the Mississippi River. When fabrication was completed, the barge was towed through the Panama Canal, up the Pacific Coast, and through the Bering Straits to the site. The unit was dragged off the barge to its operating position and six weeks later started operating. This was also an excellent example of critical timing of the delivery of equipment, as there was only a six-week window during which the barge could be brought into the Arctic Ocean site, unloaded, and towed back out before freezing would preclude its movement.

In another instance, the OC heard of a project in Southeast Asia that required a unit of equipment that was produced in the US and had a substantial lead-time. Apparently the equipment was vital to the project and the product of the project was quite vital. The equipment had to be transported by ship through shipping lanes that were considered at risk, from pirates as well as from the weather. It is purported that two units of the equipment were produced and shipped via different routes to ensure that the project was not delayed. While most instances are much less dramatic, it is quite reasonable that having a backup item would be advisable on a project.

The acquisition of equipment, especially the more expensive variety, is no doubt going to involve the purchasing department, if not several key members of general management. For example, on a new ferrous casting plant at Chrysler, the decision as to the type of melt process—cupola, induction furnace, or arc furnace—was made by the corporate executive committee. (It might be of interest to some that a major factor in that decision was a linear programming model of the melt process that incorporated process losses and controllability of the different processes. This was an early example of the role of advanced decision-making techniques related to projects.)

The significance of equipment items to a project argues for them to be incorporated into the project schedule and control system. There should be sufficient detail to give an early warning of any delays creeping into the schedule for these items. A casual "check-is-in-the-mail" approach to follow-up on these activities is hardly sufficient. Provisions should be made for visual inspection of progress for all major items and any others on which there may be a suspicion of less than full and unbiased reporting. Short of that, it may be useful to require that a responsible executive of the supplier company be assigned to your item and require that this person make periodic reports of progress in person at a meeting of key project stakeholders.

A variation of this was successful for the OC on the installation of the 911 system in Pontiac, Michigan, a purchased service. The cut-over was to be accomplished over a weekend and involved degradation of emergency communications during the changeover. The same weekend, the 911 system for Oakland County was to be cut over. Oakland County had a population of about a million while Pontiac had about 80,000. There was concern that, should there be problems, resources would be diverted to ensure that Oakland County's cut over was successful. While we had a customer representative assigned to our account, efforts to identify the person responsible for successful performance of the project were unsuccessful, short of the vice president of marketing for Michigan Bell. He was invited to visit City Hall and explain how he was going to ensure a successful cut over for Pontiac. About a week after the cut-over, the customer representative indicated that Pontiac's cut-over had been Michigan Bell's most successful 911 cut-over to date.

In addition to the previous, there is generally equipment involved in the performance of the project. For the construction project this may include cranes, forklifts, scaffolding, and so on. Consider a 100-ton crane. There are often substantial costs of bringing the equipment onto the job, setting it up, dismantling it, and moving it off the site. It may cost $500 per day, whether it is in use or not. It is wise to plan and schedule the project in such a manner as to minimize the time on site of such equipment. This is illustrated with an arena project where the crane sat with its boom on the ground for some three months before it was first used. Minimizing time on the site goes beyond this. If care is not exercised in planning and scheduling the work for which an item of equipment is required, the equipment can sit idle for considerable periods between usages. For equipment of this type, to the extent possible, those activities requiring the use of such equipment should be scheduled so as to provide contiguous requirements. Thus, some activities early in the project should be delayed as long as possible while some at the end should be moved ahead as far as possible. Another alternative is to analyze carefully the requirements to determine if a smaller capacity crane, or whatever, would suffice for some of the earlier and later work. This could incur less set-up, tear-down, and usage costs.

For equipment such as scaffolding there are different levels of technology depending on the requirements and the quantity and nature of the work for which it is required. For example, if the need is very short term, and it is feasible, it might be possible to use a platform suspended from a crane or from a structural member. In some cases it might be appropriate to use timbers to construct a temporary platform. More likely, a standard frame-type scaffold would be appropriate. If a considerable masonry wall were involved, it may well be economical to incur the higher costs of an elevator-type scaffold. The economics include the labor cost to adjust the scaffold level and the increased efficiency for the masons to be working more nearly at their optimum height relative to the current course.

For equipment requiring checkout before use, such as a computer for debugging code, delivery should be scheduled to recognize the checkout period, as well as some degree of uncertainty of success of the checkout, and the time required to obtain replacement parts and or a new unit.

Managing Materials

Managing materials on a project should also follow standard materials management practices. While this is an ideal computer application, the OC is unaware of any commercial software designed specifically to integrate these materials management practices with the needs of project management. Major design/build firms have their own quite sophisticated proprietary systems. The OC is also unaware of any significant literature specifically describing the logistic problems or of logistic systems on projects.

Classification of Materials

A major logistics practice in manufacturing is the classification of items according to ABC categories. There is no magic about the use of the three letters. More categories can be used if it is truly beneficial. The three are convenient for discussion purposes however.

In a manufacturing environment, all inventory items are classified based on the annual cost of acquisition, i.e., the annual usage is multiplied by the cost per unit. The parts are then sorted on this measure. Those having the highest annual value are placed in class "A," those having the lowest value in class "C," and those in between in class "B." The determination of the cutoff between classes is simply based on an assessment of the relative cost of managing each category. For example, class A items may be managed very closely, perhaps on a just-in-time (JIT) basis. Class C items may be managed on more of a just-in-case (JIC) basis. Class B items may be managed on a max-min basis.

Implicit in this is that class C items are very low in cost and it would not make sense to allow the project to be delayed because of a stock-out. Examples are nails on a construction project or paper to print computer code or test results on a systems project. On the other hand, it is likely that special bolts made of an expensive alloy or an unusual chemical reagent for testing drug efficacy would be in class B. Items that do not merit managing as major equipment but may be serial numbered or required for a specific activity may be in class A. The point is that all items do not require the same level of management attention to ensure that they are available.

The literature of materials management includes extensive discussion of techniques for managing inventory. They range from simple bin control through Materials Requirements Planning. The former might be used for class C parts. It typically has a bin with a partition in it. The bin contains the quantity that is deemed economical to obtain as one order, sometimes plus a safety amount. The safety amount is in recognition of the uncertainties associated with usage during the reorder lead-time and the uncertainty of the lead-time. The back portion of the bin contains the safety stock. The front part of the bin contains the remainder of the items. When the last item is taken from the front of the bin, it is a signal that it is time to reorder. This approach would be applicable for items that were used consistently throughout the project, i.e., they are not directly related to the performance of any one activity. Paper towels might be such an item. The determination of the economic quantity to order can be simply the standard packing quantity or it can be derived from an economic order quantity model.

Material Requirements Planning

Material Requirements Planning (MRP) is a computer technique for scheduling the production or purchase of items that are related directly to two or more scheduled production lots. Given that a particular item is scheduled for production at two or more times in the future, it permits the determination of how many units of a component part will be required for each production lot and for how many lots the component part should be purchased at one time. (It's a bit more complicated than that but this is sufficient for discussion here.)

Now if we substitute activity for production lot, the same concept is applicable to projects. Thus, suppose special welding rods are required on a number of activities on a project. Suppose these activities are not contiguous. Should we purchase only the welding rods for a given activity and repeat the process for each activity that requires welding rods? This strategy would require the creation of a lot of purchase orders. (Not necessarily as we might put welding rods on "open order," calling for another shipment as required, but please go along with the program for the sake of illustration here. Imagine any item you wish.) It would also require some record keeping associated with receiving each shipment. Alternatively, should we purchase the total number of welding rods early in the project? This strategy would result in tying up capital early in the project and thus add to the cost of funds employed. Someone would have to control the issue of the rods lest they "walk away." Some space would be required to store them and there might be some deterioration over time, if only due to corrosion.

There may be a better strategy that is somewhere between these two extremes. Consideration should be given to ordering the quantity required for the next activity requiring welding rods, the next two activities requiring welding rods, the next three, and so on. While the mathematical techniques to solve such a problem exist, they are not presently available in a computer program designed to meet the needs of the project environment, let alone integrated into project scheduling software. Thus, it is up to the project manager, or the designated materials manager, to consider the options manually. The good news is that the number of items that are required by more than one activity that should be handled in this manner is not great.

Proper management of materials used in a project, whether they are a part of the product of the project or simply used in performing the project, offers opportunities to reduce the cost of the project. The astute project manager should be aware of these opportunities and ensure that they are being pursued on the project.

JIT versus JIC

There are two major divergent philosophies of resource management—just-in-case (JIC) and just-in-time (JIT). Both can have a role in project management. Until about 1980, JIC was the prevailing practice in manufacturing of all kinds. It accepts producing and delivery times as being uncertain and provides a buffer inventory that allows user production to continue in spite of the uncertainty. In a multilevel manufacturing system, with buffer inventory between each successive step in the system, the investment in total inventory was very large. In addition to the cost of carrying this inventory, there were significant costs of excess and obsolete parts and material handling. JIC has been the generally prevailing practice on projects.

Just-in-time concepts were developed to a fine art in manufacturing in Japan. In part due to the close proximity of suppliers, purchased components were scheduled to be delivered to the using plant as often as every two hours. Little or no inventory was held at the user plant. This same philosophy was implemented internal to the manufacturing plant in the Kanban concept. Kanban is literally "card" in Japanese. The cards were used as authority to produce by the previous process. Often the card was replaced by a parts tray or bin that held one production lot. There might be three trays rotating between the producing process and the user process. An empty tray at the producing process was authorization to produce that quantity, just in time to supply the user process.

Just-in-time, as applied in the manufacturing environment, has relatively little risk. The items managed by JIT are in production; there is little risk that they will not be produced in time. They are typically shipped by truck, a transportation mode that is very reliable in most developed countries. There is very little uncertainty as to when they will be needed, as production schedules are determined in advance and deviations from schedule are relatively rare within the scheduling lead-time.

Just-in-time has been used on some projects in a variety of ways with considerable success and benefits. One notable example was the approach used in constructing the World Trade Center on lower Manhattan. The approach was necessitated by the almost nonexistent storage space at the construction site. A marshaling yard was established across the Hudson in New Jersey. All material was delivered there, loaded onto trucks, and transported to the construction site on a daily basis as needed. The epitome of this was in structural steel erection. The steel members for a given day's erection were loaded onto flat bed trailers in the reverse order of their erection. Upon arrival at the site, as each member was offloaded it was immediately installed. While drayage may have been a little more, handling and record keeping were minimized. Contrast that with the arena construction project where the steel for the upper stories was delivered first and sat in the open for weeks prior to arrival of the steel for the first floor.

Another similar instance of excellent materials management is demonstrated by the Bad Creek Pumped-Hydro Generating facility (Snyder and Caligan 1990). The generating room is a cavern carved out of solid rock, basically at water level of the lower lake. There was no place to store anything but components to be installed on a given day. The marshaling yard received all material and moved it into the cavern just in time to be used. This was taken to a new level, however, as the materials management operation packaged all the tools and supplies needed to install those components to ensure that the higher-paid craftspeople did not have to wait for delivery or spend time going to a "tool crib" to obtain them.

It has been reported that a chemical plant was constructed in eastern Tennessee that truly used JIT concepts by, in essence, eliminating the marshaling yard and relying on their suppliers to deliver components to the job site just in time to be installed. It was reported that considerable savings were realized. While much project work often proceeds in a JIT fashion, it is more likely due to the time pressures on projects and to happenstance rather than a conscious effort to use JIT concepts.

Costs of JIC versus JIT

The project environment tends to tilt in favor of JIC materials management, regardless of whether it is for the product or the project. The usual measures of performance on a project are—in varying order—cost, schedule, and technical performance. Very seldom are measures such as cost of funds employed, cost of excess and obsolete materials, or efficiency of equipment usage examined. On most projects, the cost of funds employed *seems* relatively small. However, on a project such as the English Channel Tunnel, with a total cost in the range of $10 billion (US), the cost of funds employed eventually was in excess of $1 million a day, even at bank prime rates. This is certainly enough to warrant attention. A careful analysis of these costs on any project would generally reveal that the cost of funds employed is significant to the client. Thus, this measure warrants some attention.

When considering the cost of bringing materials and equipment onto the project, we cannot consider the cost of funds to be the low bank prime rate. In manufacturing, it is common for the annual cost of inventory to be in the range of 30 to 45 percent of the cost of the item. Just the interest on the money itself may be in the range of 15 to 20 percent. At minimum this would be the prime rate, or it might be determined by the return that could be achieved on those funds if invested in the financial market. More realistically it is the rate of return that could be expected from investing in the most lucrative internal use of funds. Perhaps that is another project on which the return on investment (ROI) might be 20 percent. On top of that, there is a cost of space in which to store the item. This may seem free unless it has to be stored under cover or even in a commercial warehouse close to the site or in office space rented for the project. There are security costs, even if only to prevent the item from "walking away." Have you ever heard of "do-it-yourself" projects, even houses, that were done with materials taken from the project site? There is also a real possibility for excess and obsolete items to be scrapped at the end of the project or sold for a small percent of their cost, just to dispose of them. Finally, uncontrolled inventory can invite a wasteful attitude on the part of project personnel, such as cutting "fire blocks" out of new 2"×4"s rather than using up short pieces that are all around.

While all of these costs do not apply to every item, there is a real cost associated with JIC approaches to materials management. For example, consider the early delivery of a piece of equipment that will be a part of the product of the project, costing $100,000. The relevant interest rate on this would be around 25 percent or $68 per calendar day, or $2,100 per month. Or consider bringing a piece of equipment onto the project a month early that will be used in performing the project, costing $500 per day. Not only does it cost $15,000 for that month but also the cost of these funds from the time the equipment was actually needed until the end of the project would be in the order of \$320 per month. If the project lasts for another twelve months, that would be another \$3,820. For the client, the cost of funds employed, now some \$18,800, would continue for perhaps another five years until the cost of the project was recovered. Compounded annually, that could add up to as much as \$57,000 additional to the total cost for the project. Thus, these costs are not trivial on any project. (Note: This discussion assumes that all costs exceeding the conceptual theoretical minimum cost for the project are recovered at the end of the payback period. This illustrates how important this conceptual theoretical minimum cost is on projects.)

Does this mean that all project materials management decisions should be based on the JIT philosophy? Certainly not. On many projects, uncertainties are much greater, whether caused by weather or by pushing the state-of-the-art on high tech projects. The costs of delay on a project can be substantial, especially when considering the "domino effect" of delays. This occurs when a delay prevents an activity from proceeding as scheduled, thus resulting in a resource required for that activity to not be available at the new schedule time. It can add to the delay on that activity. It is likely to happen to subsequent activities until the total delay is much greater than that on the first activity delayed. This phenomenon is not provided for in the typical CPT system.

Does this mean that the JIT philosophy of materials management should be ignored? Certainly not. The moral to this discussion is that decisions relating to materials management are more complex than are generally perceived and deserve more careful consideration and improved tools for decision-making than are generally used. It also means that care should be exercised in chastising the materials manager solely for a late delivery now and then. Rather, the project manager should recognize the degree of uncertainty and create "windows of opportunity" for the delivery of certain items, arranging for alternative work to proceed with the least interruption of other aspects of the schedule possible.

Managing Services

Services are either unique or commodity. Unique services may vary from very skilled experts such as specialty physicians or niche consultants, to very specialized equipment such as concrete pumper trucks or special electronic equipment. Commodity services include such things as utilities and hauling services, such as for dirt or gravel.

Unique services are generally labor-, skill-, knowledge-, and/or equipment-intensive. They tend to have monopolistic characteristics and often serve a very limited niche market. The more these characteristics are true, the more expensive and schedule sensitive the services are. It is also relevant to consider the providers of these services as similar or unique as discussed under human resources previously. Often they have relatively limited capacity and tend to oversell their capacity. Since their earning capability is directly proportional to their billable time, they have a tendency to move on to the next job if delayed on the current job, thus exacerbating the domino effect on schedule delays.

Commodity services vary widely in their monopolistic characteristics, depending on the cost of entry into the business. For example, electrical service requires a large investment in generating and distribution facilities, while general hauling businesses often start with a used truck, and, if successful, expand to meet market opportunities.

Quality of service varies widely, often proportional to the degree of monopoly characteristics. For example, electric utility rates have been set through regulatory bodies. Quality of service, such as continuity of service and voltage maintenance for electric service, is dependent on the management of the provider. For those services that are monopolistic in nature, often the only recourse is to negotiate the terms and conditions prior to committing to the project. This is typically a major criterion in facility site selection when either building or renting.

Services for which the cost of entry is low, such as trash hauling, are sometimes fraught with unscrupulous controls to maintain prices by limiting competition. Such practices should be thoroughly understood before costing a project or even considering becoming involved in a project where this is the case. The OC once advised an employer not to enter a specific construction market without the relevant "local knowledge" for this reason.

Managing Information

Projects often require information that must be purchased. For example, construction projects often purchase weather information to assist in scheduling decisions. It would be foolhardy to schedule a major concrete pour if heavy rain were predicted or to leave a free-standing masonry wall unsupported in the face of predicted strong winds. Clearly weather information must be very timely, perhaps more frequently than daily, and very location specific.

Some projects are highly dependent upon regulatory and industry codes. One design-build firm created a business unit to establish a database of such information so it could sell a service of providing such information. In the absence of the availability of such a service, time must be allowed for the ad hoc research efforts and it should be scheduled early to minimize surprises and rework.

On some projects, especially those really pushing the state-of-the-art, information on current technological developments can prove valuable. Sometimes this information can be in another part of the same organization. A recent article reported that a significant effort to redesign a part was negated when another project team redesigned the product where the part was to be used, eliminating the need for the part.

Documentation should be considered a resource. Standard policies, procedures, and practices available from other projects or organizations can reduce the effort required to provide them on a specific project. These should be available as a database that can be accessed and changed to meet the needs of the particular project. Similarly, documenting the product of the project can be expedited if user manuals and other documents are obtained from the supplier of the equipment in computer form. They should be tailored to match the specifics of the product as delivered. It is a pet peeve of the OC to purchase a computer program or a motor home and be handed documentation that has all the options relevant to every variation of the computer or the motor home included. It is a huge assumption to think that the user is smart enough to determine which options apply in a specific instance. This is compounded when a crisis arises. Furthermore, a misinterpretation could result in very undesirable consequences. It would be a very valuable service to the client to particularize these documents to the specific model installed.

Managing Configuration

On many projects it is desirable, if not necessary, to maintain accurate and detailed records of the specific components installed in the product of the project. This is especially relevant for space and software systems projects. It is very evident when we consider what is involved in making in-flight corrections to computer programs on a space mission. Such efforts are preceded by extensive testing of the "fix" on identical hardware and software on the ground and then, when proven to work, sent to the errant vehicle. In more mundane projects it is also worth knowing the precise nature of a piece of equipment operating in a remote location so the correct replacement part can be dispatched when necessary. For critical parts it may be relevant to know all the conditions extant on a steel pour that resulted in castings for the critical part. This is particularly true if there is any potential liability associated with the failure of that part. An example might be a flywheel on a gas compressor.

As Built

Anyone who has ever done a significant repair or remodeling of a house is familiar with the need for accurate information about how the house was actually constructed, where pipes and wires were routed and even what specific outlets and fixtures are on each electrical circuit. Most of us are familiar with the occasional interruption of utility service because the as-built records were not accurate or they were ignored. On major construction projects such records are vital for both troubleshooting and revision. For the house it may be sufficient to frequently take pictures that can be compared to the final designs. On more extensive projects, it is necessary to revise the drawings to show exactly how things were built.

MANAGING INTANGIBLES

Ambient Conditions

Most every reader can imagine all the ambient conditions, and how they could vary depending upon the time of the year, that might delay the imaginary project discussed in Chapter XI involving driving from New York to Los Angeles.

Ambient conditions include weather and the changes in climatic conditions over the seasons of a year. It also includes the zero gravity conditions of outer space. Normally weather is thought of as a risk factor. It can be thought of as a resource. Work can be scheduled to take advantage of or in spite of probable weather conditions. If it is in spite of probable weather conditions, there may well be penalty costs due to delays, extra work involved, lack of efficiency, and even destruction of work already completed. For example, on earth moving fill work, a certain amount of moisture is required to achieve satisfactory compaction. Too much moisture and the equipment cannot move. Thus, scheduling such earth work to take advantage of natural precipitation patterns can permit balancing the amount of water that has to be hauled and minimize the delays due to excessive precipitation. On one construction project on a site with poor drainage, it was deemed desirable to start the project by installing the parking lot over the entire site. Even though it required digging through the pavement, the project was not bothered by muddy conditions at the site in spite of heavy rains.

In building the original Alaska Highway, many swampy areas were encountered. The only time these could be worked was during the winter when they were frozen. Similarly, some of the work on the Alyeska Pipeline required working in river beds that became swollen during the spring thaws but were nearly dry during other times of the year. The conditions extant in outer space are being researched to determine if it can affect the metallurgy, biology, or other outcomes of producing metals, crops, and other life forms.

Ambient conditions can affect office work also. Excessive noise and other distractions can cause people to lose concentration. Uncomfortable temperatures and humidity can be debilitating. Failure to keep HVAC systems free from disease inducing organisms can lead to health problems. Unsafe conditions can lead to accidents and lost time of the person(s) directly affected, as well as others who are simply curious, and most everyone who hears about it and spends time discussing it. "Bullpen" office arrangements can lead to perturbations and lost time. The OC is reminded of the effects on an essentially all-male drafting room when he walked into the area accompanied by an especially attractive female computer systems engineer. There must have been at least fifty people in that bullpen and they all stopped working. It may have been fifteen minutes before they returned to work. Similar behaviors have been experienced for mostly female work groups.

Space

First consider space as an integral part of the product of the project. The purpose of most construction projects is to create space. However, the sequence in which it is created is a serious consideration in scheduling. For example, a house must be framed and dried in before sheet rock can be hung. It would be unwise to schedule other work in the same space at the same time as dry walling. Similarly, it is generally unwise to schedule work by two or more trades in the same space at the same time. It may be undesirable to use the same laboratory to perform two different types of tests at the same time. Or, it may be undesirable to try to debug two different programs at the same time, on the same computer. Thus, specific spaces become as relevant in scheduling as the equipment, materials, and humans.

Similarly, considering space as a resource that is a part of the project, the project staff must have space in which to conduct the work of the project. Sometimes this becomes a major decision, such as whether to collocate the project team members versus have them remain in their functional areas during the project. While this becomes a very tangible consideration of space, the decision is often based on a number of intangible factors. Space for storing materials on site is also a relevant factor as witnessed by the World Trade Center and Bad Creek Pumped-Storage Hydro projects.

Time

Time is an interesting anomaly. Most people consider time as a very explicit resource in scheduling work on a project. However, time as represented by slack in the schedule is often ignored as a resource. Ownership of slack should be explicitly recognized in all project contracts and control of slack given to the project manager to the greatest extent possible. You must ensure that slack is used appropriately and not frittered away by default. For one thing, slack can be used in negotiating schedule changes. On the other hand, ill-used time can lead to extra costs. Project activities performed too early lead to increased interest costs on funds employed. Worse, it can lead to expensive rework.

Information

There is a type of information that may seem superfluous to the objectives of the project, as well as to the product of the project. This is all the records, progress reports, correspondence, and so on, that provide the evidence that the project was undertaken in a prudent manner. It may seem to be an expense that can be avoided, especially if the project is already over budget. However, if the project goes sour and ends up in court, the cost of gathering such information after the fact will be much greater. The cost of not having good quality, well-organized records can be enormous if it results in losing the dispute. Allocate the time to gather and organize this information as the project progresses. It will be much easier.

Finally, information systems seldom work effectively by themselves. They require monitoring to ensure that the information is being gathered, it is accurate and timely, and that it is being organized in a manner that enhances its value to those who need it for operating guidance as well as decision-making.

SUMMARY

We have examined the resources available to the project manager and some characteristics that are relevant in managing each of them. A mark of an excellent project manager is the ingenuity applied in solving the problems that inevitably occur on a project. This includes problems with obtaining resources.

Managing resources on a project is not a trivial problem. There are many factors to consider and it is not likely that a computer program will recognize all of these factors, let alone the opportunities. You will need systems for planning, scheduling, analyzing progress, documenting the project, and providing stakeholders with information that maintains interest and confidence in the project. You must ensure that the information is accurate, timely, complete, and accessible. If you cannot allocate time for this it is vital that you assign the responsibility to a person who has the time to spend on it *and* your welcome attention.

Managing resources will probably occupy the largest part of your time, second only to attending meetings, and most of that meeting time will be spent on human resource matters. Good luck!

Sam's list of resources was longer than expected. It was especially surprising to realize that the old Shaman had a few tricks to offer in addition to blessing the raft before its maiden voyage. The following resources were identified.

1 Matriarch (mother-in-law)
1 Shaman
3 elder men
6 elder women
39 able-bodied men
35 able-bodied women (5 of them pregnant)
10 teenage boys (one crippled)
12 teenage girls
15 small children
12 cows (2 pregnant)
3 bulls

Sam realized that calling on the Matriarch to say a "few" words to the hunters before they left might be very motivating. The Shaman revealed knowledge of a secret blend of juices of plants and animal waste that produced vines of unusual strength and flexibility. Now Sam had to see if these resources met the needs of the project.

APPENDIX XII.A
MARS PATHFINDER PROJECT

PROJECT COST/RESOURCE MANAGEMENT

The Mars Pathfinder Project faced a tremendous resource management challenge from the very beginning. As a Discovery Mission, the department was cost capped at $150 million in FY92 dollars, excluding the rover ($171M real year $). Due to this fact, Mars Pathfinder was much more of a design-to-cost project than previous JPL missions.

The baseline budget for Pathfinder was based upon a grass roots cost estimate, and was formalized and presented at the Design, Implementation and Cost Review held in July, 1993. The budget was based on a product oriented work breakdown structure. The development baseline was scoped at $131 million, with $40 million held in reserve. The project reserve was planned in detail and was time-phased throughout the project based upon estimated time of need. The high level of planned reserves was primarily due to the risks associated with developing the unique entry, descent, landing system, the new avionics and software approach, the high technology telecommunications subsystem and the complexity involved with the mechanical assembly and test of the three-in-one spacecraft design.

The Pathfinder project benefited from existing JPL multimission infrastructure, which permitted the Ground Data System and Mission Operations development to be completed for under $10 million, a substantial reduction from what had been spent historically for missions of similar scope. It also used heritage from the Cassini Project to help reduce cost and schedule in the AIM and Telecom subsystems.

Prior to budget updates, each account budget would be reviewed and pre-negotiated with project management prior to preparation of the formal budget submittals. Guidelines and target budget amounts were developed and submitted to each technical manager. An important factor in the budgeting process was the openness and honesty of the technical managers in surfacing issues affecting the budget. If proposed changes in an account budget were identified, the budget would be reviewed again, leading to either an increase or decrease.

Budgets at the cost account level were initiated and updated electronically using the JPL Resource Cost Planner (RCP) system. This system allowed for the detailed planning of workforce and cost elements for each account within the work breakdown structure, and roll-up summaries of plans at the subsystem, system and project level. This system was networked so that budget updates could be performed by Cognizant Account Managers, and then be analyzed, adjusted and approved by the Financial Manager and Flight System/Project Manager.

The project also used other electronic financial database tools within the JPL system to track planned vs. actual costs and workforce on a weekly and monthly basis. One monthly report which was particularly useful, was a workforce report that tracked planned vs. actual workforce by individual name for each cost account. This report would detect any individual charging who was not budgeted, or those charging at a higher rate than budgeted. This was very important for controlling costs on a workforce intensive project.

Another important factor in the financial success of Pathfinder was the "designers/builders become the testers/operators" philosophy, which saved documentation, was efficient in the use of people, and reduced risk. The project also worked to efficiently roll-off personnel at designated times. Pathfinder issued formal closures of work authorizations to the JPL technical divisions for each individual immediately after they rolled off to help prevent unnecessary charging. The transition of Pathfinder team members onto other projects at the end of their assignments was not usually a problem because Pathfinder personnel were in great demand around the Lab.

One of the most significant factors in meeting the cost cap was the institution of time-phased "what if" and lien lists, which accounted for real or potential cost growth requests from technical managers for which project reserves might need to be applied. The cognizant technical managers were responsible for identifying current and anticipated items of cost growth to project management, which would then make the decision to record it as "hard" or "soft." An unavoidable or high-probability cost growth item was recorded as a "hard" lien. A low-probability cost growth request with sufficient merit was recorded as a "soft" lien. A running report was maintained which could inform management at any point in time about the total amount of encumbered reserves vs. total reserves. This tool was extremely helpful in being able to status project reserve usage, as well as helping to forecast the amount and rate of reserve usage downstream.

The Pathfinder project also found innovative ways to save money for the project. For example, the Flight System Manager and Financial Manager initiated a system for generating Memorandums of Understanding (MOU's) for spare hardware transfers between Mars Pathfinder and other JPL projects, resulting in approximately $750,000 in cost credits for Pathfinder. This is a win/win relationship for both projects, leading to lower costs for Pathfinder, and lower costs and reduced schedule time for the receiving project, which acquired flight qualified hardware without the normal procurement and testing lead time and lot set-up costs. The practice of selling hardware to other projects was not without risk, since if Pathfinder had experienced trouble later, the hardware might have been needed. The MOU's had a provision for returning hardware or replacing it if Pathfinder later required it.

The project also used JPL accounting changes to its advantage by applying a reduced burden rate to Pathfinder resident field personnel at Cape Canaveral during the launch campaign, which resulted in a $300,000 savings.

Another strategy that was significant in maintaining financial control were the high percentage of fixed price contracts that were negotiated with our industry partners. This limited the amount of procurement cost growth experienced by the project.

The project also held Monthly Management Reviews (MMR's), where project management would review in detail the status of cost and schedule performance for each element of the project.

The bottom line is that Pathfinder completed its development approximately $300K under the NASA cost cap without reducing its original scope of work.

APPENDIX XII.B
MARS PATHFINDER PROJECT

PROJECT CONTRACT/PROCUREMENT MANAGEMENT

Contract and Procurement management on Mars Pathfinder was part of a new way of doing business at JPL. Although Pathfinder was awarded as a JPL in-house development, there were significant portions of the work that were performed by our industry partners. Thus, there was an important need to develop a sound procurement plan and implementation.

A Hardware Acquisition Team was established to provide end-to-end tracking and problem solving on subcontracts and other procurements. The team was led by a senior technical person from the Pathfinder project staff (designated Hardware Acquisition Team Manager) and a Procurement Manager from the JPL Procurement Division. These managers were accessible to the entire team for status and resolution on procurement issues. Other members of the Hardware Acquisition Team consisted of JPL contract technical managers, procurement negotiators and project element managers (responsible for delivering hardware). Regularly scheduled monthly meetings were held with each participating division, where each procurement status would be reviewed. These meetings were supplemented by weekly follow-up meetings when necessary.

The project also conducted RFP Pre-ship Reviews for major procurements. Pathfinder used a "concurrent engineering" approach in these meetings, whereby all interested parties (including those needed for approval) were in the meeting to review the RFP's and resolve any outstanding issues. Taking this approach saved a tremendous amount of review time, and helped eliminate unnecessary cost driver requirements. ...

A major contributor to completing the development under the cost cap was the ability of project management and the acquisition team to negotiate a high percentage of fixed-price contracts with industry in an environment which has historically executed cost-plus contracts.

101

Approximately 70% of major procurements on Pathfinder were fixed price. This reduced the financial risk to the project considerably.

There was also an electronic parts expert from Mission Assurance assigned as Parts Manager who was responsible for the procurements and deliveries of small electronic parts for the project. This freed up the acquisition team to focus on the major subcontracts and other large procurements. Many smaller procurements on the project were purchased under blanket requisitions, which also saved a significant amount of processing time.

Chapter XIII

Project Scheduling

Sam was worried about the availability of the resources at the times they would be needed. The review of the total resources available in the family revealed that there were more than anticipated but so many of them were obligated to daily routine that the remaining pool seemed tight. It was time to analyze more carefully exactly what the requirements would be by day and adjust the schedule to meet the availability.

INTRODUCTION

For many inexperienced project managers, project scheduling and project schedules are among the least understood aspects of projects. This is an interesting anomaly as we are constantly engaged in scheduling in our daily life. Much can be learned about project scheduling from reflecting on simple projects undertaken by ourselves, alone or as part of the family.

When doing a project alone, the implications of resource availability are abundantly clear. Paraphrasing Pogo, "We have recognized the resource limitation; it is me." We learn that there are often perturbations to resource availability, sometimes dictated by our spouse or family. We learn that the simple act of scheduling a task leads to a greater likelihood that it will be done, especially if it is a task that we are not especially anxious to undertake. We soon learn to group different tasks to enable us to perform them more efficiently. For example, applying finish—paint, stain, varnish—requires considerable make-ready and put-away effort. The environment needs to be dust free, arrangements must be made to protect other items in the area (especially if spraying) and tools such as brushes or spray guns must be cleaned up afterwards. The OC has learned well that planning in considerable detail can facilitate scheduling tasks to gain such efficiencies.

When doing a project as a family we become even more aware of the conflicts for resources and the desirability of cooperation among various individuals, i.e., a team approach. For example, a simple weekend outing starts with personal hygiene in the bathroom. Most families can relate to the problems of utilizing a single bathroom. Not only can young people take an interminably long time to shower, they may deplete the supply of hot water in the process, thus further delaying the next person. Consideration of all the tasks that are required just to get everyone in the car, ready to go, leads to a realization of the complexity of and need for scheduling.

While undertaking a major do-it-yourself project of adding two bedrooms to our house, the OC was well aware of some other aspects of scheduling. Various members of the family were capable of performing some of the tasks. In general, they were only available on weekends. Thus, to take maximum advantage of these resources required some scheduling of other tasks. To begin with, a task that was to be performed by another family member had to be available to be done on the planned weekend. That meant that several preceding tasks had to be completed prior to the weekend. The materials and equipment required for their task had to be available. The space in which the work was to be done had to be clear. Thus, to effectively utilize these resources, the OC was required to accomplish certain tasks prior to the weekend.

In building a house, the same technique was used. Periodically, a detailed project network diagram (PND) was developed for the work to be accomplished in the next few weeks. Each activity was coded as to the best resource (skill level, least cost, and so on) to perform that activity. Often additional activities were identified that were necessary to ensure that a specific activity could be done at all or be done more efficiently. Several advantages were gained from this process. Generally, we were able to use the least cost resource to perform an activity. We were able to have the tools, material, and work space available before the activity started so there were no delays. Perhaps the subtlest advantage was the opportunity to benefit from "carpe diem." In spite of the best-laid plans and schedules, things do not always go as planned on a project. The weather is uncooperative. A supplier does not deliver as scheduled. A worker is unexpectedly absent. By having the major activities clearly scheduled and by constantly updating the PND, we were able to adapt quickly to schedule perturbations and minimize the unproductive time for the resources.

Perhaps the most important lesson is the realization that accomplishing a project on time and within budget is primarily a function of how well resources are utilized. This is more than adequate justification for understanding the concepts of scheduling and ensuring that your project is scheduled well and performed to that schedule to the extent possible.

Thus, from these simple projects, a lot of lessons can be learned about scheduling. Most of all, it becomes clear that calculation of early and late start and finish times is merely preparation for scheduling.

WHAT IS SCHEDULING?

First, what is a project schedule? *A Guide to the Project Management Body of Knowledge (PMBOK® Guide) – 2000 Edition* defines a project schedule as "the planned dates for performing activities and the planned dates for meeting milestones" (Project Management Institute 2000, 206). Thus, it is a statement of intent. It may be more than that. Note that included in this definition are "the planned dates for meeting milestones." In general, milestone dates are more important than other events in a project. A milestone is defined as "a significant event in the project, usually completion of a major deliverable" (Project Management Institute 2000, 203). Thus, while there may be some flexibility on planned dates for most activities, there is often very little flexibility for a milestone. They generally represent a commitment comparable to project completion. Sometimes, milestones are more demanding on scheduling than project completion. Failure to have all necessary activities completed prior to a high-level executive review of the project to date can sometimes be more serious than not having all activities completed by the scheduled project completion date.

Schedules are developed by "analyzing activity sequences, activity durations, and resource requirements to create the project schedule" (Project Management Institute 2000, 34). Inputs to schedule development are identified as "project network diagrams, activity duration estimates, resource requirements, resource pool description, calendars, constraints, assumptions, leads and lags, risk management plan, and activity attributes" (Project Management Institute 2000, 73–75). The implications of these two sentences could be the subject of a book. We will limit our discussion to fit into this chapter.

A major tool used in scheduling resources is the "resource profile." It shows graphically the number of units of a given resource required on each day of the project. (See Figure XIII.2, A Typical Resource Profile.) Using this information it is possible to move activities in time to reduce the maximum resource requirement for any given time period.

OBJECTIVES OF SCHEDULING

The most important objective of scheduling is to ensure the *feasibility of completing the project by the required date*. This is most vivid when considering the launch of a space mission to Mars. There is a very short window of time during which the relationship between Earth and Mars makes such a mission possible. The next window might be years away. It is also vivid when considering the launch of a new product. There may be a trade show at which it is critical to display the new product. Failure to meet that date could lead to economic failure of the product. Less obvious is the satisfaction with the project by the client, a major factor in determining the likelihood of repeat business. Not to be overlooked is the importance of timely project completion to the career of the project manager.

Project cost is directly related to the effective use of resources. Using the right resource to perform an activity avoids unnecessary costs. Summing all the costs of the project ensures that it is feasible to complete the project within budget limitations.

Availability of resources when needed ensures timely performance. Availability of the right resources minimizes costs for performing an activity. Availability of sufficient resources enables the use of the best methods for performing an activity. Knowing the availability, or unavailability, of key resources minimizes the possibility of delays while awaiting critical decisions or approvals. Making the best use of scarce or expensive resources minimizes delays due to bottlenecks at these resources.

Coordination of participants ensures that all participants are playing the same music. A project team without adequate coordination is like an orchestra warming up before a concert. It does not make beautiful music. A well-coordinated project team builds its own enthusiasm and focus for the project.

Ability to measure performance is dependent on a carefully constructed PND and a realistic schedule. Without a meaningful measure of performance there is no basis for determining where corrective action is required or what corrective actions are appropriate. This is one of the major differences between modern project management (MPM) and the old way of doing things. In the past, if there was a suspicion that the project was in trouble, the corrective action was often to "put everyone on overtime," an expensive and often dysfunctional solution. With MPM, which includes effective scheduling, it is feasible to determine where problems exist and determine which of many alternatives provides the best solution. Often this is not overtime.

Effective adaptation to circumstances (i.e., carpe diem) is much easier because the effect on other parts of the project can be readily assessed and changes made. This minimizes the unnecessary costs of unproductive time.

TYPES OF SCHEDULING

There are three basic types of scheduling; time-constrained scheduling, resource-constrained scheduling, and critical chain scheduling. We will use the project defined in Figure XIII.1, A Project for Scheduling, to illustrate each of these.

Time-Constrained Scheduling

This approach should be used when time is the most important objective for the project. The major assumption is that whatever resources may be required in a given period can be made available. It does include a leveling process to minimize the peak resources required and may include a capability to minimize the variations in resource requirements that can result from unadjusted critical path type calculations. Both of these tend to minimize the costs of hiring, firing, training, and orientation.

Resource requirements are best understood when they are depicted graphically as a resource profile as shown in Figure XIII.2, A Typical Resource Profile. The Gantt chart on the top depicts the schedule for a set of activities requiring a given resource. Above each bar is the number of units of that resource required by that activity. The bottom graph simply depicts the sum of those units of resource required on any given day. The x-axis portrays the time periods during which the project is in process. The y-axis portrays the number of units of the resource required. Thus, on day 4, activity B requires 3 units and activity C requires 3 units for a total of 6 units. In the Gantt chart, each activity is shown by a bar extending from its earliest start to its latest finish. The resources required by an activity are shown by the numbers in the bar on the days that activity is scheduled.

Note the characteristic curve. Relatively few resources are required in the early stages of the project, increasing to a peak, and then decreasing until the project is completed. First, it is important to understand two basic resource profiles, the early schedule and the late schedule.

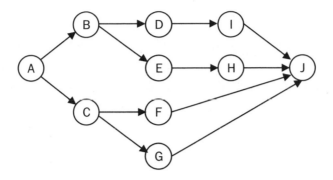

Act	Foll's	Dur	EARLY		LATE		Slack	Res's Req'd
			St	Fin	St	Fin		
A	B, C	3	0	3	0	3	0	2
B	D, E	2	3	5	3	5	0	3
C	F, G	5	3	8	5	10	2	3
D	I	2	5	7	10	12	5	4
E	H	6	5	11	5	11	0	2
F	J	4	8	12	10	14	2	4
G	J	2	8	10	12	14	4	3
H	I	3	11	14	11	14	0	2
I	J	2	7	9	12	14	5	2
J	–	2	14	16	14	16	0	3

FIGURE XIII.1

A Project for Scheduling

The early schedule profile simply schedules all activities at their earliest possible times as shown in Figure XIII.3, Early Schedule Resource Profile. This can result in a rapid increase in resources required, a rather high peak requirement, and a rather gradual decline. The peak resource requirement is for 11 units for one day.

In addition to the excessive maximum resource requirement, there are some other problems associated with such a schedule. The rapid increase in resources means that a lot of time is required to orient all those resources and ensure that they are productively employed doing

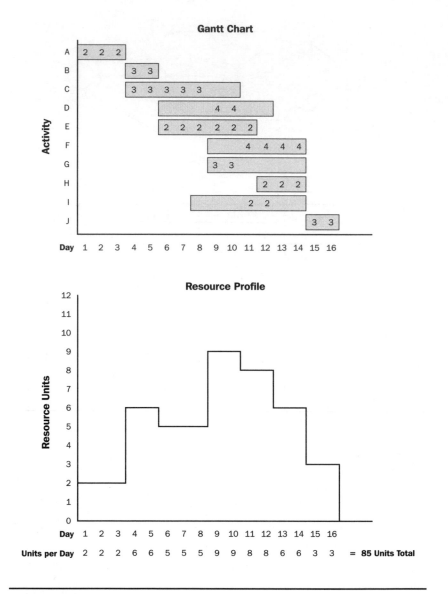

FIGURE XIII.2
A Typical Resource Profile

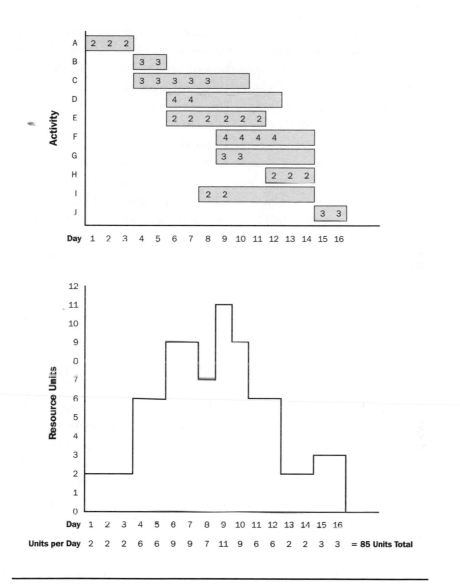

FIGURE XIII.3
Early Schedule Resource Profile

the right things the right way. Rushing through the formative stages of the project provides little time for the project manager and team to think through some of the details of the processes involved. This can often lead to errors, late recognition of opportunities, and excessive rework. Thus, it can be a relatively expensive approach to a project. It is also expensive in terms of the interest on funds employed. Its use should probably be limited to crisis management where human safety or minimizing further loss to physical assets is involved. Even then, crisis planning should be considered before the crisis actually happens. It might be used on a subproject or in the early phase of a project on activities for which the outcome is highly uncertain and the nature of subsequent subprojects or phases of the project are dependent on the outcome.

The late schedule profile simply schedules all activities at their latest possible times as shown in Figure XIII.4, Late Schedule Resource Profile. This results in a more gradual increase in resource requirements, a high peak, and a rapid decrease. The peak resource requirement is for 10 units for one day.

It has other types of problems associated with it. Probably the most serious problem is that all slack is used up before an activity is started. Thus, if any problem occurs in performing an activity, it is likely to delay the project completion. Similarly, all personnel should know exactly what they are to do to minimize the chances of any rework, for that would surely delay the project completion. The major advantage of this approach is the conservation of funds employed and thus, the cost of funds employed. Thus, it might be applicable when the cost of funds involved is relatively high. It might also be used in a competitive situation where it is desired to keep the intentions of the project secret until the last possible moment, such as in warfare or introducing a new product to the market while minimizing the opportunity for competition to react. In any case, there should be very little uncertainty about the time required or the outcome of any of the activities in the project.

Given an understanding of these two alternatives, it is relatively clear that, for most projects, a better alternative is something in between the early and late schedules. It is feasible to start with either. For example, if it is desired to hew to the late schedule, one might examine activities for

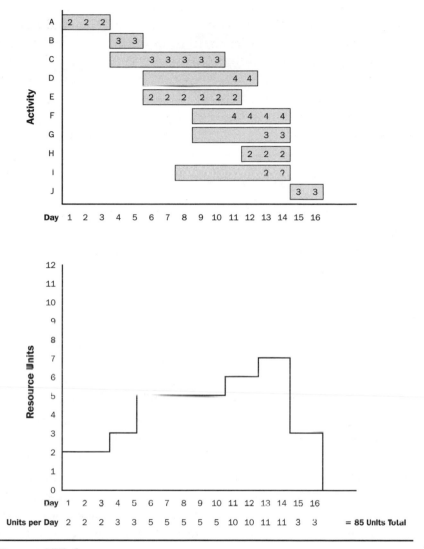

FIGURE XIII.4

Late Schedule Resource Profile

uncertainty and assign them earlier target completion times. Having done this, a recalculation would show further possibilities. It might be reasonable to consider the cost of the individual activities and assign the lowest cost activities to earlier times. Successive iterations of this type

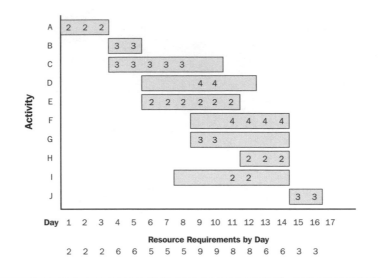

FIGURE XIII.5
Leveled Resource Requirements—Time Constrained

can substantially reduce the peak resource requirements while reducing the risk and delaying the employment of funds.

Alternatively, it may be desired to minimize the risk of being late by starting with the early schedule and delaying activity start and complete times as required. In this case, periods of peak resource requirement are examined to determine which activities are candidates for delaying. Generally, this involves examining the slack on the activities. Those with little or no slack should be scheduled at their early times. The greater the slack, the more an activity can be delayed. This is illustrated in Figure XIII.5, Leveled Resource Requirements—Time Constrained. Later, we discuss the simple procedure by which this was derived.

Using a computer program to perform the calculations and portray the resource requirements on successive iterations, it is possible to reduce the peaks rather quickly. Alternatively, the computer program may contain logic that makes the decisions and presents a leveled resource schedule very quickly. Care must be exercised in using such a capability to be sure that the decisions are appropriate, given your project and your objectives. The simplest capabilities may achieve the leveling desired but not schedule activities in the manner you may wish. It may be necessary to lock in the schedule date for the most important activities and let the computer program schedule the rest.

Whatever you do, be sure you understand the logic used in the scheduling process. It may do unexpected things to you if you don't. It has always been the conviction of the OC that *one should never use a computer program to perform a task without understanding the logic the program uses.*

Resource-Constrained Scheduling

Resource-constrained scheduling works in a similar manner except that there are real limits on the number of units of a given resource available, such that the project cannot be completed by its earliest completion date. The project must be scheduled in order to make best use of these resources and to delay the project by the least amount of time. The logic is similar but easily gets more involved such as, when there are two or more activities that can be scheduled, sometimes it works best to schedule a short one requiring several units of the resource and sometimes one of longer duration requiring one or a few units of the resource. It is analogous to stacking rocks to make a rock wall of a specific height. Sometimes it requires trying several alternatives to get the best fit. Figure XIII.6, Resource-Constrained Schedule, illustrates the schedule given a maximum of six units of resource. Note that staying within this limit results in lengthening the project by two days.

Critical Chain Scheduling

A recent concept in project scheduling has generated a great deal of interest and discussion. It is commonly known as Critical Chain Project Management (CCPM). It is really a variation on or extension of Critical Path Method (CPM) as it uses the same PND, the early and late calculations, resource analysis, and so on. It seems most applicable in a new product development environment where the projects are similar and the objectives in scheduling are to complete the project in the shortest possible time and provide reliable estimates of when the

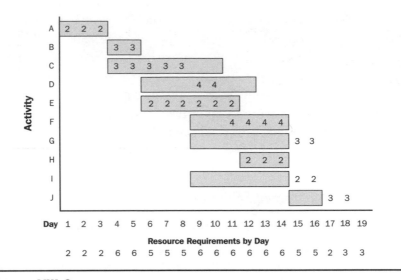

FIGURE XIII.6
Resource-Constrained Schedule

projects will be completed. The former is important as a competitive strategy as the project is often awarded to the organization that can deliver first. The latter is important so the client can be given a delivery date that is very likely to be met. Application on other types of projects has led to reports of success, however, most such reports are anecdotal. Therefore, it is not clear exactly what led to the successes (Leach 2001; Webster 2002).

CCPM recognizes that activity durations are not certain. They have some degree of variability. In most of the CCPM literature, it assumes that the variability is directly related to the duration; specifically that it is 50 percent of the duration, a questionable assumption. There are alternatives to this. Furthermore, it assumes that the estimated duration is the expected value as defined in probability theory, permitting them to be added along a path. There is reason to argue that people tend to estimate the most likely, or most frequently occurring, value. There are alternatives available here.

Critical to this estimating is the expectation that the activities will be performed within their estimated duration most of the time. To the

Activity	A	C	F	G	Path Duration
Durations for CPM	2	5	4	2	= 13 Days
Duration Estimates for CCPM	1	3	3	2	= 9 Days
Variation Estimate for CCPM	0.5	1.5	1.5	1	
Variances Squared	0.25	2.25	2.25	1	= 5.75
Buffer (At One Sigma)					2.4 Days
Path Duration with CCPM					11.4 Days

TABLE XIII.1
Some Concepts of Critical Chain

extent that more time is required, it is absorbed in a buffer. This is a critical assumption if the estimating is to be done by the person who will perform the activity. If that person anticipates a bad consequence should the activity require more time than was estimated, the estimate is likely to be padded to avoid the bad consequences. Thus, for CCPM to be effective, there must be a high degree of trust that management will behave in a manner consistent with getting unpadded estimates. This is a critical assumption in CCPM or any other approach expecting to get unpadded estimates.

Some of the essential concepts of CCPM can be illustrated using the example project. Suppose that analysis indicates that the chain A, C, F, and G form a critical chain. Table XIII.1, Some Concepts of Critical Chain, provides the data to illustrate the differences in applying CCPM.

In the examples up to this point, we have used fixed values for durations, much as if they were commitments. Thus, it is argued quite plausibly that the persons responsible added some padding to their estimates to avoid trouble if they require all their estimated time. Durations under CCPM are assumed to be made without that threat and, therefore, are more realistic. Recognizing that there is a chance of some of these activities taking longer than the estimate, an estimate (50 percent of the duration) is also made for the variation in each of them. Using Central Limit Theorem principles (rather loosely applied), the estimated durations and the variations are added (note, the variations are squared to make them additive). This gives an estimated duration of 9 days for the critical chain and a path duration of 11.4 days, including 2.4 days (square root of 5.75) for the buffer.

The starts and finishes of these activities are not provided to the person responsible for the activity. It is understood that the critical chain activity will get priority over all other work as soon as its predecessor is completed. Furthermore, it is understood that each responsible person will devote full attention to his activity until it is finished (no multi-tasking). If this is done, any activity that consumes extra time will eat into the buffer duration. At some point in buffer reduction, the manager is to take action to ensure it does not get worse. The real benefit is that if an activity is finished in less than its estimated duration, that saving in time is passed on to the next activity, and so on, generally reducing the duration of the total project. So not only is the project scheduled for a shorter time, but also any time saved along the way is retained for early project completion.

CCPM recognizes that in any project, there is likely to be (at least) one resource that is a bottleneck. This resource is identified as the "critical resource." Basically, it should never be idle, as that would delay all projects requiring that resource. To minimize the chances of idle time for the critical resource, an analysis of paths leading to an activity requiring that resource identifies a "critical chain" of activities. The durations for that chain are analyzed for variability and a "buffer" is established at the end of the chain, i.e., just before the activity requiring the critical resource. This provides some assurance that the critical chain will be completed before it is anticipated that the critical resource will be ready to work on the activity of concern and that the critical resource will not be without work to perform.

CCPM recognizes that projects seem to require more time to complete than is predicted by the critical path. Some activities exceed their estimated duration, resulting in delays to succeeding activities. Using conventional CPM, when activities are completed early, seldom are the time savings passed on to succeeding activities by performing them earlier than scheduled. This results in a bias for projects to be late as compared to their anticipated completion date. To overcome this bias, CCPM introduces the "relay-race" mentality. In this, an activity on a critical chain is to be started as soon as all the preceding activities are completed. Thus, if the preceding activities are completed earlier than expected, those gains are captured for the project. CCPM advocates argue that using priorities in the typical manner has not been effective, whereas an activity identified as on a critical chain is unambiguously given highest priority. It is assumed that any conflicts between two or more activities identified as on critical chains are resolved by some higher authority.

Also essential to the relay-race mentality is a major change in communicating expectations to the performers of the activities. In conventional CPM, the performer is provided a start and finish date for each activity. Since past behavior of management has often been punishment for completing an activity early (by expecting it all the time), seldom are the early completions reported. Furthermore, progress is typically reported in terms of percent completion, a figure that has, in more than a few instances, been determined by the percentage of the estimated duration that has been used to date. Thus, the opportunity to save time has not been realized. CCPM does not publish the start or completion dates but, rather, provides the person responsible for an activity the relevant information needed to determine the status of all immediately preceding activities. Then, with this knowledge, the activity is expected to be started as soon as the predecessors are finished and report progress by indicating when they will complete their activity. This requires a high degree of trust in the project team member by management, and vice versa.

Thus, the organizational climate, as reflected in the behavior of both management and the project team members, seems to be crucial to the success of CCPM. Indeed, it is questionable whether CCPM should be adopted without the commitment to such an organizational climate.

While this is a very brief discussion of CCPM, it does convey the essentials. It is in its early stage of adoption. Many of its features will be adapted and incorporated into the standard practice of MPM. Questions remaining unanswered at this time will be resolved. In the meantime, it should be used with caution, recognizing the assumptions, some of which are tenuous. Nevertheless, some of its features can be adapted and adopted, in part, with considerable benefits in project performance. For a thorough discussion of CCPM see Leach (2001).

CONSIDERATIONS IN SCHEDULING

While we are all experienced in scheduling projects—it is inherent in daily life—most of us have not reflected on the many considerations we apply. Generally we approach scheduling in an ad hoc manner and apply many of these considerations subconsciously.

Before discussing these considerations let us think about some bad practices. In discussing scheduling with a representative of a major think-tank operation, he explained how he liked to schedule. He liked to work at a chalkboard. First he would put the project start date on the far left and the desired/required project completion date at the far right. Then he would divide the board horizontally into equal time units, depending on the overall time available in which to perform the project. If there were major milestones between the start and finish, he would reflect a bit and put those in at specific dates. Then he would start drawing bars to represent activities to be accomplished to perform the project. Again, he would reflect on the time available based on the project start and finish and milestone dates, allocating time to the activity based on his judgment as to the time that was available in which to perform the activity. The chalkboard was convenient for this, as it allowed him to revise those activity durations in order to "crowd" all the work into the time frame available.

If this sounds like the way you schedule projects, cease and desist immediately! This is a sure path to project failure! Just some of the problems with this approach are:

❏ Activity durations determined in this manner have no relationship to the actual time required to perform them!
❏ There is no way of knowing what activities are really on the critical path!
❏ There is no consideration of the resources required in total or by time period!
❏ There is no consideration of the minimum cost to perform activities!

Indeed, a project schedule developed in this manner is nothing but wishful thinking!

In case you did not notice the use of exclamation marks above, take heed, as they are a polite way of expressing expletives that the editor would delete. That is how strongly the OC feels about this approach! Now, let's discuss some more rational considerations.

Activity Characteristics

Availability for Scheduling

Effective scheduling is enhanced by flexibility, as represented by the number of activities that are available to be scheduled at any point in the scheduling process. In a serial project, when one activity is completed, there is only one activity available for scheduling. If the number of units or type of resource varies from one activity to the next, there will be a series of changes in the number or type of resources required as the project progresses. A burst node provides flexibility to select the next activity to schedule based on its duration, number of units of resource required, or other criterion. Thus, when scheduling, it is useful to consider the number of activities available for scheduling and the number of activities that will be added to that availability list by each of the alternatives. Thus, the scheduler can elect to increase the flexibility by selecting a burst node with the greatest number of followers.

It is possible to develop information that will aid in making selections from the availability list by ranking the activities. This provides insights into the flexibility in scheduling at different stages in the PND. It is explained in Appendix XIII.A.

Activity Dimensions

It may seem strange to think of an activity as having dimensions like a brick. However, when scheduling, it is useful to consider the process like laying up a brick wall. Since bricks tend to be uniform in size, perhaps it is better to think of laying up a rock wall. One protocol in laying up a rock wall is to place those that are largest on the bottom and use smaller ones to fill in to achieve a uniform height of the wall. This is also applicable in scheduling project activities.

The two most important dimensions of an activity are the duration and units of resource required. Thus, using the "largest first" decision rule, the activity that is in the availability list that requires the longest time or the most units of resource should be scheduled first. Note, there are several similar decision criteria that can be derived, such as the activity having the largest resource-days requirement, the activity requiring the most scarce or highest cost resource, the activity with the greatest uncertainty associated with its successful performance, etc. Alternatively, it may be desirable to delay the scheduling of the activity having the highest total cost, or at least scheduling it at or nearer to its latest dates.

As the scheduling process proceeds, smaller activities can be used to fill in between the activities with the larger dimensions to most effectively utilize the resources available.

This discussion assumes that each activity requires only one resource type. This is often not realistic. Many activities require several different types of resources. This substantially increases the complexity of the scheduling process. One way to deal with this is to prioritize the resources as to criticality in scheduling. This can be done informally or it can be done rigorously by computer. A rigorous approach is discussed in Appendix XIII.A.

Work Content

One model of the work content of an activity is to simply multiply the duration by the resource application rate. Implicit in this model is an assumption about the methods and technologies to be used in performing the activity. Most activities can be performed using a number of alternative methods and technologies. Sometimes the choice is obvious but sometimes it is important to examine the economics, as well as other considerations, to select the best for your particular project.

Methods

Methods that are employed on a task not only determine the time for and cost of performing the task, but may also determine when it can be performed. For example, in the extreme, had the processing plant for the Endicott Oil Field been constructed on site, both the total duration and cost would have been greater. The weather would have hindered progress and some of steps required to mitigate these weather effects would have added considerable extra costs. On a less grand scale, the introduction of jigs and fixtures where an activity involves repetitive tasks can reduce both time and cost. It is a general observation of the OC that many craftspeople and other project personnel have little or no specific training in the industrial engineering techniques for improving work methods.

Technologies

Technologies employed can make a considerable difference in the time and cost of performing an activity. For example, in pouring concrete on a construction job, a choice could be made between using a bucket and crane versus a pumper. Selection of the programming language on a computer system project may have either positive or negative effects on the project. The early phases of coding will probably go slower on a new language, speeding up as the project progresses. One language may result in less total code to be written. On the other hand, a new language may result in some inefficient code due to lack of experience, there are likely to be more errors, and, if there are any bugs in the new language, there could be delays in resolving them or determining suitable workarounds. A careful analysis of the costs, duration, and uncertainties must be made. Often there may be an impact on the quality of the product of the project.

Real Work

It may seem strange to speak of "real work" in a project. It implies that there is something that might be called "false work." The concept here is derived from what is generally referred to as "assembly line balancing," the assigning of work elements to work stations on a progressive line. It is easily recognized that, if a worker is assigned a set of tasks, each of which requires using a different tool, the worker will spend considerable time putting one tool away and getting the next one. In this setting, putting a tool away may mean putting it in a holster, and getting the next tool may mean getting it out of a holster. While these may seem trivial to most project persons, when these are repeated 50 to 100 times per hour, they represent a significant part of the total work content. On the other hand, if the worker were assigned only tasks requiring the same tool, there would be no time required to put a tool away or get it out. Thus, all the work performed would result in a change of the product being worked upon. In line balancing parlance these are known as "make-ready" and "put-away" work elements. This is also a well-known phenomenon in job shops, leading to sequencing work to minimize the total set-up costs.

The same phenomena are involved in project work. On a construction project, building a scaffold does not change the product of the project. It simply facilitates the work that will be performed, such as laying blocks, while the worker stands on the scaffold. Suppose the block wall is going to be stuccoed. There are at least two alternative plans regarding the scaffold. The scaffold can be left in place until the stuccoing is done or it can be removed after erecting the block wall and rebuilt for the stuccoing. The erecting of the scaffold is make-ready work and the removal is put-away work. Clearly, the make-ready/put-away work will be minimized by the first alternative. In construction, this is often referred to as set up and tear down.

The same phenomenon occurs in intellectual activities. For example, a person writing a report has to get the necessary references out, find the file for the report, and "initialize the brain," i.e., internalize the subject of the report, the relevant facts, the relevant politics, and other aspects of the report, *and* get in the mood, before actually putting the first word on paper or on the computer. Any interruption, be it a phone call, lunch, a meeting, or whatever, can require a repeat of some of these elements before productive writing starts again. If the report cannot be completed in one sitting, the "mood" may change quickly and it may be necessary to refile everything. This is especially true if we reach the end of a day or week. The longer the absence from the task, the more relearning will be required. Thus, there is make-ready and put-away work associated with intellectual activity. Interestingly, getting in the mood to write seems to be the most difficult and time-consuming effort for this OC.

From this it is clear that, to the extent possible, work should be scheduled to minimize the make-ready and put-away work as much as possible and, by so doing, maximize the amount of work that can be called "real work." This implies not starting significant tasks near the end of a day or week. Rather, start them at the beginning of a day or week and minimize the times that make ready and put away recur.

Recognizing these opportunities requires two things in scheduling. First, it is almost essential that subsets of activities be scheduled into a schedule block, for example, a block of all activities for which the scaffold is necessary or desirable. Schedule this subset of activities and then schedule the block as a unit. Secondly, the ability to utilize the frequent or occasional small block of time at the end of a day or week illustrates the advantage of having a punch list of small activities that can be used to productively utilize these blocks of time.

Multitasking

One of the essential concepts in CCPM is avoiding multitasking of resources. In general, this is a very desirable objective. CCPM literature emphasizes how this lengthens the durations of most projects, if not all, by consuming a greater elapsed time for the activities being worked on. In addition, few people are unfamiliar with the notion that once you get going well on an activity, you progress faster if you are not interrupted. Indeed, there is make-ready and put-away work as discussed above. In fact, it seems to be worse on project activities that involve critical thinking. One must recall where they were when they last stopped on the activity, get in the proper frame of mind, and overcome the inertia that is often involved, especially if the activity is not a favorite.

Thus, multitasking should be avoided to the extent possible. Often, the major deterrent to avoiding multitasking is convincing management that it is dysfunctional.

On the other hand, sometimes there is a limit to how fast one can progress on a given activity. In those cases, it is certainly desirable to work on another activity, so long as there is a clear understanding of priorities between activities, and work on lower level priority activities will be stopped to permit return to the top priority activity as soon as it is available again.

The relevancy of this is more clear when the objective of CCPM is clearly understood. The objective of CCPM is to complete the highest priority project in the shortest possible time. It is claimed that, as a result of using the principles of CCPM, all projects are completed in less time and that more projects can be processed by the same resources. What has not been researched is what are the unintended consequences of pursuing this objective, seemingly at the exclusion of all other objectives.

Technical Criticality

A project should be planned to provide a high probability of achieving time, cost, and performance objectives. Activities should be included to enhance these probabilities. It may be useful to explicitly identify some of these activities as to how critical they are to project success. For example, we might categorize activities as must do, should do, would be desirable to do, and could do. It would be unnecessary to explicitly identify the must do activities or precedences. The other three categories should be identified so that they might be eliminated, modified, or delayed if necessary to properly schedule the project. Similarly, they could be ranked on a three-point scale identifying their importance in achieving technical objectives. Any of these actions have the potential of increasing risks on the project and so, therefore, should always be identified and documented to provide the rationale for the action in the event of adverse consequences. These bits of information might be used to reduce project costs or total duration, or to draw your attention to activities you should monitor closely.

Precedence Criticality

Similarly, precedences should be included to enhance these probabilities. It may be useful to explicitly identify some of these activities and precedences as to how critical they are to project success. For example, they might also be categorized on a scale such as must do, should do, would be desirable to do, and could do. As before, three categories should be identified so that they might be eliminated, modified, or delayed, if necessary, to properly schedule the project. These actions also have the potential of increasing risks on the project and should always be identified and documented.

Resource Characteristics

Appropriate Resources

Assigning appropriate resources to perform a specific activity is essential to achieve both effectiveness and efficiency. The wrong resource will often result in errors, more time to perform the activity, greater cost, or all three. Errors will result from lack of knowledge, skill, or experience. These will also lead to more time required and often to greater cost. Frequently, a resource that is overly capable will result in a higher billing rate that results in greater cost. The latter may be an appropriate action if the activity is critical, either in time or some other sense. The OC saved considerably in labor costs for building a house by paying close attention to this aspect of resource scheduling.

Available and Ready to Use

Ensuring that all resources are available and ready to use cannot be ignored. Anyone who has ever done a do-it-yourself project has surely experienced the frustration of discovering that a minor item, such as the right size of screw, was missing (probably after all stores were closed, late on Sunday afternoon) and therefore the project could not be finished. On more significant projects, such a discovery could lead to significant delays and considerable costs. Thus, while the management by exception principle is quite useful, management of the trivial may prove essential, also.

Attention must be given to human resources to ensure that they will be available when needed, have the appropriate skills or are trained, and that they have the necessary tools and equipment. Materials need to be checked to ensure appropriateness. Equipment must be maintained to ensure that it is operational when needed. Each of these requires the time and efforts of someone—time and efforts that can easily be overlooked in considering total resources and costs.

Similar versus Unique Resources

The difference between the scheduling of similar resources versus unique resources is subtle. For similar resources we are typically concerned with the number of units required per time period. Thus, we may be concerned with how many carpenters, welders, pipe fitters, or the like are available versus required per time period. For unique resources, we are typically concerned with what percent of the time that a single unit of resource is committed. It is not uncommon for a unique resource to be assigned to work on one task four hours per day and another task for two hours per day. Thus, they would be "loaded" at 75 percent. Sometimes the loading may be greater than 100 percent implying that the resource will have to work overtime. Note that multitasking is not recommended if it can be avoided.

The unique resource problem is further exacerbated when considering the use of alternative resources, either human or nonhuman.

Alternative Resources

One of the most complex types of decisions is the consideration of alternative resources. There are often multiple technologies and methods for performing specific activities. When considering the availability of resources, it may be relevant to choose a technology or method that is less than optimum simply because the resources are more readily available, especially at the time they are needed. The essence of this problem is exemplified by the "drafting room problem" mentioned earlier, a special case of the assignment problem.

The assignment problem is quite simple as presented in operations research/management science (OR/MS) texts and articles, as it assumes that both the tasks and resources are all immediately available or, alternatively, that the time for starting the tasks is immaterial. Unfortunately, in the drafting room problem time is relevant. Furthermore, the tasks and the resources are not immediately available. Therefore, this becomes a three-dimensional problem for which a solution technique did not exist and may still not exist. The dimensions are the date of availability for the task to be performed, the date of availability of the resource, and the relative efficiency of each resource to perform each task. The supervisor of the drafting room could consider each of these three dimensions mentally but we did not know how to solve it on a computer even if we had all the data. Getting all the data was another problem. Since the problem was three dimensional, data was required for each cell in the matrix, a formidable task for the supervisor. However, the mental solution only required the supervisor to roughly estimate values for a subset of the cells where decisions were relevant. Thus, the effort to schedule the drafting room evolved into a tool for the supervisor to check the schedule he developed mentally for logical consistency with the PND data.

Automatic computer scheduling seems very attractive. Certainly some project management software packages have such capabilities.

One of the earliest such packages was called Resource Allocation and Multi-Project Scheduling (RAMPS), developed by CEIR around 1963 (Moshman, Johnson, and Larsen 1963). While its features were attractive, it required too much information to be input to make it a desirable program to use. There are some real limits to the desirability of depending on the computer to answer all of your scheduling problems. The preceding and, especially, the following discussion illustrate how many things there are to consider in developing a really good schedule.

There are many opportunities for consideration of alternative resources on project activities. It is probably unreasonable to expect anyone to quantify all those opportunities for a realistic project. However, you should always be looking for opportunities to consider alternative resources, technologies, and methodologies when scheduling a project.

Adaptive Scheduling

Adaptive scheduling is a term applied to a wordier expression, "taking advantage of the opportunity of the moment" or carpe diem. It stems from a realistic acceptance of Murphy's Law, "If something can go wrong, it will." Indeed, it is the OC's firm opinion that Murphy has a permanent roost on every project manager's shoulder. People will not show up as scheduled. Equipment will break down at the worst time. A sudden change in weather will preclude performing some activity. The necessary screw will be missing. The well-prepared project manager will be conscious of the alternative uses of the resources that are available and will be able to make the necessary decisions to redeploy those resources to productive efforts with the minimum delay. It can be awesome how fast the bill for unused resources can build up in such circumstances. It can make a substantial dent in project reserves.

Alternatively, occasionally Murphy will be outwitted and an opportunity to accomplish something advantageously will present itself. For example, another project may be stymied and have excess resources that are available cheap, if not free. A subcontractor may be delayed in moving to a next job and offer to perform some work at a good price. A piece of equipment may arrive early and be available at low (or no) cost for a period. The ability to react quickly to utilize this opportunity can result in budget improvements, if not project duration reduction, also.

The single most important technique to assist in this is having available a "to-do" list of work that is available to be worked on at any given time. When resources are unexpectedly available, reference to this list can result in quick and effective decisions. The second useful technique is to schedule in such a way as to ensure there are a suitable number of available activities on that list. The third technique is to "manage by walking around" so you are intimately familiar with the status of the project and know what is really possible.

To permit quick response, the project manager, and probably all the key managers, need a report showing the work that is available to be done at any point in time. It needs to be sorted by plannable constraining factors such as materials, equipment, information, and so on, as well as unplannable constraints such as weather, human resources, and the like. Those activities or tasks that have no plannable constraints should be first, followed by those that do have constraints. The project manager should regularly review this list to attempt to move activities or tasks up to ready to be done. Then, when the unexpected happens, quick decisions can be made, action taken, and the resources diverted to productive status as quickly as possible.

Any of the above considerations can apply to either human or non-human resources.

Special Considerations in Human Resource Scheduling

Some special considerations in scheduling human resources include:
- ❑ *Work periods and workday length* can be quite varied. The normal might be five eight-hour days Monday through Friday. The hours could be more or less and the days different. It is not unusual to have four ten-hour days. These might be accompanied by three twelve-hour days if a seven-day-a-week operation is desired.
- ❑ *Shift patterns*, in addition to length, may vary substantially. For example, they might normally include two, four-day, ten-hour shifts with four-hour periods for equipment maintenance accompanied by limited work on a three-day, twelve-hour shift for some crafts.

❑ *Overtime allowances* may vary from one project to the next and between different crafts on the same project. It is not uncommon for specific union contracts to be negotiated for major projects. Normally we think of overtime as increasing costs. A careful examination of the cost drivers for labor may indicate that the first hour of overtime may be at substantially less than average hourly costs for straight time. This is because labor costs often include a substantial amount for benefits that are applicable only to the forty-hour workweek. For some equipment the overtime cost may be less if there is a daily (monthly or weekly) rate.

❑ *Physical and physiological* constraints are generally dealt with as human factors or human engineering. An example of such a consideration is the limitation of parcel size and weight by many parcel delivery services. These services are designed to be performed by one person acting alone with no special equipment. Thus, it makes sense to limit the weight that can be safely carried by one person. A physical problem that has received considerable attention lately is carpal tunnel syndrome, perhaps a consequence of computer usage. In addition, there are a variety of capabilities of humans that have limits, or at least reductions in performance levels. A broad knowledge of human engineering concepts can improve sensitivity to these factors.

❑ *Psychological* factors can have an effect on the general efficiency and attitudes of humans. One study dealt with, in effect, the impact of boredom, job variety, and other such factors. It found that within electrician tasks, people employed solely as wire pullers became bored and both less efficient and less concerned about the quality of their work. Many such lessons about human behavior on projects can be imputed by more extensive research in mass production industries, such as the famous Western Electric studies.

❑ *Social/Cultural* constraints include such things as holidays, some of which require no work and others that entail a premium cost. They may have to be excluded from the project schedule or simply recognized for their premium cost. Many projects employ people from a variety of cultures. The holidays of each must be recognized. Some cultures have unique religious rites for which provisions must be made.

❑ *Legal* constraints include overtime requirements, minority contract requirements, and noise and pollution limitations, especially if they vary by time of day or other such factors. They may also include some implications of Equal Employment Opportunity and labor relations legislation. Some holiday arrangements also have legal implications.

Project Characteristics

There are considerations that are essentially at the project level.

Required Dates

Required dates are a fact of project life. However, they should be evaluated carefully as to whether they are really required, desired, or a remnant of old-fashioned approaches to project management. Required dates may be relevant for many projects. Space missions often have feasible time windows that are short and far between. The success of a new product may be dependent upon introducing it at a trade show. A new facility may be required to produce a new model year product.

Sometimes the required date is simply as soon as possible (ASAP), such as the development of a new medical instrument or medicine necessary to save lives. The restoration of critical infrastructure facilities after a disaster, such as an earthquake or hurricane, must be completed ASAP.

On most projects, however, the driving force leading to target completion dates is simply the desire to start recovering the capital invested in the project and/or receiving the return on investment. On these projects, a more deliberate approach should be taken to determine target completion dates. An executive level project plan, expressed as a PND, should be developed. It should reflect the least cost approach to performing the project. Then, using the time/cost tradeoff model discussed in Chapter XIV, and considering other costs such as interest on invested capital, effect on market share, and other such costs, a target date can be set that truly has the potential of maximizing return on investment. The same approach should be used in setting target dates for major milestones.

The OC foresees a day when an organization will consider its portfolio of projects, its resources available, and other such factors to analyze tradeoffs between projects in setting target dates. Those capabilities need to be developed and would fill another book.

Space

Space required for the performance of work is easily ignored. Often we concentrate on the human resources required for the work. It is well understood that scheduling two or more trades into the same space on a construction project may be asking for problems. Similarly, collocating a noisy activity, even if it only involves telephones ringing frequently, with an intellectually demanding activity can be very dysfunctional. On construction projects, it is often necessary to be careful to provide clearance to install major items of equipment. For example, on a new high school, major concrete beams had to be installed in the center of the structure. It required two 100-ton cranes to lift the beams. Getting the cranes in place and their booms erected required considerable space. Thus, many other activities had to be delayed to provide for this, including completing the pouring of the basement wall where the cranes entered and exited.

Risk

In any scheduling process there are likely to be compromises. For example, it may be desirable to proceed on excavation or writing code before all the specs have been written. Clear recognition of these risk decisions should be documented and evaluated for risk management. Furthermore, a conscious review of the schedule should be made to consider risks that were not recognized in the process of scheduling. It may be relevant to have one or more persons experienced with this type of project review the project plan and schedule before it is given final approval.

Buffers

One way to deal with uncertainty and risk is to provide buffers in the schedule to absorb the perturbations that may occur. CCPM uses buffers extensively to account for the variability of activity durations. Schedulers have long recognized the importance of this by including "water," "cushion," or "contingency" allowances of time. While the theory has been extant for years, seldom has the basis for these allowances been more than an "intelligent guess." With CCPM concepts, combined with Monte Carlo Program Evaluation and Review Technique (PERT), it is both becoming more popular and more rigorous as discussed later under Burst and Merge Nodes.

Project Plan Characteristics

Feasibility

A review may reveal circumstances that lead you to question the feasibility of the schedule. This would be a judgment based on experience both as a project manager and with the particular organization(s) involved. For example, the resources of a certain functional manager may be crucial to the schedule. Past experience with that functional manager may lead to doubts that the resources will be made available at the time required or in sufficient quantities to complete their activities per the schedule. The OC remembers well making a presentation to a top executive committee, making a commitment based on receiving five additional people and then facing the reality when the boss provided 1.5 people for the project.

On the other hand, don't be too quick to reject the project or schedule out of hand. For example, the manager of profit planning approached the OC one day asking for help. It seems that the vice president of finance was not satisfied with receiving the annual profit plan some five months after the start of the model year. He wanted the profit plan no later than the beginning of the model year. The manager of profit planning wanted the OC to assist in developing a project plan for the annual profit-planning project that would prove it was impossible to take five months out of the process. The OC agreed to help but only on the condition that the objective of the project planning effort would be to see if we could take the five months out. The first project plan took three months out of the schedule. The next year the other two months were taken out. That made both the vice president and the manager of profit planning happy. Clearly the OC was happy too.

If you are short on experience on the project you are scheduling, it may be wise to ask a more experienced project manager to take a look at your plan and schedule with you or to conduct a formal project plan review relying on the experience and wisdom of several senior project managers.

Burst and Merge Nodes

The simplest PND is strictly serial, i.e., one activity following another. As the PND gets more complicated, we start to see activities with more than one follower or more than one predecessor. These are called burst nodes and merge nodes, respectively. In general, burst nodes are desirable from a scheduling point of view, as they make more than one activity available for scheduling, thus creating more alternatives to find the activity that best utilizes available resources. Burst nodes typically occur following major progress meetings, for example, when the purpose of the meeting is to make a go/no-go decision on continuing the project.

Merge points are of greater interest, however, as they have some different characteristics. They often are major milestones or major review meetings involving high-level executives. An example of the latter is new product review by the executive styling committee. This type of milestone is probably more significant in scheduling because of the "status" of the individuals involved and their personal schedules. It is not likely that such meetings can be delayed by a few days. They are often put on the calendar a year in advance.

The schedule manager in the styling staff had a simple approach to this phenomenon. He simply inserted an activity preceding the executive committee meeting that he called "water." This activity had no work content but typically had a duration of a couple of weeks. He theorized that with so many activities coming into this merge node, at least one would be late. Therefore, by building in some "water" before the meeting, there was a good chance that any stragglers could be completed before the meeting.

Actually there is a theoretical basis for this that relies on the same probabilistic model as reliability. Indeed, the discussion of reliability in Chapter III of *PM 101* is relevant. Consider a set of activities, each

Column 1 Number of Preceding Activities	Column 2 Pr(c) = 0.99	Column 3 Pr(c) = 0.95	Column 4 Pr(c) = 0.90
1	.0100	.0500	.1000
2	.0199	.0975	.1900
3	.0297	.1426	.2710
4	.0394	.1855	.3439
5	.0490	.2262	.4095

TABLE XIII.2

Probability That at Least One Activity Will be Late for Varying Numbers of Predecessors of a Merge Node

having the same probability of being completed by a certain date. Suppose that probability is 99 percent. System failure is comparable to at least one activity not being completed on time. Table XIII.2, column 2, shows the probability that at least one activity will be late. Thus, for only one preceding activity the probability is simply 0.01. As the number of predecessors increases, the probability of at least one activity being late increases, becoming nearly 5 percent for five predecessors. Suppose the probabilities of those activities being completed by the required date are 95 percent, then for five predecessors there would be a 23 percent chance of not being ready for the meeting. For a probability of 90 percent, there would be more than a 40 percent chance of not being ready.

Now suppose we add an activity, "water," between the merge node and the critical meeting with a duration of one week, which might be equivalent to moving from column 4 to column 3. If a 23 percent chance of not being ready for the meeting gives you an anxiety attack, perhaps a second week of "water" would be appropriate which might be equivalent to column 2. It should be clear that the individual probabilities for all the predecessors being completed by a certain date need not be equal, as they seldom are. Also, note that we have not determined the one week or two weeks theoretically. The ideal way to do this would be by Monte Carlo PERT. Alternatively, ordinary PERT logic would provide a quick and dirty solution.

Now the validity of this model can be questioned. It is a ceteris paribus model, i.e., all other things being equal. In other words, it implies that you, as project manager, can have no effect on the probabilities of completion of these activities. Clearly, there is a range of alternative interventions from getting a longer bullwhip to rolling up your sleeves and helping on the activity that is in trouble. Certainly, your concerned interest in the progress on any problem activities will have an impact. The point is that most activities are performed by human individuals who are subject to motivational actions that may cause them to expedite their work. On the other hand, if the pressure is too great, they are likely to take short cuts that could lead to errors, rework, and even extreme embarrassment. Thus, while the above is a ceteris paribus model, it can provide a guide as to how much "water" to provide and where to use management attention to counter the ceteris paribus assumption.

Critical Path

This is the most obvious set of activities to consider in scheduling. Any delays on this path will delay the completion of the project, ceteris paribus. Indeed, you should review these activities to consider putting a little challenge on those responsible for these activities to save some time in the early stages of the project and build a little cushion into the critical path. Note that such a challenge should not be done by arbitrarily reducing activity duration. Rather, it might take the form of a "perk" if these activities are completed in less time than anticipated. Note also that emphasis on time alone may lead to sacrificing other objectives. Care must be taken that the project team maintains a balanced focus on all objectives of the project.

Critical Resources

Some resources are obviously critical because they are scarce or costly. For example, one or more activities may require efforts of a specific person with unique knowledge or skills. That person may be available only at certain times. Thus, the schedule will have to recognize this condition. If possible, it is often desirable to have all activities requiring that unique resource scheduled consecutively. Too often, when such a resource leaves the project, their return becomes a source of considerable uncertainty.

Costly resources are often characterized by being rented or leased. Even if they are owned by the parent or related organization, they are cross-charged to the project. Often they are also expensive to move on and off the job site. Consider delaying any activities requiring such a resource early in the project and advancing any activities late in the project to minimize the time that resource is charged to the project. Those activities in between should be examined to minimize conflicts in the use of the resource to preclude the need for multiple units of such a resource.

A tool that the OC has used to gain insight into scheduling resources is the "upper/lower envelope." The OC takes no credit for the concept. It appeared in a journal or proceedings in the early 1960s. In spite of extensive search, the article has not been located again. This concept and its use are discussed and illustrated in Appendix XIII.A.

SUMMARY

In this chapter, we have tried to provide some insights into the problems of scheduling. The most important lesson is that neither the early nor late calculations are likely to provide a really acceptable schedule. They only provide the outer limits within which a schedule can be developed, *given the existing plan and target dates*.

Scheduling resources on a project is not a trivial problem. There are many factors to consider and it is not likely that a computer program will recognize all these factors, let alone the opportunities. Thus, really good scheduling requires the attention of the project manager, or at least the attention of a person who has the time to spend on it *and* the welcome concern of the project manager.

Sam plotted all the activities on a flat rock side of a cave (so it would not get washed away by the rain), just as the older elder had instructed. It looked like this. Not having computer capabilities, the analysis was limited to total resources, resorting to intuition to identify any problems with individual resource types. Note that the start times represent the end of the indicated day, thus time zero is the beginning of day one.

From this, Sam realized that the worst problem was on days 37, 38, and 39. Sam decided that it would be wise to limit the total resources employed on any one day to 15. Thus, the initial decision to use the viners to help find animals would not work. Instead, Sam decided to dispatch the hunters on day 2, supplemented by only two of the viners. This would add back 5 days to the duration. The 2 viners for 18 days would add back the equivalent of 9 days and, if the team was not having success by day 30, overtime could be authorized. Sam also delayed GMV another 3 days. With these changes, Sam was satisfied that the project could be done on schedule with the resources available.

Sam was also very appreciative of the advice from the elder to draw it in a cave. It was really a job to draw all those lines and add all those tic marks. Sam hoped that the schedule would be followed, as the very thought of doing this again caused a bad headache.

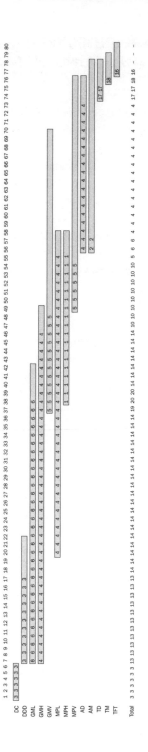

SAM'S RESOURCE ANALYSIS

APPENDIX XIII.A
COMPUTER SCHEDULING OF RESOURCES

Most project management computer software includes provisions for scheduling resources. Most of the algorithms are proprietary, but many rely on rather simple concepts. The following discussion provides some insights into the general processes for scheduling. For further detail, the reader should examine the user's manual for a specific software package of concern and/or read some of the literature that reported research into the efficacy of the variety of algorithms (Davis and Patterson 1975).

ANALYTICAL PROCEDURES

One of the best rigorous discussions of project scheduling is contained in Moder, Phillips, and Davis (1983). It relies heavily on mathematical notation and, thus, requires considerable effort to read and comprehend. In short, it examines a number of heuristics, i.e., problem-solving protocols or sets of decision rules, for scheduling. It demonstrates that different heuristics achieve differing objectives. From this, it is possible to choose a heuristic consistent with the objectives of the project. Generally, these objectives are time related and they are applied throughout the duration of the project. It is the OC's opinion (that means there is no rigorous research supporting this proposition) that most projects can be scheduled better using a mix of these objectives and the decision rules in different orders. In addition, there are other objectives and decision rules that are not well explored in the literature. (It has been a practice of project management software vendors to not publish details on their proprietary approaches to scheduling.)

To select the best heuristics, we need to understand some characteristics of the PND for a specific project. That means we need some analytical procedures for measuring these characteristics. In the previous discussion, we have mentioned a number of considerations in scheduling. The applicability of these varies depending on the characteristics of the PND. For example, the occurrence of burst nodes creates opportunities for increased flexibility and merge nodes tend to restrict flexibility in scheduling. A simple distribution of these by rank provides insights into where there are segments of the PND where one decision rule would be more appropriate than another. Other characteristics that can add insight to scheduling are the size of the activities (both time and resources), the occurrence of specific critical resource requirements, and space requirements.

Activity Rank

Activity rank is often used in computer-based scheduling heuristics, as well as in calculating early and late times. Activity rank can be calculated by simply making the duration of every activity in the PDN equal to one (1). Now perform the early calculations. The activity, A_R^{fmax}, with the highest rank, R, will be at the end of the chain of activities having the largest number of activities in that chain. Thus, that activity will have at least R-1 predecessors. While it is comparable to the critical path, it is not the same. We can be more specific by identifying the rank obtained in this manner as the forward rank, R^f.

The same process can be used to calculate the backward rank, using the late calculation routine. It is useful to set the backward rank, R^b, of the activity having the highest forward rank, A_R^{fmax}, at the value of the highest rank, i.e., R^{fmax}. These calculations are shown in Figure XIII.A.1, Activity Rank.

You may now recognize that slack calculations may be performed giving what might be called "rank slack." This is a measure of the scheduling flexibility available in the PND.

To the OC's knowledge, there is no project management scheduling software package presently available that presents this type of information to the scheduler. It may well be used in proprietary scheduling routines and, perhaps, may be available as a sophisticated option in some. Nevertheless, understanding these concepts should enhance the understanding of the nuances of scheduling and, therefore, result in its consideration, consciously or unconsciously, when resolving tough scheduling problems.

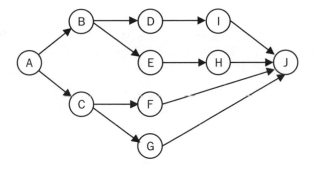

			Forward Rank		Backward Rank		Rank
Act	Pred	Dur	ES	EF	LS	LF	Slack
A	–	1	0	1	0	1	0
B	A	1	1	2	1	2	0
C	A	1	1	2	2	3	1
D	B	1	2	3	2	3	0
E	B	1	2	3	2	3	0
F	C	1	2	3	3	4	1
G	C	1	2	3	3	4	1
H	E	1	3	4	3	4	0
I	D	1	3	4	3	4	0
J	I, H, F, G	1	4	5	4	5	0

FIGURE XIII.A.1

Activity Rank

Availability List

A way to think about the scheduling problem is illustrated by the availability list. Make a list of those activities that are available to be scheduled, i.e., those activities for which their predecessors have been completed. To begin with, the available list has only those activities that can start at the beginning of the project. For example, consider the simple PND in Figure XIII.1, A Project for Scheduling. Start with time zero. The only activity that can be scheduled is A. Step forward in time, one unit of time per iteration, until that activity is completed. At this point, A is removed from the list and activities B and C are

143

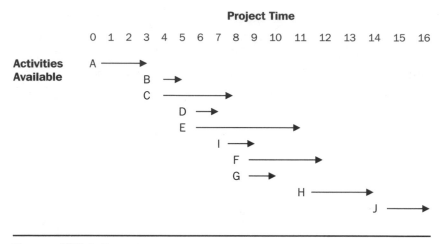

FIGURE XIII.A.2
Availability List

added to the availability list. When B is completed, it disappears from the availability list and activities D and E are added. When C is finished, activities F and G are added. And so on as shown in Figure XIII.A.2, Availability List. They are shown on the assumption that the project is scheduled at the earliest times. If any activity, say activity C, is delayed, its followers would not become available until it is finished. This can be seen in Figure XIII.A.6, Logic for a Time-Constrained Resource Requirement. Note that activity H is not available until both of its predecessors, C and E, are completed. Activity J is not available until all four of its predecessors, F, G, H, and I, are completed.

When A is completed, a decision must be made between B and C. This is done by a rule that is commonly referred to as a "decision rule." For example, the decision rule could be, "schedule the activity with the least slack." Another decision rule might be, "schedule the activity with the shortest duration," or, "schedule the activity with the longest duration." Alternatively, we could use "schedule the activity with the largest requirement for the resource, subject to it being less than or equal to the number of units of resource available." From this simple example, it can be seen that the problem of scheduling resources is not simple.

Upper and Lower Envelopes

The analysis of resource requirements is an excellent example of an analytical procedure. It provides information about the maximum and minimum units of resources that can be used on any given day.

First, consider the lower envelope as shown in Figure XIII.A.3, Lower Envelope. This also shows a resource profile, however, it includes only the resources that are absolutely required on any given day. That is, if an activity has slack equal to or greater than the duration of the activity, there is no day on which that activity must be in process. Each activity is shown on the Gantt chart as starting on its latest start date and finishing on its earliest finish date. Thus, activities with slack greater than or equal to their duration are not included. For example, consider activity C with a duration of five days and slack of two days. It could be scheduled on any five consecutive days out of the seven days on which it might be performed. It cannot be moved off of the third, fourth, or fifth days; therefore resources must be available on those days.

The significance of the lower envelope is that it clearly indicates the absolute minimum resource units that are required on any given day, for that plan. If they are not available, the activity(s) involved will certainly be delayed and thus, the project will be delayed. From the lower envelope we can see that we must have 2 people the first three days of the project and 3 the last two days. We will use that information later.

Now, consider the upper envelope as shown in Figure XIII.A.4, Upper Envelope. It is simply a resource profile that indicates the greatest number of units of a resource that could possibly be used on any day given the current project plan. It is developed by assuming that each activity starts at its early start time and runs continuously until its latest finish time. Clearly, this results in more resource days than are actually required. The total resource days in the upper envelope (141) divided by the total resource required in the project (85) is a measure of schedule flexibility.

The important information is in the valleys of this profile. This can be seen on days 1–3 where the maximum units that can be used are only 2. That coincides with the same information from the lower envelope.

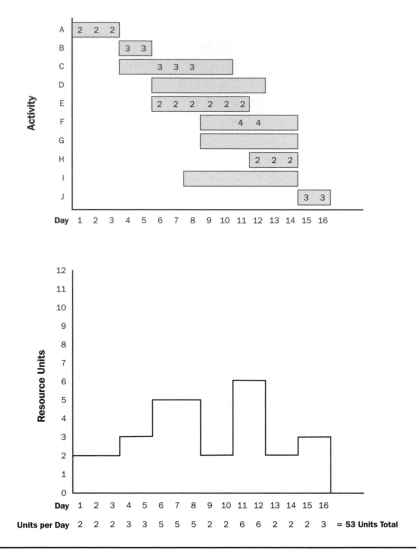

FIGURE XIII.A.3

Lower Envelope

Assume that it was planned to bring 6 units onto the project. The extra units should not be brought in until at least day four. The same is true for the last two days where the upper and lower envelopes both indicate 3 units of resource.

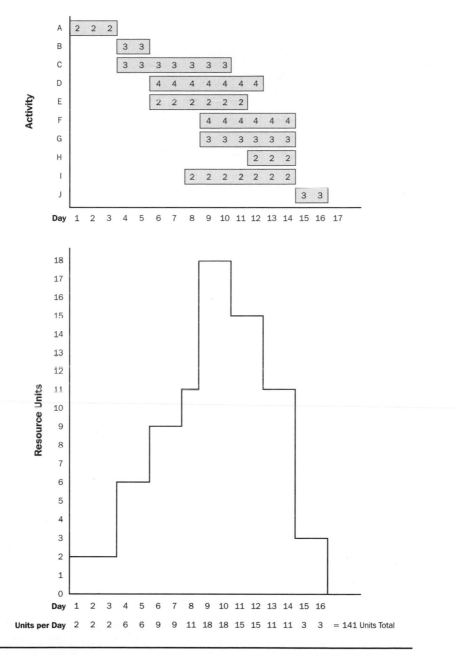

FIGURE XIII.A.4
Upper Envelope

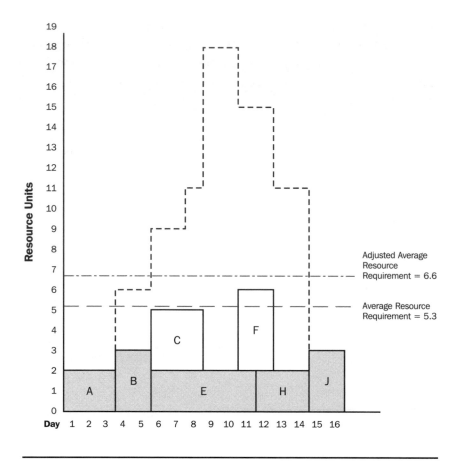

FIGURE XIII.A.5

Combined Upper and Lower Envelopes with Average Resource Requirements

The information in the upper and lower envelopes can be enhanced by showing the planned resource profile on the same chart as shown in Figure XIII.A.5, Combined Upper and Lower Envelopes with Average Resource Requirements. This will make clear if there is a discrepancy between requirements and what is intended to be provided for the project, either too few given the lower envelope or more than can possibly be used given the upper envelope. Considering this information, decisions can be made to bring in more units of a resource at certain times or delay bringing them in when they cannot be used continuously until after a valley in the lower envelope. Temporary peaks might be provided for by overtime, for example. Alternatively, the project plan can be reviewed to see if changes in it will make better use of the resources.

We can use the information in Figure XIII.A.5 to determine the number of units to consider in provisioning the project. The total units of resources required is 85. When divided by the project length, that gives an average of 5.3 units per day. Drawing that on the graph we see that there will be wasted resources on days 1–3 and 15–16. Subtract the resource days required for activities A (6) and J (6) from the total (85), then divide by the remaining duration (11), and we get an adjusted average resource requirement of 6.6. It is clear that it will take a little more than 6 units, but we will schedule to 6 and see what can be done. Note that the activities making up the lower envelope are plotted here to see their impact on these requirements. This will be used in the next step.

Now, using just that lower envelope plot (marked in light and dark gray) it is easy to see the alternatives in Figure XIII.A.6, Logic for a Time-Constrained Resource Requirement. The activities on the critical path can be scheduled at their calculated times. These are shaded (lightly) on the resource profile. In addition, from the lower envelope, we know that parts of activities C must be scheduled on days 6, 7, and 8, and activity F on days 13 and 14. This leaves decisions for activities C, D, F, G, and I. These decisions are shown below by squares on the days that might be chosen. Consider activity C. It must be scheduled for another two days on either days 4, 5, 9, or 10. Since it fits well on days 4 and 5, we can schedule it there. Activity D fits well on days 9 and 10. The remainder of activity F fits well on days 13 and 14. This leaves activities G and I for which there are no gaps to fill in their respective times available. Thus, they have been scheduled on days 9 and 10 and 11 and 12. Clearly, there is another alternative, to schedule activity I on days 8 and 9 and, G on days 10 and 11. Either would be acceptable.

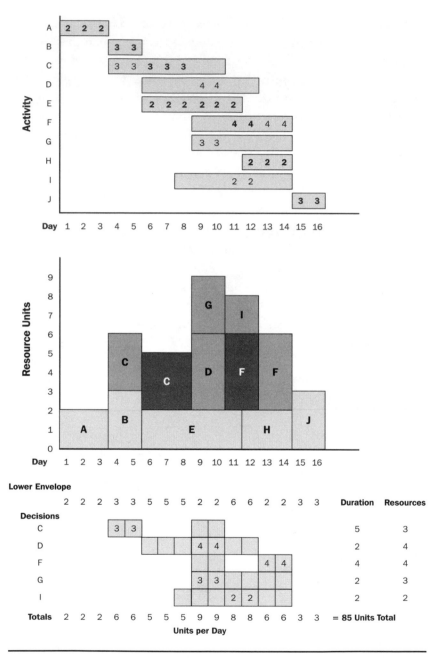

FIGURE XIII.A.6

Logic for a Time-Constrained Resource Requirement

Note that this schedule is as good as can be achieved for this project plan, i.e., the logic as expressed in the PND and the time and resource estimates for the activities. Another project plan might offer advantages. For example, suppose activity G could be done by 2 units of resource in 3 days. It could be scheduled after activity I, resulting in a peak resource requirement of 8 units (instead of 9) for four days, as well as using a unit of resource on day 8 that might otherwise be wasted. Another alternative might be to delay completion by two days, permitting both activities G and I to be done on days 15 and 16 and slipping activity J to days 17 and 18. Note that this is the solution shown for the resource-constrained schedule in Figure XIII.A.7. Other changes might be made to the original plan that would reduce the total project cost.

Similarly, Figure XIII.A.7, Logic for a Resource-Constrained Schedule illustrates a simple procedure for developing this schedule. At the bottom, the availability list is shown. Thus, in the beginning only activity A is available. When it is finished, Activities B and C become available. When B is finished, D and E become available. Note that H is not available until both E and F are finished. E was selected to schedule before D because it required three or less units of resource and it had the longer duration.

The previous analyses are based on a very simple project. You can imagine how complex the analysis would be for a realistic project. Doing it with any precision would certainly require computer capability. Even then it would be very complex. However, there are some simplifications that can reduce the complexity. One of these is using concepts such as the ranking procedure illustrated above to subdivide the project into segments, each of which can be scheduled separately. For example, had the histogram of ranks been bimodal, it would suggest that each mode could be scheduled separately, the results combined and checked for feasibility. Similarly, if the upper envelope had been bimodal, that would have suggested the same conclusion. Reviewing the lower envelope might reveal that a specific resource is critical over a period of time. It might be appropriate to schedule that resource, identify the resultant set of activities as a block, and then treat that block as a single pseudoactivity for the rest of the scheduling process. Identifying such a block could be the basis for establishing a

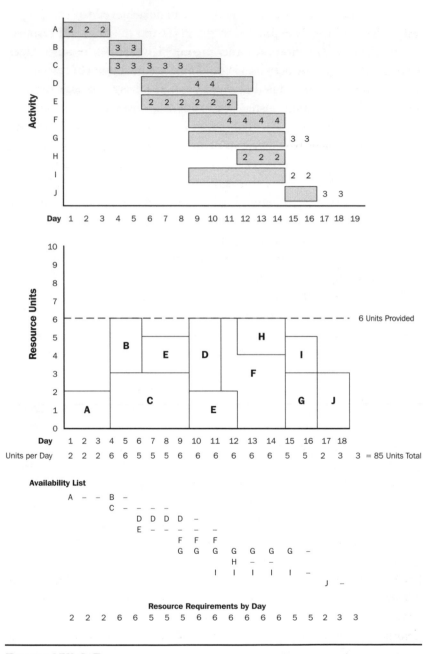

FIGURE XIII.A.7

Logic for a Resource-Constrained Schedule

critical chain. These are just examples of the many approaches that might be used in scheduling.

While it would be unwise to attempt to perform these analyses manually, understanding the procedures can help you recognize opportunities to affect a computer-developed schedule. For example, any schedule is based precisely on a specific project plan and estimates, including the methodologies and technologies used. Often it will become clear from analysis of the resource schedule that one activity, or a certain type of activity, is causing a scheduling problem. A change in any of these can often solve the problem. As a last resort, you may decide to add resources or overtime to crash one or more activities. Many times the overtime will be at no increase in cost for the work, after considering the effects of the benefits. Similarly, the extra resources needed for a few days can often be hired off the street for the short period of time required.

At the time of writing this book, the OC is not familiar with any project management scheduling software that provides this upper and lower envelope information. Being familiar with the concept, however, a scheduler can manually consider the values on certain days where it appears there may be a problem.

MULTIPLE RESOURCE SCHEDULING

To this point, we have assumed that there is a single resource type involved in the project. The problem becomes far more complicated when there are multiple resource types required. A complete explication of this subject goes beyond the scope of the present volume, however, it is relevant to provide some insight into the nature of the problem.

Focusing on one resource at a time is one alternative. Optimizing the scheduling of one resource often leads to unsatisfactory requirements for one or more of the other resources. On the other hand, it makes some sense as it permits focusing on the most critical resource. A critical resource may be defined in more than one way. It may be the most expensive resource or it may be the one that is in shortest supply.

These characteristics are not mutually exclusive. One rule, derived from job-shop scheduling, is that a critical resource should never be idle. This can be achieved by yet another scheduling rule such as, "Select the activity that has the most immediate followers." This rule tends to provide the greatest flexibility in further scheduling. Alternatively, "Select the activity that has the most follower activities that require the critical resource."

Studies of various decision rules have been reported in literature. Clearly, each decision rule has positive and negative consequences. For example, a negative consequence of the decision rule, "Schedule the activity with the shortest duration," is that longer activities will be delayed interminably. This could be a very serious consequence, as these activities may well have high uncertainties and could thus delay the entire project. This, of course, suggests another decision rule, "Schedule those activities with the greatest uncertainty as soon as possible."

One interesting aspect of these decision rules is that any one rule often leads to ties. This requires the specification of a subsidiary rule that is a tiebreaker. Sometimes a third tiebreaker is required. The OC has had a long-standing interest in researching the characteristics of projects to determine if there might be a way of determining the circumstances under which alternative decision rules could be selected and the order in which they should be sequenced for tie breaking. While such research may exist, the OC is unaware of it. This may be because such rules are proprietary and imbedded in project management scheduling systems.

It may be apparent from the previous paragraphs that no one decision rule will give the best results for all activities in a project. An examination of one's own behavior in scheduling a project will reveal that many decision rules are actually applied. For example, on do-it-yourself projects at home, the OC often uses a rule something like, "Perform all those activities that precede activities requiring the purchase of more supplies." This tends to minimize the total number of shopping trips, as well as the purchase of the wrong items or the right items in the wrong quantities.

APPENDIX XIII.B
MARS PATHFINDER PROJECT

PROJECT TIME/SCHEDULE MANAGEMENT

The Level 2 Master Schedule was published in the Mars Pathfinder Project Plan document in February, 1994. This schedule was originally developed and implemented at the Design, Implementation and Cost Review (DICR) held in July, 1993. The controlling project milestones and the major milestones from each system were included in this schedule. More detailed Level 3/Level 4 schedules were developed and maintained in MS Project at the system and subsystem levels.

Maintaining the launch schedule for a mission to Mars is extremely critical due to the orbital relationship between Earth and Mars. There is only a 30 day launch window that occurs every 26 months for a successful trajectory to Mars. In other words, a launch slip of more than 30 days would mean a 26 month postponement of the mission.

The Level 3 Master network schedule was maintained by the Flight System Manager and Project Scheduler, and tracked events such as RFP's, contract start and end dates, design reviews, fabrication deliveries, deliveries of major subsystems, and completions during assembly, test and launch operations (ATLO). A major item delivery database was developed to connect the Level 3/4 schedules into two performance assessment metrics; one for total planned vs. actual Flight System events and another for planned vs. actual major testing and delivery events. This provided a good indicator of ahead- or behind-schedule condition. In addition, a procurement performance matrix for subcontractors and vendors was maintained by the Pathfinder contract manager.

Schedule reserve was budgeted for each phase of the project based upon the degree of perceived schedule risk. For the 37 month development schedule, approximately 20 weeks of schedule margin was planned. The margin was distributed as follows:

Development/Procurements	40%
Assembly and Test	45%
Launch Campaign	15%

During the course of the project, schedule margin was utilized for completing the mechanical assembly of the flight system and in final delivery and test of various elements of the entry, descent and landing system, including airbags and rocket assisted deceleration systems. The project was able to manage within its budgeted schedule margin, and was ready to launch on December 2, 1996 (the first day of the launch window). Due to weather and other considerations, the actual launch date of Mars Pathfinder was December 4, 1996.

	Original Date	Actual Date
Commencement Date:	10/01/93	11/01/93
Project Defined:	07/20/93	07/20/93
Client Approval:	11/01/93	11/01/93
Project Closeout	08/04/98	04/19/98

APPENDIX XIII.C
MARS PATHFINDER PROJECT

PROJECT SCHEDULE

| | JPL OFFICE OF FLIGHT PROJECTS | | MESUR PATHFINDER | P 1/1 |

Project schedule table (JPL Office of Flight Projects):

- ACHIEVEMENT: A. SPEAR
- PROJECT SCHEDULE — LEVEL 2
- MESUR PATHFINDER — P 1/1
- STATUS AS OF: Mar 1, 1994
- BASELINE DATE: Jul 20, 1993

ACTIVITY	FY93 (1993)	FY94 (1994)	FY95 (1995)	FY96 (1996)	FY97

1 MILESTONES
2 INCREMENTAL DEVELOPMENT DEMOS
3 ATLO SYSTEM TESTS
4 FLIGHT SYSTEM
5 ENTRY, DESCENT AND LANDING
6 ATTITUDE AND INFORMATION MGMT HARDWARE
7 MECHANICAL INTEGRATION HARDWARE
8 POWER, PROPULSION AND TELECOM
9 SCIENCE & INSTRUMENTS
10 LANDER IMAGER
11 ATMOSPHERIC STRUCTURE/METEOROLOGY
12 APX SPECTROMETER
13 APX DEPLOYMENT MECHANISM
14 ROVER
15 PROTOTYPE DEVELOPMENT
16 SYSTEM INTEGRATION MODEL
17 FLIGHT UNIT
18 GROUND DATA SYSTEM
19 SOFTWARE DEVELOPMENT
20 HARDWARE PROCUREMENT/INSTALL
21 MISSION OPERATIONS
22 DESIGN & DEVELOP
23 TEST

Legend:
- AC = Attitude Control
- AM = Analytical Model
- BB = Breadboard
- CDR = Critical Design Rev.
- DTM = Development Test Model
- EDL = Entry, Descent & Landing
- EM = Engineering Model
- FC = Flight Computer
- FSR = Flight System Review
- FU = Flight Unit
- LRR = Launch Readiness Review
- MSA = Mission Support Area
- PSR = Pre-Ship Rev.
- SAF = Spacecraft Assembly Area
- SIM = System Integration Model
- SRR = System Requirements Rev.
- TDR = Technical Definition Review
- TSR = Technical Status Rev.
- MOSRR = MOS Readiness Review
- ◇ = Delivery to Testbed

157

MARS PATHFINDER FLIGHT SYSTEM SUMMARY

Mars Pathfinder Flight System Summary

ID	Task Name	Dur.
1	SYSTEM I/F & MILESTONES	828d
2	Subsystem PDR's	31d
13	Flight System DDR	2d
15	EDL Peer Review	2d
16	Project CDR	2d
19	ATLO S/S integration	40d
20	EDL Peer Review	2d
21	IRR	2d
23	Shelf Vib. & Centrifuge Prep & Test	34d
24	Sys. Test #1 Prep & Test	45d
25	Sys. Test #2 Prep & Test	27d
26	Sys. Test #3 Prep & Test	46d
27	Acous/Spin & Cruise STV prep & test	45d
28	Pyro/ Entry Spin Prep & Test	19d
29	Sys Test #4 Entry/ Lnded in Chamber	10d
30	Landed STV Prep & Test	14d
31	Sys Test #5 End-to-end	10d
32	Final Preps to Ship (including 19 day cor	29d
35	ETR Assy & Test	45d
36	LAUNCH	0d
37	EEIS MILESTONES	405d
38	EEIS Phase 1 Demo	20d
39	EEIS Phase 2 Demo	25d
71	LANDER	523d
81	Petal DTM Fab/Assy	115d
82	FAB/ASSY FLT Base Petals	145d
84	FAB/ASSY FLT Side Petals	160d
104	CRUISE STAGE	535d
107	FAB/ASSY FLT Cruise	156d
138	FLIGHT CABLING	315d

Mars Pathfinder Flight System Summary

ID	Task Name	Dur.
140	CABLING DRWNGS	97d
144	FAB/DEL FLT Base Petal Cables (W510	105d
202	AIRBAGS	682d
212	Prototype Airbag Drop Tests @ Plumbro	20d
216	FSD Airbag Drop Tests @ Plumbrook	9d
222	Qual Drop Test	20d
243	EDL SYSTEM TESTS & ANALYSIS	403d
244	DTM B/S, Lndr,Bridle Sep. Tests	35d
245	DTM Cruise, B/S Sep. Tests	22d
252	Model Correlation/Evaluations	20d
261	PROPULSION	541d
269	PROP INTEG W/CRUISE STAGE	71d
300	RADIO FREQ. SUBSYSTEM	573d
310	SSPA EM Dev/Test & DEL	186d
317	TMU #1 FLT Assy/Test/DEL	17d
318	RFS INTEG & TEST	60d
343	AIM LANDER ELECTRONICS	431d
347	Dev/DEL EM Lndr Elec to FST/P	90d
349	Dev/DEL FLT Lndr Elec to FST/P	182d
353	AIM FLIGHT SOFTWARE	571d
365	DEV/DEL Ph C FLT SW to FST/P	55d
368	DEV/DEL PH D FLT SW to FST/P	85d
373	DEV/DEL PH 2.1 FLT SW to FST/P	20d
394	FLIGHT COMPUTER (MFC)	426d
399	DEV/DEL MFC BB	38d
400	DEV/DEL MFC EM to FST/P	180d
402	AIM S/S INTEGRATION & TEST	519d
405	EM ASSEMBLY LEVEL TESTS	130d
406	FLIGHT ASSY LEVEL TESTS	150d
414	DEL Phase 2.1 S/W to ATLO	45d

Chapter XIV

Time/Cost Tradeoff in Scheduling

Sam was still concerned that the project would not be completed before the rains came. There was a family up the river a ways. Perhaps they could be called on for help. They had a reputation for being very mercenary, so it would surely cost an arm and a leg to get them to help. Therefore, Sam wanted to be sure of two things before contacting them. First, where might they contribute to the timely completion of the project? Second, how much would their help cost per day saved? Sam looked again to the elders for advice.

INTRODUCTION

One of the major concepts in the original development of critical path techniques (CPTs) was time/cost tradeoff. It was developed as a joint effort between Univac and DuPont companies. While it was a significant development that provided real value, it had two shortcomings; it was computer processor intensive and it was labor intensive.

In the late 1950s and early 1960s, computers were slow and memory was expensive. Thus, there were relatively few computers with adequate capabilities and the cost of using them was high. Critical Path Planning and Scheduling (CPPS) required more data on each activity than the simpler Critical Path Method (CPM) at a time when the network approach to project planning was just being introduced. CPM required more data than previous planning methods. Thus, there was considerable resistance to providing even more data for CPPS. As a result, the cost benefit ratio was deemed to be negative and time/cost tradeoff, as a computer technique, fell out of favor.

Three major changes have taken place in the interim that suggest that time/cost tradeoff may well return to favor. First, computers are far more powerful and much less expensive today, substantially reducing the computing cost of using this capability. Second, CPTs have gained acceptance across industries as modern project management (MPM) has become de rigueur. Third, the number of sophisticated users of CPT has increased to the point of "being ready for" the next level of sophistication of techniques. In addition, better understanding of the mathematical logic of the concept has lead to simpler requirements for its use. Thus, it is predicted that time/cost tradeoff, as a computer capability, will become popular in the near future.

More importantly, even without computer capabilities to apply time/cost tradeoff, the logic is a fundamental part of the process of scheduling to meet a target duration. It can be expected that the first plan developed for a given project will indicate a longer project duration than is acceptable. Indeed, it is argued that to plan otherwise will inevitably lead to less than the optimum plan for the project. Thus, a variety of steps must be taken to reduce the duration. In Chapter XI we discussed fifteen ways to improve project performance, especially with regard to project duration. One of these was "applying additional resources" for which time/cost tradeoff can be useful. While manual application of the technique is not likely to be as precise or complete as the computer application, it is relatively easy to perform within the limits of the usual requirements. Thus, it is important for every project manager to comprehend the concepts involved.

HISTORY

The DuPont Company recognized that in the maintenance of their chemical process facilities, downtime for maintenance had a direct and tangible opportunity cost as measured by the contribution margin per unit of the product that was not produced during that downtime. (Contribution margin is the selling price per unit minus all the direct costs of producing the unit.) This was more serious in this industry than in most because facilities were generally operated at maximum capacity 24 hours per day, 365 days per year and there was a market for all they could produce. Thus, the longer the unit was out of service, the greater this opportunity cost. They also recognized that they could perform this maintenance in less cost by incurring overtime or other increased cost methods to expedite work. However, the calculations necessary to determine these costs were very complex.

The same problem existed in the construction of new facilities. Seldom were facilities built to produce a new chemical compound without having a ready market for that compound. Thus, every day spent on creating that facility incurred a loss of the marginal contribution from the production and sale of that compound.

The advent of computers presented an opportunity to perform these calculations in a relatively timely and affordable method. Developments in a mathematical technique called linear programming provided the logic for the calculations and developments in modeling construction projects using project network diagrams (PNDs) provided the framework on which those calculations could be performed.

Thus, DuPont sought the assistance of Univac, a producer of early computers, to develop a computer program that would perform the necessary calculation. The story of this effort is presented in *The Origins of CPM: A Personal History*, by the two persons primarily responsible for this development, James Kelley and Morgan Walker (1989). They were successful and proved the efficacy of the technique as documented in *Critical Path Planning and Scheduling System* (CPPS) in 1958 (Kelly and Walker 1959). Basically the concept was as follows.

THE BASIC CONCEPTS OF CPPS

Consider a simple project composed of four activities as shown in Figure XIV.1, Activity Cost Data for a Simple Project.

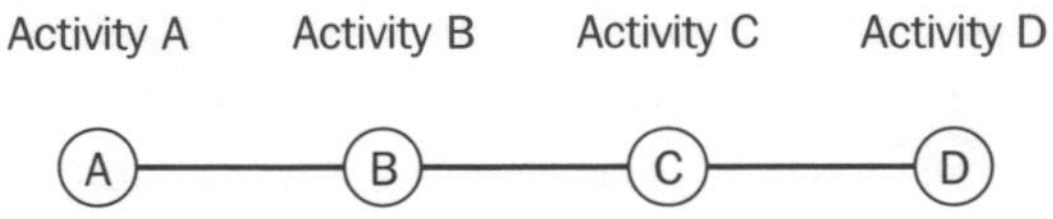

	Activity A	Activity B	Activity C	Activity D	Total
	(A)————(B)————(C)————(D)
Normal Duration	5 Days	7 Days	10 Days	4 Days	
Normal Cost	$100	$300	$500	$200	$1100
Crash Duration	3 Days	2 Days	6 Days	2 Days	
Crash Cost	$200	$850	$660	$380	$2090
Time Reduction	2 Days	5 Days	4 Days	2 Days	
Cost Increase	$100	$550	$160	$180	$ 990
Cost per Day (Slope)	$50	$110	$40	$90	

FIGURE XIV.1
Activity Cost Data for a Simple Project

Each activity requires a period of time for its performance. This period of time, its duration, is variable, but at different costs. Each activity has a normal duration (t_n) that represents the time that would normally be required and a normal cost (c_n) that would be incurred for that duration. The activity can be performed in less time, the crash time (t_c), but at an increased cost, the crash cost (c_c). The time/cost relationship is then represented by a straight line connecting these two points and is illustrated below each activity in Figure XIV.2. The cost curve has a slope (S_i). For example, activity A would normally be performed in five days at a cost of $100. It can be performed in three days at a cost of $200. This is a cost increase of $50 per day, i.e., the slope of the cost curve.

The crash time does not necessarily represent the least time in which the activity can be performed; it can represent simply a reasonable reduction in time. Note that the amount of the time reductions has no relationship to the normal time for the activity. Similarly, the slopes of the cost curves may all be different, as in this example. The objective of CPPS is to determine the minimum cost curve for the project as a function of the total duration of the project.

Addition of the normal times for the four activities indicates that the normal duration (D_n) for the project is 26 days and the normal

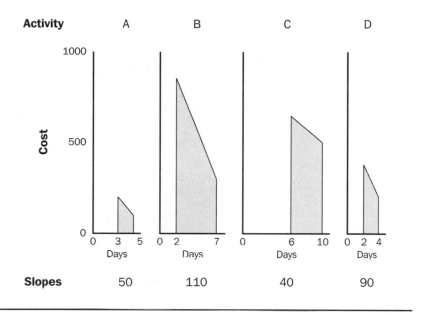

FIGURE XIV.2
Cost Curves for a Simple Project

cost is $1,100. Similarly, the project can be done in as few as 13 days at a cost of $2,090 if all activities are crashed to their crash duration. Thus, we can save 13 days at an additional cost of $990, or an average cost of $72.31 per day. But, that is the average cost per day, not the least cost curve.

Closer examination reveals that the first 4 days of reduction in project duration can be achieved at a cost of only $40 per day. The next 2 days will cost $50 per day. The next 2 days cost $90 per day, while the last 5 days cost $110 per day. These values represent the least cost curve for crashing the project as shown in Figure XIV.3, Least Cost Curve for a Simple Project.

Now, suppose the product of the project has the potential of generating a contribution margin of $105 per day. How much should we spend to reduce the project duration and what should that duration be? Since the average cost per day is $72.31 for the thirteen-day reduction in time, it might be argued, "Put everybody on overtime!" a

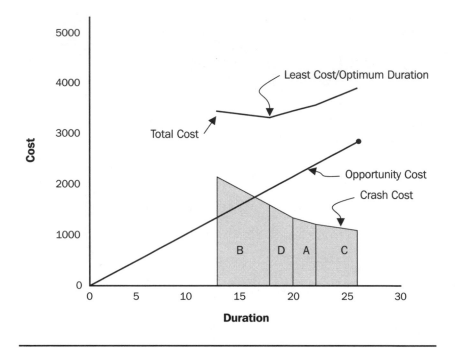

FIGURE XIV.3
Least Cost Curve for a Simple Project

not infrequent response. However, closer examination shows that for the first four days of time reduction the daily cost is only $40, resulting in a saving of $65 per day, a total of $260. The next 2 days of reduction can be achieved at a daily cost of $50, resulting in a saving of $55 per day, a total of $110; and now a grand total of $370. The next 2 days will cost $90 dollars per day, a savings of $15 per day or $30, and a grand total of $400. Crashing activity B would cost $110 per day, resulting in a net cost of $5 per day and thus reducing the grand total to $375. Looked at in this manner, it does not seem wise to spend $110 to save $105. Thus, the project duration should be reduced by 8 days at a cost of $1,540, saving a net of $400. Compare this to the "everybody on overtime" alternative that would complete the project in 13 days and cost $2,090, saving only $375.

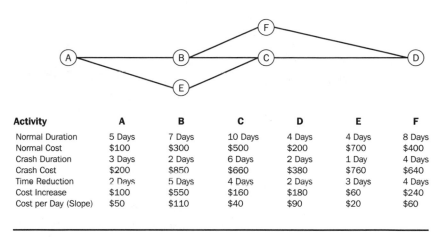

Activity	A	B	C	D	E	F
Normal Duration	5 Days	7 Days	10 Days	4 Days	4 Days	8 Days
Normal Cost	$100	$300	$500	$200	$700	$400
Crash Duration	3 Days	2 Days	6 Days	2 Days	1 Day	4 Days
Crash Cost	$200	$850	$660	$380	$760	$640
Time Reduction	2 Days	5 Days	4 Days	2 Days	3 Days	4 Days
Cost Increase	$100	$550	$160	$180	$60	$240
Cost per Day (Slope)	$50	$110	$40	$90	$20	$60

FIGURE XIV.4

Cost Data for a More Realistic Project

The Complicating Effect of Realistic PNDs

The preceding example makes the concept quite simple as, indeed, it is. However, we have illustrated it on a very simple PND. To understand why a computer program is appropriate for realistic PNDs, we introduce two more activities that are in parallel to some of the other activities in the original problem. Activity E can start at the same time as activity A, but must be completed before Activity C can begin. Activity F can start as soon as Activity B is completed, but only has to be finished for the project to be completed. The PND and the relevant data are shown in Figure XIV.4, Cost Data for a More Realistic Project.

Consider the results of crashing this project one day at a time as shown in Table XIV.1, Crashing a More Complex Project, and look at the cost curves as shown in Figure XIV.5, Cost Curves for a More Complex Project. Next we must find the least cost curve, as shown in Figure XIV.6, Least Cost Curve for a More Complex Project. You may wish to use paper and pencil to draw the PND at various stages to confirm that you understand what is happening.

We start with the minimum cost for performing this project according to the current plan and estimates. Since there are only three

Project Duration	Project Cost	Path Durations			Action Taken
		ABCD	AECD	ABFD	
26	2200	26	23	24	All Activities at Normal Duration
25	2240	25	22	24	C Reduced 1 Day @ $40
24	2280	24	21	24	C Reduced 1 Day @ $40
23	2330	23	20	23	A Reduced 1 Day @ $50
22	2380	22	19	22	A Reduced 1 Day @ $50
21	2470	21	18	21	D Reduced 1 Day @ $90
20	2560	20	17	20	D Reduced 1 Day @ $90
19	2660	19	16	19	C & F Reduced 1 Day @ $40 + $60
18	2760	18	15	18	C & F Reduced 1 Day @ $40 + $60
17	2870	17	15	17	B Reduced 1 Day @ $110
16	2980	16	15	16	B Reduced 1 Day @ $110
15	3090	15	15	15	B Reduced 1 Day @ $110
14	3220	14	14	14	B & E Reduced 1 Day @ $110 + $20
13	3350	13	13	13	B & E Reduced 1 Day @ $110 + $20

TABLE XIV.1

Crashing a More Complex Project

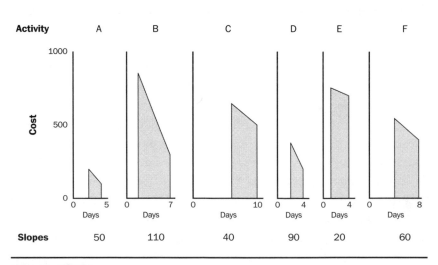

FIGURE XIV.5

Cost Curves for a More Complex Project

166

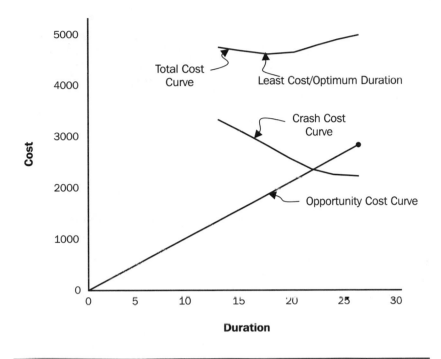

FIGURE XIV.6

Least Cost Curve for a More Complex Project

paths through this PND, it is easy to calculate the duration of each path. Clearly the critical path, ABCD must be shortened to reduce the total project duration. Activity C is the least cost alternative; therefore, we take two days out of activity C.

Now there are two paths that are critical, so time must be taken out of each of them. The alternatives can be seen easily in Table XIV.2, Crash Alternatives with Two Critical Paths. Activity A is in both paths so its cost is only incurred once. The same is true for Activities B and D. Activities C and F are each in only one of the paths; therefore, they both must be crashed and their costs combined. From this it is clear that the least cost per day is to crash Activity A. Thus, two days are taken out of Activity A. Note that this also takes time out of AECD.

Paths		A	B	F	D
	Crash Costs per Day	$50	$110	$60	$90
A	$50	$50			
B	$110		$110		
C	$40			$100	
D	$90				$90

TABLE XIV.2
Crash Alternatives with Two Critical Paths

This still leaves the two critical paths and so Table XIV.2 is still applicable. The next least costly alternative is Activity D. Two days can be taken out of it. The next alternative is to take time out of Activities C and F. There is still slack on the path AECD, so we can take time out of Activity B. As its duration is reduced, path AECD stays at 15 days until the duration of all three paths becomes 15 days. At this point, time must also be taken out of path AECD. To show all alternatives would require a three-dimensional matrix, which is tedious in two-dimensional space. You should be able to visualize such a matrix. Fortunately, for this example, Activities A, C, and D have been crashed as much as possible so only Activity E can be crashed in this path. Thus, crashing Activities B and E results in a cost of $130 per day. Note that this still leaves Activity E with one more day it could be crashed, but it would not reduce the duration of the project. Similarly, Activity F could still be crashed, but with no reduction in project duration. Thus, even if we crashed to the shortest project duration, we would save $140 on Activities E and F as compared to "putting everyone on overtime." Using the same marginal contribution of $105 per day, we should stop crashing at a project duration of 18 days.

Crashing Realistic Project Networks

Experience in developing and cursorily analyzing a large number of PNDs indicates that, on most projects, most of the time, only a small percentage of activities will actually be candidates for crashing. The above illustration suggests a procedure that can be used on any project to get the majority of the savings of time with close to the minimum cost increase. Let us review that procedure.

First, analyze the opportunity costs and other costs that vary with the duration of the project. This will be necessary to judge when to stop the crashing process, as well as looking at other alternatives for reducing the project duration.

Then, carefully analyze the project, looking for less expensive opportunities to improve performance on the project. Use the alternatives outlined in Chapter XI under Ways to Reduce Project Duration and consider making a few extra computer runs to calculate the network. Start with analyzing the activities on the critical path. You might want to estimate the value of the slope of the time/cost curve. That could require more time than you wish to allocate. At minimum, assign a value from 1 to 10 to represent the increasing relative slopes of the cost curves. Crash the activities you have assigned a value of 1. If this does not make another path critical, continue for those activities you have assigned a 2. When the time reduction on the original critical path changes the critical path, perform the same analysis on the new critical path. Repeat this process until you judge that the cost of additional crashing is too high. Remember that as the number of critical paths increase, you will have to reduce the durations of more than one activity, perhaps requiring data such as in Table XIV.2.

To determine when to stop, periodically consider in more detail the slope of the cost curves of the activities you are considering crashing. Again, remember that you will eventually have to crash more than one activity at a time, so you must consider their combined costs. This should give you an idea of whether the slope of the least slope activity or combined activities have exceeded the opportunity and other costs associated with the length of the project duration.

This procedure will not ensure the optimum solution to the crashing problem, but it will give a good approximation and requires minimum additional effort for estimating and recording the required inputs for a better solution.

FACTORS AFFECTING THE OPPORTUNITY COST

The original statement of the problem in the case of DuPont focused on how much of a marginal contribution might be achieved from a product if the facility had been producing the product during the period of maintenance or construction. Thus, if the facility could have produced 1,000 gallons of product per day, the selling price were $1.00 per gallon, and the variable costs of production were $0.925 per gallon, the marginal contribution would be $0.075 per gallon, or $75.00 per day.

There may be other costs associated with the facility being out of service that are directly related to the duration of the project. For example, we have discussed the cost of funds employed in Chapter XII. This cost is certainly directly related to the duration of the project, and should be included along with the marginal contribution.

On any project, there are some indirect costs, i.e., they are not directly related to any activity. An example is the cost of the project manager. That is directly related to the duration of the total project. A careful examination of the project budget should reveal that these costs are appreciable. Their cost per day should also be included with the marginal contribution.

There may be other costs, some of which may be less tangible. An example might be the cost of future business lost as a result of not being able to meet customers' needs for the product that is produced by the facility that is the product of the project. Each project should be analyzed carefully to isolate all applicable opportunity costs. This is probably best accomplished during the feasibility phase of the project.

FACTORS AFFECTING THE ACTIVITY'S COSTS

In the presentation of the basic concepts of time/cost tradeoff earlier, we assumed that the activity time/cost curve was linear. This was justified by the focus on, not the total cost curve, but rather a realistic segment of this curve. It is relevant to examine the cost curve of a typical activity to understand its actual shape and the factors affecting its shape and slope. For example, it is posited that the activity cost curve

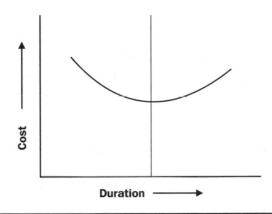

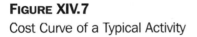

FIGURE XIV.7
Cost Curve of a Typical Activity

is actually nonlinear and that it has an optimum duration for any given method, technology, and staffing. On each side of the optimum duration, the cost increases. Thus, as shown in Figure XIV.7, Cost Curve of a Typical Activity, there is a penalty cost of taking too long to perform an activity, as well as in performing the activity in too short a time.

Taking Too Long

Four factors contribute to the cost increasing as the duration exceeds the optimum duration. First, cost of funds employed is involved just as it is for the project as a whole. Second, there is always a possibility of deterioration of the work product as time goes by, if, for no other reason, than gathering dust and corroding.

Probably the most serious cost is "relearning." Generally, a result of taking longer than the optimum duration for performing an activity is repeated stopping and starting of work effort. Every time work on an activity is started there is make-ready time required to get the object ready to work on, reviewing exactly what has to be done, and getting equipment and tools ready. This can readily be observed on a do-it-yourself project that extends over several weekends. Or consider a task at your desk at home over a period of evenings. Even though everything is left as it was last night, there is some time required for reorientation before productivity reaches the normal level. If your worksite at home happens to be the kitchen table, there may be a requirement to clean off the table every night, thus requiring put-away time.

Finally, just getting into the frame of mind necessary to perform the task is likely to result in nonproductive time for all but the most disciplined. If it is a "chore," such as preparing annual tax filing, getting into the right frame of mind may take longer each night. On some occasions, "attitude adjustment" has led to a very low productivity rate for the rest of the evening.

Going Faster

The simplest way to apply additional resources on an activity is for the same person or team to work longer hours. Indeed, it can be shown that, in many organizations, in spite of overtime pay, the first hour of overtime may be "free," considering that benefits and some other costs do not increase because of that extra hour. Generally, benefits do not increase when going from an eight-hour day to a nine-hour day. Space rent does not change. Supervision is generally not paid extra, and so on. Thus, the optimum duration may be something more than the normal eight-hour day.

Beyond nine or ten hours per day, it can be expected that humans will feel the need for nourishment. A nonpaid meal break, a paid break, or eating while working are alternatives. Each has some, albeit different, costs in terms of productivity and costs to the activity. Some time after that, the lengthening of the workday is accompanied by a decrease in productivity. This may not be apparent for very occasional overtime. Industrial engineering studies have demonstrated that after only a few weeks of steady overtime, productivity deteriorates to the point of only achieving the productivity of a normal eight-hour day. Thus, the cost curve increases at an increasing rate. These effects may be moderated in a project environment that is characterized by intense commitment to the project and its objectives. Nevertheless, they will be present.

Furthermore, the person's family will not likely share the same commitment and enthusiasm, probably leading to effects on the person's behavior in other ways after some period of protracted overtime. In the extreme, whether scheduled or just permitted, project environments can become so intense and the motivation to accomplish objectives so high that people may well extend themselves physically to the detriment of their health and, sometimes, their continued existence. A responsible project manager must be concerned about this personally, and for the entire project team.

Another way to reduce the duration of an activity is to add resources. Suppose an activity is such that a second shift can be added. Often, two people performing the same task will have slightly different ways of doing them. This can be seen in tasks as disparate as using calipers to measure and writing a section of computer code. For example, on a machine tool, one operator may move a tool from right to left in making the final adjustment while the other makes the same adjustment from left to right. Any slap in the adjustment device will lead to slightly different measures that may have to be corrected later. Differences of style in coding can lead to confusion and lost time. Even if this is absent, there is time required between shifts to communicate the status of the activity and plans for the next steps. If the two people are not the most cooperative, miscommunication and errors may be introduced. Thus, unproductive time is probably inevitable.

Adding resources can be achieved by assigning two people to the task. One may be a helper at a lower cost, in which case the reduced productivity of the helper may be acceptable due to the increased productivity of the lead person. If two people of equal skill are involved, there will likely be unproductive time discussing how they are going to work together and while one waits for the other to complete his or her share of the task. As additional people are added, the effects are compounded. The only exception to this concept is that some jobs can be done faster with more than one person. A simple example is that two people could manhandle an ungainly object that one person would have to move using a dolly or lifting device.

Thus, with a few exceptions, the cost of performing an activity will generally increase at a continuous rate as we attempt to perform the activity in less duration. In addition, the uncertainty associated with an activity's duration probably increases as the actual duration decreases from the optimum. It seems that most people are more likely to make mistakes as a function of increasing time pressure. Thus, there is an increasing likelihood of rework that was not allowed for in the original duration estimate.

SOME EXTENSIONS

There is the potential for some interesting extensions of the time/cost tradeoff concept as people, already sophisticated with project management software, recognize the opportunities. One in particular was documented in the 1960s (Bildson and Gillespie 1962). The article discussed the combination of CPPS and PERT to assess the increase in cost to increase the probability of completing a project by a specific date. This would be very useful knowledge to have when bidding on a fixed-price contract with a penalty cost, for example.

It seems quite reasonable that this concept could be extended to analyze alternatives for accelerating a project that has gotten behind schedule. It would be useful to assess the potential costs of accelerating a project to meet an earlier target date, such as bringing a product to market a year early.

It is expected that other extensions will be recognized as both practitioners and researchers apply this concept to real projects. One of these may well be in the strategic management of the portfolio of projects within an organization.

SUMMARY

The time/cost tradeoff capability, which was the origin of CPM, has great value in the planning and management of projects, whether performed on a computer or intuitively. It is likely to become a popular tool in the not too distant future. In the meantime, users must recognize some caveats.

First, failure to understand the time/cost tradeoff concept can lead to unnecessary costs that result in a blanket, "put everyone on overtime!" directive. Most activities in the typical project do not require crashing. *Do not* try to crash activities while in the planning stage. Very few people have the ability to anticipate the most economical alternatives. Develop your plan to represent the best way you know how to complete the project. Make a computer run of the CPM calculations. Review the output to ensure that the plan is what you expected it to be. Then, start making modifications based on the first ten items in the list of Ways to Improve Performance on Projects. After those are exhausted, consider adding resources using the time/cost tradeoff analysis.

Second, even though there are additional costs and computer time involved in applying the time/cost tradeoff, the above presentation has shown that familiarity with the concepts and a little extra analysis time can achieve most of the available savings of a rigorous computer analysis. Focus on the activities that are critical as the target project duration is reduced and make informed judgments about the crash costs for relevant activities.

Third, any computer application of time/cost tradeoff is performed based on the stated plan for the project. More significant improvements in project performance may be available from a different plan. Thus, this concept should not be applied unthinkingly. On the other hand, it should always be considered, at least intuitively, when considering improving the performance of a project.

Fourth, the application of additional resources is in the eleventh position in the list of Ways to Reduce Project Duration as discussed in Chapter XI. While that is a judgmental ranking, it implies that adding additional resources certainly should not be the first course of action.

Fifth, if there is any degree of uncertainty associated with an activity, it is argued that the uncertainty increases as the activity is accelerated. At minimum, the uncertainty is not likely to decrease as the time is compressed. Indeed, it is argued that as the duration of the activity is compressed, the likelihood that it will be completed earlier than planned decreases while the likelihood that it will be late increases, resulting in an increasingly skewed probability distribution of completion times. Again, whether performed on a computer or intuitively, this phenomenon must be recognized.

Finally, because projects are unique, any planning is fraught with uncertainties. Thus, the applications of any of the techniques discussed in this work are, at best, the best estimates of what will, or can, happen. Failure to manage the execution of the project will negate the best planning efforts.

Regardless, as the precision of project management increases, the best project managers will employ the best tools. Time/cost tradeoff is certainly one of those tools, whether done on a computer or intuitively. Users must be aware of, not only the concept, but of the underlying phenomena that actually affect the real work on a project as a function of crashing.

> Sam reviewed the plan and calculations that were prepared to date, and decided that it was unnecessary to call on the neighbors at this time. Sam reserved this option for consideration if the project actually started slipping.

Chapter XV

Cost Management

Sam considered the conditions for determining success of the project. The concept of monetary cost of the project would not be introduced until several centuries later. All of the materials were essentially free for the taking. The labor would be supplied by family members. Only if the neighboring family was asked to help would there be any exchange of things valuable to the family. Nevertheless, Sam was concerned about how much of the family's resources, in terms of labor hours, would be necessary to complete the raft. "Oh my," thought Sam, "something more to learn and to do before this project really gets underway."

Cost management must be pervasive throughout the project. It starts with the original statement of requirements and may, if not should, extend through the life of the product of the project. The latter is associated with life-cycle cost management, recognizing the estimated costs of operating, maintaining, and decommissioning the product of the project. This implies a much larger scope for project management than is portrayed in most college texts and in many sources on project management itself.

Probably the most important concept in cost management is recognizing that most costs are determined, at least in their minimum value, in the planning stage. Thus, cost management is much more than the popular concepts of earned value, as important as that may be. (Earned value is discussed later in this chapter.)

There are many cost drivers in a project. Some of the key drivers and, therefore, areas for cost management include scope, design, purchase and subcontract, schedule, materials, labor, methods, equipment, change, and overall. To discuss these concepts, we are relying heavily on a project to build a house, an experience many readers have had or will have. Thus, regardless of career area, it should be somewhat familiar to any reader. The concepts are equally applicable to any project. Some project types have special tools to add precision and accuracy to the process, most notably computer systems projects. Those interested in any of these project types should seek references that explicate those special tools.

SCOPE COST MANAGEMENT

Consider the example of the house introduced in *PM 101* Chapter VII, Scope Management. The first step in defining project cost is to assess the general deliverables we desire. We said we wanted a house with 3,000 square feet of floor area on three floor levels (basement, first, and second) with ten rooms and a three-car garage.

A homebuilder or architect might use a general estimating factor such as $100 per square foot of heated area plus garage space at $50 per square foot, indicating that we are immediately talking about a $330,000 house. Or, if it is warranted, they might use $80 per square foot for basement space, $90 for second floor space, and $130 per square foot for first floor space.

$$80 \times 1000 = \$80,000$$
$$130 \times 1000 = \$130,000$$
$$90 \times 1000 = \$90,000$$
$$3 \times 50 \times 200 = \underline{\$30,000}$$
$$\$330,000$$

General
Exterior
Interior
Floor Plan
Utilities
HVAC
Spaces
Detail Floor Plans

TABLE XV.1
Product Breakdown Structure of Physical Features
(Abbreviated from *PM 101*, Chapter VII)

A more refined estimate could be generated by recognizing that bathrooms and kitchens are the most expensive rooms and make adjustments on this basis. The overall style could result in higher costs if it requires more than ordinary manual work.

Thus, with very little definition of the product scope, a planning estimate can be developed as the basis for major tradeoffs. This may be sufficient to reduce our "wish list" by giving up the second floor, reducing the total area to 2,400 square feet, and getting by with a single-car garage resulting in an estimate of $262,000. If this is in the right ballpark, further planning can proceed.

$$80 \times 1200 = \$96,000$$
$$130 \times 1200 = \$156,000$$
$$1 \times 50 \times 200 = \underline{\$10,000}$$
$$\$262,000$$

At this next level, the estimates might be more refined to recognize the cost of raw space versus the major determinants of costs, such as the number of lineal feet of counter space and cabinet space, cabinet wood and finish, type of counter surface, and type of appliances. Perhaps at this level of planning we can start to recognize the impact of our wish list of Product Design Characteristics in Table XV.2. Each of these has cost implications and may be the basis for further tradeoff decisions.

Security—protection from outside threats

Safety—protection from inside threats

Environmental Friendliness—the degree to which the product impinges on the environment

Performance—the *ilities*

   Usability: the ability for the typical user to use the item for normally intended uses; often called *user friendliness*

   Availability: the percentage of the time the unit is available for intended uses. This is often described by *mean time to failure* or similar measures

   Repairability: the ability to access the item to make repairs and the (inverse of) degree of expertise required to perform repairs

   Maintainability: The relative ease of keeping the item in good operating condition and appearance

---

TABLE XV.2

Product Design Characteristics (Abbreviated from *PM 101*, Chapter VII)

Clearly, cost management begins with scope management in terms of overall requirements, features, and functions.

DESIGN COST CONTROL

Given these planning estimates as the basis for scope management, we are now prepared to begin the actual design process. If we have proceeded to the level of planning discussed above, there are targets for general layout, construction concepts, detail design of each room, and design of all utilities serving the house. Before each of these segments is completed, they should be costed and compared to the targets. If a target is exceeded, the design must be modified or tradeoffs made with other features of the house. If savings are realized while still achieving all the scope requirements, those savings can be used to enhance the subject feature or some other feature in the house. By carefully managing this process, the costs inherent in the final design can be controlled to ensure that the house can be built within the stated budget. Failure to manage cost at this stage will almost guarantee a higher total cost of the house.

SCHEDULE COST MANAGEMENT

The discussion of time-cost tradeoff in Chapter XIV should suggest the nature of this phenomenon. Indeed, some attention to that concept in strategic planning for the project might be a good guide in establishing a target schedule. Trying to push a project too fast will inevitably lead to higher cost, unless it is in the best interests of members of the project team to meet that schedule.

Some building contractors have profited by using modern project management techniques to accelerate the schedule, not only saving on cost of funds employed, but also creating a competitive advantage in the marketplace. One of the best examples of accelerated schedules is in businesses that rely on multiple small sites, such as fast food and other retail outlets. They have standardized the designs, materials purchase and delivery, and methods, as well as schedule control, to seemingly open a new outlet overnight.

One way to minimize the time required to complete a project is to control the resources that perform core tasks. Thus, a building contractor that specializes in masonry structures might acquire the resources and people to perform masonry related tasks. For tasks that are not core technologies, the prime project performer might team with other organizations to form a relationship such that attention to schedule is to their advantage also. Some advantage in schedule can be gained by carefully tailoring contract terms to increase the motivation of key suppliers to perform to schedule.

Equally as important as setting realistic target dates, is the maintenance of schedule. In Chapter XII we introduced the "domino effect" on schedules. Missing one target date may result in a key resource diverting to another project, making them unavailable at the new target date. This may result in further perturbations to the schedule that extend project completion far more than the original delay. The effects of this can be reduced by including some "water," i.e., a buffer, in the original schedule, applying additional resources selectively to accelerate activities that get behind schedule, by avoiding design changes during project execution, and by avoiding errors that lead to rework.

SUBCONTRACT COST MANAGEMENT

It may seem acceptable to "hire good subcontractors and let them do their job" with minimum supervision. However, when we examine the typical motivations of the subcontractor, we gain a better insight into what is necessary to manage the relationship.

First, subcontractors provide services to a variety of clients. They need to line up at least enough business to cover their fixed costs, to keep their people employed, and to make their desired profit. Thus, it is to their advantage to bid on and accept at least as much work as necessary to meet these objectives. Additional work, performed satisfactorily, provides them a cushion against a future bad year, permits them to buy additional equipment, and perhaps allows them a bit of special pleasure. Thus, there is an incentive to commit to more work than they can accomplish in a given time period. Interestingly, this is probably exacerbated by both an under- as well as an oversupply of the services provided by the subcontractor. Unless there is a special incentive for the subcontractor to perform to schedule for a specific client, chances are the subcontractor will give preference to the job that generates the greatest profit for them, fits into a time slot they have, or some other such characteristic. It would be foolish to expect a subcontractor to unilaterally respond to how badly they are needed on your project.

Secondly, anyone who depends on bidding, especially where the low bid gets the job, to get his work is immediately in a conflict. Subcontractors must bid low enough to get the work, but that limits their net on the job. Thus, they must rely on innovative ways to reduce the costs of performing the contracts they win to enhance their profitability. Some of these "innovative ways" may be dysfunctional for the client. Thus, lacking other bases for confidence in the integrity of the subcontractor, it is wise to take steps to ensure that the work is done properly and that sufficient resources are committed per schedule to accomplish the work in a timely manner. This may include contract terms such as penalties/incentives, requirement for scheduling and reporting that assure the client of planned and actual progress, routine and nonroutine inspections of progress, and even a full-time representative of the client present where the work is being performed.

Some clients have been known to resort to less than the most upright behaviors, such as "forgetting" to turn in a check request to pay a cash-strapped subcontractor or allowing a preceding task to be performed in such a way as to be inconvenient to the subcontractor. (Interestingly, attempts to further elicit such practices met with feigned innocence from the interviewee. Surely there are other techniques.) These are not recommended. More appropriate is a leadership style that is based on sufficient experience that permits the quick suggestion or, better yet, demonstration of feasible solutions to a problem that is causing a delay. The OC has observed and used this technique often. The most powerful effect of this leadership style is its "halo" effect. Once used, it prods the responsible person to look for her own solutions before being shown up on another problem.

Each subcontractor and project has its own characteristics and requires different methods for managing. Considerable ingenuity is required on the part of the project manager to select the most effective method for managing that subcontractor. Generally, however, the most effective method is to make clear exactly what is expected before signing a contract, establish a pattern of checking on performance and correcting errors early on, act honestly and with integrity, and take action quickly when cooperation is lacking. Clearly, having alternatives makes the latter most effective.

MATERIALS COST MANAGEMENT

Perhaps the most important job of the project manager is taking action to ensure that members of the project team *can* perform their assignments when scheduled. This means removing barriers where they appear but, better yet, minimizing the chance that a barrier to progress does appear. Past management practices have focused attention on the "big things," those that are most costly, have the longest lead-time, or have the greatest uncertainty. The tales of failure are replete with examples of races being lost due to the failure or absence of a "two-bit" item. These require even more attention today with the pressures of just-in-time (JIT) inventory management.

The discussion of materials management in Chapter XII provides insights into alternative ways of managing materials inventory. Additional aspects include purchase costs, transportation and communication costs, and materials usage.

Purchase Costs

The costs of materials and equipment for the product of the project are largely determined by the purchasing function. Once the specifications for these items have been determined, the base costs of these items are largely determined. If the specs for an item are so tight, as to preclude all but a single provider, purchasing has little opportunity to consider alternatives. The less lead-time provided to purchasing, the less time they have to shop the item and negotiate. The higher the required technical performance of the item, the fewer the providers capable of supplying the item. Thus, the success of the purchasing function in buying these items is largely determined by the project team, in how tightly they write the specifications, how much lead-time is provided, the technical performance required of the item, and what commitments they have made to suppliers in the design process.

Specifications

It might be a wise policy for the project manager to review all specifications for items that include provisions that restrict the applicability of standard items. Sometimes it may be important to question specifications for standard items to ensure that they do not include requirements that are not relevant on the current project. For example, if the standard calls for a vehicle engine to operate while fording a stream of three feet in depth, and the current project is to design a golf cart, the standard specification just may not be applicable.

Similarly, specifications may be restrictive by eliminating all but a specific brand. By excluding competition, the cost of such items will likely exceed that which may be feasible. On the other hand, it is important to have a means of ensuring that the item actually obtained will meet all requirements. Thus, it may well be desirable to specify the operating requirements and environment, if for no other reason than to provide a legitimate reason for rejecting items that are not acceptable. Sometimes it may be relevant to specify certain production methods to ensure the item has required properties, such as metallurgical, and quality control methods to ensure that deficient items are not allowed to be supplied to the project. All of these requirements will add cost to the item, but deficient items may well result in far greater costs, if not disastrous effects.

Technical Performance Required

In general, the higher the technical performance that is required of an item, the higher the cost. It may require special design efforts, it may be produced in low volume, there will probably be a higher scrap rate, it may require special equipment to produce, and there will likely be fewer suppliers capable of producing it. All of these factors lead to higher costs.

Lead-Time

Timing of the project can have significant impacts on costs and schedule. In general, the more time spent in the design/development phase, the more costs can be reduced. On a major casting plant, it was determined that another month for design would permit completion of $5,000,000 more of the design for the bid package, which could save $1,000,000 in latter field orders and change orders.

Allowing time for innovation can lead to reduced costs. In a small way, the OC recently experienced this in some small projects at home. The original design concept was complicated, with considerable work content. Allowing time for creative thinking led to innovative solutions that were substantially simpler with much less work content. The innovation process can be accelerated by active application of value engineering at various levels in the project. It is applicable to the analysis of features and functions of the product of the project, as well as to the processes of the project. It is applicable at the macro as well as the micro level. It often has side effects. For example, on a major building, two 100+-ton beams were required. Original plans called for them to be cast in place. The alternative of precast, prestressed beams, cast at the site, was considered. It proved both schedule and cost effective, even though other changes to the construction schedule were required. Access had to be maintained to the basement floor level to permit concrete trucks to deliver concrete during the casting process and egress by two cranes capable of lifting and setting the beams after the support columns were in place.

Commitments Made to Suppliers

One of the risks inherent in developmental projects is dictating the supplier of an item, due to a close working relationship with a supplier in developing a critical element of the product of the project, or process to be used in performing the project. Unless the supplier is compensated for all efforts expended on the development, and ownership of the resultant product or process by the client is clearly established, the supplier has a reasonable expectation of receiving a contract to supply the results of the development. In such a case, competition is excluded and cost is determined by other factors. Thus, an organization should have a policy that determines the conditions under which such close relationships can be developed. It should not preclude such relationships, but should provide guidance to the project team in how to manage the process to ensure the best results for the project and the sponsoring organization. Too restrictive a policy can stifle the innovation that leads to progress and competitive advantage.

Transportation/Communications Costs

At first glance, these two technologies may seem incongruous, however, when we recognize the degree to which modern projects rely on, if not are based on, the transmission of information, their similarity becomes more obvious. Many projects today are international in scope, whether developing a product for use in many areas of the world or using resources from many areas of the world in performing the project. Regardless, the transportation of physical goods or information is a complex subject. If the project requires much of either, specialists should be employed to ensure that the best technologies are used, the equipment is adequate (especially for the environment where it is to be used), and that other cost drivers are considered in planning the project. Even such details as location of certain facilities may be important in determining costs. For example, most metropolitan areas have transportation rates that are based on location within the metro area. If a major logistics facility and marshaling yard is required, one site may have definite cost advantages over another. For communications, if site location is optional, one having conventional cell phone service might be advantageous over one that required satellite service. This would be especially true if videoconferencing were involved. Even having sites in the same conventional telephone service areas would avoid extra service charges.

On a more micro scale, project layout can reduce the amount of transportation required and the problems associated with it. On a construction project, careful planning of staging areas where materials are placed in temporary storage can reduce the need to move them later to where they can be accessed with minimal additional effort. By using JIT concepts a little less rigorously, structural steel can be laid down within reach of the crane that will lift them into place. Bricks and blocks can be located to minimize forklift travel, and so on.

For projects in an office environment, analysis of paper flow and communications requirements can assist in collocating people who need to work together. Use of electronic technologies can reduce the paper flow but cannot substitute totally for the need to communicate face to face. On some projects, an open environment can be used to enhance communications. However, the open environment may reduce productivity due to the increased probability of disturbances affecting everyone. If the work is highly cerebral, it may be important to provide isolation, either in the design of workspaces or in the provision of alternative workspaces where people can seek quiet when they need it.

Materials Usage Management

Misuse of materials can result in excessive costs from using the wrong materials and from being unconcerned about costs of materials. Using the wrong materials may result in using something that performs better or worse. For example, using a stainless steel welding rod when an ordinary rod would be acceptable may result in a stronger weld or one that is more subject to corrosion due to metallurgical interactions. Using premium paper to print a disposable listing of computer code may look better, but not provide any real additional value over a less expensive type. On the other hand, changing paper may be more costly than the extra costs involved in a few pages of output.

When safety and quality are concerned, there should be no compromise of either. When convenience is the only relevant consideration, attitude is most important. The project manager should work to instill a cost consciousness on the part of all team members on the project. This can be in the simplest things. For example, the OC corrected a laborer who was dumping wheelbarrows of dirt in a location where it would have to be removed later, rather than moving it to a location a few feet away where it would be required later. On another occasion, the same concept was reinforced when a laborer was attempting to break a rock instead of simply moving it. Soon, this attitude was instilled in most workers so that they thought about what they were about to do before expending a lot of effort doing something that was "stupid."

Another aspect of attitude adjustment was in the use of materials that would otherwise have been scrapped. A carpenter was cutting, with an electric handsaw, "fire blocks" out of twelve foot 2"×4"s, rather than using the shorter pieces laying all around him. The OC demonstrated that it was faster and more economical to use the table saw with a jig. Clearly, using scrap can incur more labor cost than it is worth. Having someone at a low labor rate keep the work area clean and neatly organized can enhance the productivity of everyone on the job. More importantly, ignoring poor practices actually encourages the use of other poor practices.

LABOR COST MANAGEMENT

Projects are inevitably labor intensive. Being unique, there is not the degree of opportunity to mechanize or automate many of the tasks.

Uniqueness also leads to greater variation in the tasks being performed by individuals under a single supervisor. This can readily be seen when comparing work performed on a project versus work performed in a job shop or progressive line environment, where the work is generally much more repetitive. Thus, on projects, there is a greater reliance on the individual knowing what to do and how to do it, and being motivated to do it well without close supervision. Managing people in a project environment is generally different and more demanding than in most manufacturing environments. Thus, leadership skills are more important.

The base cost of labor for the project is largely determined by how it is managed. What factors are really managed? To a large extent, the unit rates for each resource are determined by the market. Craft wage rates may be set by union agreements. Professional wage rates are generally negotiated individually. For most purposes then, they are set for the duration of the project and the project manager has little impact on them. There are two aspects of labor costs over which control can be exercised—assignment and labor productivity.

Assignment

Assignment relates to having the right person(s) performing each task. Assigning a person who is more skilled than is required by the task results in a rate premium. Assigning a person who is less skilled results in lower productivity, greater possibility of rework, and a requirement for closer supervision. This is not a simple task because the right person is often not available at the same time that the task must be performed. This is readily apparent in the drafting room problem mentioned before. When an activity became available to be worked on, the drafting room foreman would sometimes assign a less skilled person. Sometimes he would delay the start of the activity until the best person was available. Sometimes he would look ahead and have the best person work on a less demanding or less critical activity until the subject activity became available. Tradeoffs are often required between delays of some activities, idle (or underemployed) resources, and losses in productivity (due to over- or underskilled resources being assigned).

189

Labor Productivity

Effective and efficient labor usage requires planning. One of the most common causes for labor inefficiency is idleness. The causes are many but include waiting for instructions, materials, or equipment; having more people assigned to a task than can work on the task at the same time; previous activities not completed on time or inadequately; and interruption of work because of external influences.

Waiting for instructions can be a result of inadequate supervision of either the workers or the supervisors. It may go all the way up to the project manager. One person in this path who does not delegate or plan properly can create a bottleneck for instructions flowing to the people who must perform the activity. Thus, the project manager must be sensitive to the timeliness of decisions and communication throughout the project, but especially in the project manager's office. One project manager made the entire project team conscious of this at a weekly project team meeting when he stated simply, "Gentlemen, this meeting is to report on, not to do, your homework!" That statement, and some changes in the reports used in the project management system, reduced the time spent in these meetings from about four hours per week to about two hours every other week. This added appreciably to the time available for these team members to supervise and plan in their respective areas of responsibility.

Waiting for instructions can also result from a dysfunctional leadership style. People do not like to be "chastised." The surest way to destroy initiative is to chastise people for having exercised initiative because the wrong action was taken. If any supervisor, from project manager on down, really wants to maintain a spirit of initiative, i.e., an attitude of workers to find something to do rather than stand idly by, they must avoid chastising, especially in public, those who take initiative. Rather, errors of commission should be made into learning opportunities. Take time to counsel the person or group who took initiative on what they might have done, what should have been considered, the possible consequences of alternative actions, and how to decide if they have the information necessary to proceed. Regardless, all project personnel must be made very conscious of the need for safety. Ensure that adequate training has been provided and that it is understood, and then be swift and sure in exercising discipline when safety rules are violated. Above all, the project manager and every member of the immediate project team must follow these rules assiduously. More than any other area of responsibility, leading by example in matters of safety is essential.

Time lost waiting for materials can be reduced by an effective materials management operation as discussed in Chapter XII. Necessary materials should be delivered to the work site in a timely manner—neither too late nor too much in advance. The consequences of late delivery may result simply in idle time or time spent seeking the materials. The consequences of too early delivery may be a cluttered workspace, but may also result in misuse or misplacing the materials.

Equipment can often be a bottleneck. The cost of equipment is very visible as it shows up as a real cost in both budgets and monthly expenditure analyses. There is a tendency to provide no more equipment than is absolutely necessary, expecting that this will minimize costs. The cost of waiting for equipment is less obvious and can be mistakenly attributed to general labor inefficiency. Likewise, the cost of preventive maintenance is very obvious while the costs of equipment breakdown are less obvious. One way to assess the actual cost of waiting for equipment, as well as other losses in efficiency, is to perform work-sampling studies. These use statistical sampling methods to collect observations of what the status of people or equipment is at specific instants. These observations are assumed to be an accurate reflection of the actual time spent on productive work versus being idle for specific reasons. Work sampling is a technique that should be applied by a person skilled in and knowledgeable about its use. Lack of skill can lead to erroneous conclusions. Lack of knowledge of how to use it can result in adverse labor reactions including grievances, slow downs, and even work stoppages. On the other hand, well used, it can provide the project manager with important information that can reduce unnecessary costs to the project. More information on work sampling can be found in the *Industrial Engineering Handbook* (Hobson 1992).

For a given provisioning of equipment to aid in performing the project, scheduling its use is vital. It can help reduce the time that the equipment is required on the job as well as help ensure that it is available for the most needed uses at any point in time. For example, a crane may be essential for structural steel placement. It may also be used to move other materials to where they are required. Moving the materials might be done during periods other than when structural steel is being installed, such as during breaks. It might also be done before the regular shift begins or after it ends. Thus, it might be desirable to have another crane operator and a skeleton crew for materials handling scheduled for overtime or on an alternative workday schedule to facilitate such tasks. These might be very inexpensive alternatives when compared to the cost of another crane. Similarly, not all materials handling needs to be done by the same size crane. A small, more mobile crane could handle many tasks and could be used to marshal materials that must be moved with the larger crane. While this example is construction oriented, any other major piece of equipment could be substituted for crane, regardless of the project type, and the concept would be just as valid.

As unfair as it may be, there seems to be a stereotype of public works projects that there are more people watching than there are working. Having more people assigned to a task than can work on the task at the same time will inevitably have this result. Exercise care in determining the number of people required to perform a task and assign only that many. To do this effectively, it may be necessary to subdivide an activity to isolate those tasks that are most limiting. Often there are make-ready and put-away tasks associated with an activity. For example, make-ready tasks may include taking measurements, checking materials, moving equipment into place, and other such tasks, that can be performed prior to the main crew arriving. Perhaps key personnel can be scheduled to start an hour before the crew. Similarly, as the activity nears completion, there are tasks that must be performed such as cleaning the area and tools, returning equipment and unused materials, and securing the area. These often do not require the entire crew. One or a few people might work overtime to accomplish these tasks and the majority of the crew could be moved to the next activity if there is still time left in the shift. On the other hand, do not provide less than the number of persons required to perform a task. Many tasks can be performed much more economically by a proper size team.

Projects are very time sensitive. The start of each activity is dependent upon the successful completion of predecessor activities. Inability to start an activity as scheduled not only invites idle time for its resources, but also is likely to result in the domino effect on following activities. It is very likely that an activity that is not started on time will not be finished on time. Thus, the project manager must be as concerned with the start of activities as with the completion of activities.

Successful completion of activities means that the work product of that activity is consistent with the needs and expectations of the follower activity. It may, or may not, be acceptable to publish a drawing, specification, instruction, or the like that includes a statement such as, "details to be provided later." If that precludes the follower activity from starting, the predecessor activity is not completed. On the other hand, if the people responsible for the two activities have coordinated adequately, it may be a way to gain some time in performing the two activities. This concept is at the heart of the modern quality concept, modified slightly for projects, "The customer is the next activity in the process." If that customer is not satisfied with the product of the preceding activity, then it most assuredly is not a "quality product."

The project manager must be concerned about interruptions of work because of external influences. Some are controllable and others require contingency planning. Visitors to the project can interrupt the flow of work in unexpected ways. The OC will never forget the day a whole man-day of work was lost in a large drafting room of mostly men when an especially attractive young lady walked from the entrance of the room to a meeting room. That was at a time when females were not a significant presence in such a workplace. Visiting VIPs can have a similar effect. If the VIP is an important stakeholder, you may grin and bear it. Otherwise, arrangements should be made to minimize the impact of visitors. For example, on the Northumberland Bridge (from New Brunswick to Prince Edward Island, Canada) project, a special visitors area limited their impact on traffic to the site, presentations in that facility answered most questions, and bus transportation of visitors around the site eliminated visibility of them, as well as foot traffic where the work was being done. A small fee for the tour defrayed the costs of this very valuable public relations activity.

Control of other visitors to the project is important. Sales and other representatives can be a disturbing influence. A reception area can provide control of their entrance to work areas and provide a place for project personnel to meet with visitors in a more manageable environment. Ending a visit is much easier if the meeting is in such a location rather than in the project team member's office. On many projects, control of visitors is a must due to security requirements.

Traffic flow to and from the project site can result in delays of all types, as well as lead to bad attitudes. Not only are the arteries leading to the site critical, but vehicles are often parked in the wrong places and driven in unsafe areas. This is a particular problem if there is a need for emergency vehicles to access the site. For some emergencies, it is important to evacuate the project site. Contingency planning cannot only facilitate this, but also enhance decision-making to minimize the adverse effects on labor usage. Weather is often a cause of work stoppage, or at least inefficiency. Sometimes it can call for evacuation, or at least moving people and equipment that may be at risk. Again, contingency planning can minimize the effects. For example, it may be possible to conduct training, safety talks, or other project related activities during such an interruption that might otherwise have to be scheduled during work periods. Reliable weather information can enhance the possibilities.

Methods Management

In volume production operations, industrial engineering techniques are employed extensively to reduce the work content of repetitive tasks. While projects are unique, many of the tasks performed on projects are repetitive. As such, they can be analyzed using industrial engineering techniques and the work content reduced, and/or the quality of the work improved substantially. The OC has observed many such opportunities and has taken advantage of them repeatedly. However, it has been a source of consternation that so much project work is done by rather inefficient methods.

One excellent example of the application of methods improvement is scaffolding in construction. In some areas of the world, scaffolds are constructed of bamboo poles, a highly labor intensive method. Memory still exists of scaffolding constructed of lumber; still highly labor intensive and wasteful, as the lumber was often scrapped. Then came modular tubing scaffolding; much less labor intensive and reusable. These were supplemented with elevator scaffolding; valuable because it increased the efficiency of both the scaffold installation and the masons working on it, by raising the scaffolding in smaller increments. It allowed the masons to work at the optimum height relationship between the mason and the wall being worked upon. There are many other excellent examples. Software development has benefited by the development of better tools that reduce the work content required to create code for a specific computing task.

Yet, examples abound of work being performed by inefficient methods. In part, this is explained by the dependency upon the individual worker to know how to do the task. In part, it is explained by the seeming lack of knowledge of work methods by project management personnel. Something can be done about the latter consistent with the former. Training in the fundamentals of work methods analysis should be provided to project personnel to improve awareness of causes of inefficiency and opportunities to improve methods. Simple understanding of basic elemental motions, and the ability to perform certain motions simultaneously, would surely lead to better work methods. If learning new technologies, such as alloy welding or the use of structured programming, are important, then surely some training in technologies, such as work methods analysis, should be considered important.

Such training should focus on methods analysis; use of jigs, fixtures, and templates; and the allocation of tasks among crewmembers to avoid idle time. Even the performance of nonrepetitive tasks can be improved by just a consciousness of methods analysis.

One approach to modifying these characteristics of work on projects is to look for opportunities to change the mode in which particular tasks are performed. Whenever an activity involves performing the same operations many times, there is an opportunity to perform that activity in either job shop, progressive line, or continuous flow mode. For example, on the English Channel Tunnel project, the linings of the tunnel were designed to facilitate precasting on a progressive line outside the tunnel, rather than pouring in place in the tunnel. On a lesser scale, the 80,000 seats in the Pontiac Silverdome were installed using progressive line methods, with the workers moving from one seat to the next, rather than the line moving. On a grander scale, the very large components (piers and spans) of the Northumberland Channel Bridge were precast in progressive line mode, and transported to their individual sites by a very large "forklift" constructed on a barge. (This was a concept that was truly hard to believe without actually seeing it.) Using concrete pumper trucks to place large quantities of concrete is almost a mundane example of continuous flow mode. Where volume is less and/or the variability in the components greater, the job shop mode may be useful. For some activities, it may be desirable to go to the other end of the spectrum and perform an activity in true craft mode. This is especially true on prototypes, whether physical or abstract, such as in computer systems prototyping.

EQUIPMENT COST MANAGEMENT

Equipment is used as both a substitute for labor and to augment labor. Substitution for labor is often referred to as automation. Opportunities for automation are rather limited on project work, but should not be ignored. Equipment to augment labor is essential on many projects. Using a word processor to write a book is quite obvious. It permits easy correction of mistakes, analysis of grammar, and search for alternative words along with many other benefits. Modern construction could not proceed without cranes to lift heavy objects, welding machines to join metals, and many other items of equipment. The examples across project types are endless.

The economics of equipment determine its viability. This is most easily understood by comparing the cost-volume relationship of using equipment versus manual methods, as shown in Figure XV.1, Cost versus Volume. In general, the fixed cost of acquiring the equipment is higher than the fixed cost of acquiring a manual approach. However, the unit operating costs are often much less. As a result, the cost

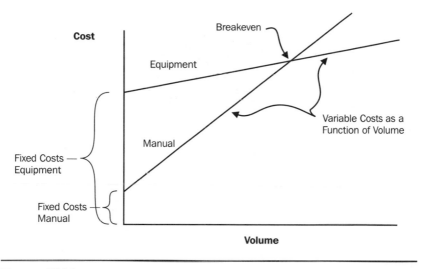

FIGURE XV.1

Cost versus Volume

curves intersect at the break-even point. If the number of units of production is less than that of the break-even point, it is more economical to use a manual approach. If the volume is greater than the break-even point, it is more economical to use the equipment. This poses a problem for projects, as volume is typically low and sometimes only one. Thus, projects tend to be labor intensive.

Several alternatives are used to revise the cost curves. One is for an organization to specialize in work for which the equipment is applicable. Such an organization can have a competitive advantage for that type of work and can increase its volume until it is above the break-even point. This assumes that a sufficient volume of that type of work is available within a reasonable market area. Making the equipment more mobile can increase the market area. Similarly, another organization can rent or lease the equipment to the project as it is required. This transforms the relevant cost curve to be more like Figure XV.2, Cost versus Time. A given project has a fixed volume of work for which the equipment is applicable. Thus, the shorter the time required to perform that work, the less the cost of the equipment to that project. This places a premium on scheduling work requiring the equipment into the shortest time span possible.

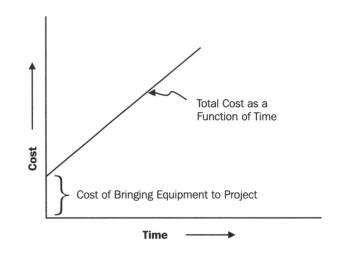

Cost

Total Cost as a
Function of Time

Cost of Bringing Equipment to Project

Time

FIGURE XV.2
Cost versus Time

Two alternatives offer opportunities to modify this relationship. One is to use a less costly piece of equipment to perform as much work as possible before bringing in the more expensive equipment. The less expensive unit may also be used to reduce the time required to perform the work that requires the more expensive equipment. Thus, a small mobile crane could be used to marshal materials into loads that can be picked up quickly by a very large crane. Of course, this assumes that the activities requiring the materials can use them at the accelerated pace.

The other alternative is to design the product of the project to take greater advantage of the availability of the equipment and, thus, increase the volume of work for which it is required. A building might be designed to use precast wall panels, rather than brick, using the large crane to lift the panels into place. Of course, this assumes that using the more expensive equipment in this manner has an economic, or other, advantage to the project.

Both of these, and other aspects of using equipment on a project, argue for the project manager to be closely involved in the design of the product of the project to enhance the opportunities to use the equipment in a cost effective manner. The project manager must also ensure that the use of the equipment does not introduce scheduling constraints that increase the project duration or cost. One manufactured housing contractor has a policy of having a bulldozer on site when heavy equipment and the manufactured modules are brought onto the site, just in case they need assistance if they get bogged down in mud or loose dirt. Another paved the site to eliminate similar problems encountered when moving equipment.

Clearly, this is a very cursory discussion of the role of equipment in performing a project. The intent is to make the reader more aware of some of the considerations involved in this very important cost element of projects.

CHANGE COST CONTROL

An oft-stated maxim of organizations that operate in the project mode is, "Bid low and make it up on changes." Seldom is this maxim followed by corollaries such as, "Unless carefully managed, changes will cost more than they earn." The OC heard an abbreviated version of this statement recently at lunch. "Changes cost more than they earn." The speaker went on to say that, "Typically, the whole crew will stand around watching as one person makes the change." Clearly, this could generate a lot of unproductive labor cost quickly. Managing change implies careful examination of *all* the consequences of the change— including effects on the project schedule, careful planning of how the costs of implementing the change are to be minimized, and negotiating for payment of a fair amount for making the change.

Consequences of a change can be elusive. A small change in a computer program may seem easy. However, that change may interact with another aspect of the program in such a way that it does not show up until after the program is released for productive use. The person making the change may not have a broad view of the system and, thus, not recognize the consequences. The test procedures for verifying the program modules and the final system likely will not be changed to recognize the change, let alone test it. Suddenly, the system fails and extensive efforts are required to identify the cause and fix it, all in rush mode at premium costs. And that says nothing about the other work that would otherwise have been accomplished by the resources used to fix the problem.

More obvious changes usually have consequences on the project schedule. Murphy's Law suggests that change will generally be on the critical path. Thus, other activities may be delayed, again initiating the domino effect on the project schedule. Often, the simplest change will lead to unexpected work or unanticipated problems. The OC is reminded of a small change in a minor redecorating project. The spouse asked for a broken tile in the shower to be replaced. The wallboard behind it was rotten. That extended to the wallboard behind a number of other tiles. Before that change was completed, the entire wall in the shower area had been removed, the wallboard replaced, and new tile installed. Only a small change in a small "honey-do" project extended over several weekends, rather than just one Saturday.

On smaller projects, it is not uncommon for the project manager, after having agreed to the change, to say to the appropriate crew leader, "Just do it!" There may be nothing more than a crude sketch and the change may be contrary to common practice. In such cases, it may well result in the rest of the crew standing around watching while the crew leader makes the change. This certainly is not managing the change. For example, it would probably be more economical to pay one person to make the change on overtime than to pay for the unproductive labor. At minimum, other work should be found for the resources that are not required to make the change.

Negotiating reimbursement for the cost of the change requires documenting the costs in a manner that is persuasive to the client. The less sophisticated the client in the concepts of project management, the more difficult this will be. Since this is often done while in a mental state of extreme exasperation, it may be difficult to apply the energy necessary to do this well. Nevertheless, careful thinking is required to identify all the costs, including costs of the time spent in negotiating the change itself, preparing the cost estimate, and examining the effects on the schedule.

Finally, because clients tend to have short memories, change control requires careful documentation of the change, its cost, and the agreement of the client.

The previous discussion implies that all change is due to client requests. Much of it can be traced to errors in executing the project. These lead to rework, a major contributor to cost overruns.

Rework Costs

Rework can be caused by client changes. Most of that should be reimbursed if the change control procedures are adequate. The rework costs that result from errors by the project team are seldom reimbursed.

Consider the impact on one construction project error. A utility tunnel was being constructed to enter a new building just inside a corner of the building. Suddenly, after much of the concrete had been poured and even more rebar installed, someone recognized that it had been laid out to arrive at the building just outside that corner. The cost of the rework of correcting this error, purportedly, eliminated the planned profit on the project. Of somewhat less magnitude, an error on another construction project was discovered just before pouring the concrete wall. The wall was to be faced with brick, but was laid out just the thickness of a brick too far out. Then, in removing the forms, the forms and rebar all fell over. It was on that same project that the structural steel for the top stories was delivered before that for the first story.

Then there was the computer project where two mating subsystems were developed with a difference of one bit in the logical definition of a number series between subsystems. Clearly, they would not work together when merged.

It would certainly be interesting, instructive, and perhaps entertaining (for all but the responsible people), to collect examples of other horror stories. There must be many of them. They all probably led to rework, claims, judgments, and, in some cases, the failure of an otherwise successful enterprise. (If you have a favorite, or more, the OC would enjoy receiving them at fmwebster@aol.com.)

Quality control is often focused on the product of the project. Does it meet the customer requirements or, more specifically, the specifications of those requirements? Quality control of the processes for performing the project is at least equally important if the project is to be successful in meeting schedule and cost targets.

All of the above affect the cost of the project. They must be exercised in a timely manner while, or preferably before, the work is being performed. They determine what will be reported as the actual cost of the activities of the project.

OVERALL COST MANAGEMENT

One of the major forces behind the quest for better project cost management practices has been the United States Department of Defense (DoD). A major share of its budget goes for new weapons systems development. Those projects have been notorious for their cost and schedule overruns. These have reflected poorly upon the DoD and particularly in their relations with the Congress in getting approval for new projects, not to mention funds to cover the overruns. Thus, the motivation to find a better way was high.

An early effort in this direction was called PERT/Cost, the wedding of project accounting to the newly developed technique called Program Evaluation and Review Technique (PERT). It was amusing to be a part of the audience of defense contractors listening to DoD personnel laud the benefits of PERT/Cost and then, during breaks, listen to those same defense contractors wail about the onerousness of these demands. Actually, the wailing was because PERT/Cost threatened to expose and curtail the very machinations that the DoD wished to eliminate, and by which the contractors made defense contracting a lucrative business (spell that "cost overruns"). Then Secretary of Defense, Robert McNamara, ordered each service to conduct tests of PERT/Cost on a major weapons system program. The results were less than satisfactory and PERT/Cost fell into disfavor.

The quest continued, resulting in Cost Schedule Control Systems Criteria (C/SCSC or C(SC)^2) based on the concept of earned value.

Furthermore, the DoD learned from PERT/Cost that it could not impose such controls on the contractors, but could make it competitively advantageous for the defense contractor to subscribe to C/SCSC. This concept has gained acceptance and has proven to achieve the benefit sought by the DoD, better cost management of projects.

The C/SCSC, in the DoD Instruction 5000.2, established certain criteria by which a contractor's cost/schedule control systems will be judged. If the system conforms to these criteria, regardless of how implemented, the contractor is "certified" and, thus, has an advantage in winning DoD contracts. The concept is very well presented in a book by Quentin Fleming (1992), a well-recognized expert on C/SCSC. This book is somewhat amusing to read as, in explaining the criteria, Fleming alludes to practices by the DoD contractors that were eliminated by complying with the criteria. (An example of this can be found on pages 152–3 in his discussion of Interdivisional Work.) Fleming also wrote a shorter treatment focusing only on earned value (Fleming 1996).

The important concept to understand at this point is earned value.

Earned Value

Earned value, very simply, is the project equivalent of standard costing for job shop accounting. Job shops generally perform a relatively small set of operations on a somewhat larger set of parts. Because these operations are performed repeatedly, one can establish a standard unit cost for performing an operation on a specific part. By using industrial engineering techniques, such a standard can be determined with a relatively high level of precision, if not accuracy. Thus, when a part is produced, the standard cost for an operation is multiplied by the number of parts produced to determine the standard cost earned for that operation. The sum of these standard costs represents the standard cost earned for producing the part.

Concurrently, the actual costs expended in producing that part are collected. If the actual costs exceed the standard costs, there is an unfavorable variance. If the actual costs are less than the standard costs, the variance is favorable. Further analysis can identify the cause

PM 102: According to the Olde Curmudgeon

of the variance as to either a price variance or a volume variance. A price variance might be as a result of paying the operator at a higher rate than used in establishing the standard. A volume variance could be as a result of producing more or less scrap parts than assumed in establishing the standard. Having determined whether it was a price or volume variance, deeper analysis can lead to a precise cause.

Much project work is nonrepetitive. This leads to four problems.

❑ First, for much project work, the uniqueness of the activities does not warrant spending much time or effort establishing a precise estimate or determining the cause of a variance. Therefore, the cost of performing an activity cannot be established with anywhere near the precision of the standard in the job shop. Thus, it is generally very difficult to establish what the cost of an activity really should be.

❑ Second, because of the variability of the work content of project activities, it is more difficult to determine the precise cause of a variance.

❑ Third, activities are considerably longer than the typical operation in the job shop, and the activity often produces only one unit of work product, so we must estimate the amount of the activity's value that has been earned at the point in time when a cost report is prepared.

❑ Finally, the duration of a project is typically much longer than the typical job in a job shop. Thus, the status of the project at intermediate points in time must be measured by the accumulation of costs from a variety of activities.

The OC ran into another problem upon implementing a proprietary version of a project cost management system when the client, a vice president for car assembly, exclaimed, "Finally, the engineers, contractors, and accountants can talk the same language." He realized that prior project control systems were a conglomeration of costs collected, based on differing premises from which it was nearly impossible to reach any conclusions about project cost and schedule status before the post-project audit was completed.

Regardless of the difficulties of measuring, it is important to have some measure of the work that has been accomplished to date on the

204

project that can be compared to the work that was intended to be done and the costs that were budgeted for that work. To accomplish this, we make some assumptions to develop the general concept.

❑ First, we assume that the estimated cost of the work performed on an activity is a measure of the value earned in its performance.

❑ Secondly, we assume that the person responsible for performing the activity can estimate with reasonable accuracy the percentage of the activity that has actually been accomplished.

It should be noted that more sophisticated versions of earned value modify these assumptions to correspond with reality, if appropriate.

Given these assumptions and a scheduled start and completion date for each activity, one can develop a time-phased budget for the project. Due to the nature of the application of resources to a project—a buildup of resources being applied rises to a peak, followed by reductions in resources applied until project completion—the budget follows that same pattern. The accumulation of these costs by period results in a cumulative budget presentation that resembles an s-curve. Thus, at any point in time, we can see how much should have been spent if the project progresses according to schedule. This value is referred to as "the budgeted cost of work scheduled" (BCWS) and is illustrated in Figure XV.3, Budgeted Cost of Work Scheduled.

Seldom are projects performed exactly to schedule. Thus, following the same accumulation process, we can develop another s-curve that represents the cost that should have been incurred based on when the activities were actually performed. This is referred to as "the budgeted cost of work performed" (BCWP). Any differences between BCWS and BCWP values represent a schedule variance. This is illustrated in Figure XV.4, BCWS versus BCWP.

It is also unusual for a project to be performed exactly to budget. Thus, it is useful to accumulate the actual costs incurred to develop "the actual cost of work performed" (ACWP). Any difference between BCWP and ACWP is a measure of cost or spending variance. This is illustrated in Figure XV.5, BCWS versus BCWP versus ACWP.

Because these values are calculated for every element of the work breakdown structure (WBS), a variance for the project as a whole can

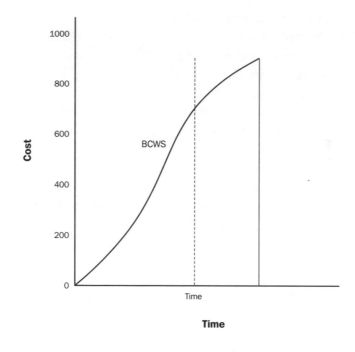

FIGURE XV.3
Budgeted Cost of Work Scheduled

be traced down the WBS to determine the cause of the variance. This is illustrated in Table XV.3, Analysis of Variances. When an element lower in the WBS is identified as the cause of a variance, detail listings can be analyzed to determine the precise cause of the problem. This permits determination of alternatives for resolving the problem and selecting corrective action.

Using these three measures, we can calculate two measures that summarize performance to date. The Schedule Performance Index (SPI) is simply:

$$SPI = BCWP/BCWS$$

Clearly, if this value is greater than 1, the project is ahead of schedule. A value of less than 1 is bad news.

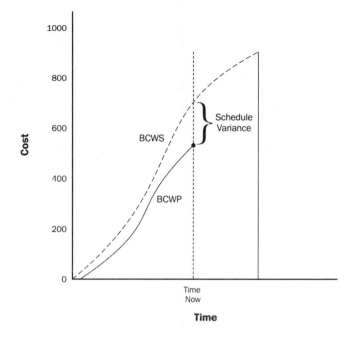

FIGURE XV.4

BCWS versus BCWP

The Cost Performance Index (CPI) is:

$$CPI = BCWP/ACWP$$

A value of greater than 1 indicates favorable cost performance, while a value of less than 1 is bad news.

Given all this information, there are techniques for developing an "estimated cost at completion" (EAC). If the variance is unfavorable, one assumption might be that there will be no further unfavorable variances. This is probably a *naive* assumption. Alternatively, we might assume that the variances to date will be reversed by better performance of the rest of the project. This is probably a *very naive* assumption. A more realistic assumption might be that the percentage variances will continue to project completion. This is supported by

207

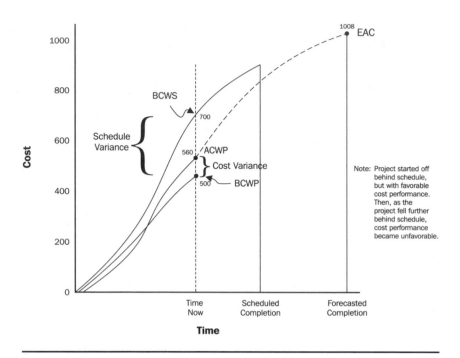

FIGURE XV.5
BCWS versus BCWP versus ACWP

research that shows that both schedule and cost performance indices are relatively stable over the duration of a project. It is justified, in part, by the domino effect. There are a myriad of other causes, not the least of which is the deterioration of the morale of the project team.

It is important to have a balanced perspective on the value of earned value. There is no question of its value on projects such as those commonly performed by the DoD. Typically, most of the work is performed by other organizations. Most of that work is performed under contracts where the DoD bears a substantial portion of the cost risk, i.e., cost reimbursable contracts of some type. Thus, the DoD is very concerned about cost overruns. They are also very concerned about schedule overruns; perhaps mostly because of the typical direct correlation between schedule overruns and cost overruns. Because of the many activities in process at any one time, it is impractical to

Work Package	Budget	BCWS	BCWP	ACWP
Total	900	700	500	560
A	100	100	100	150
B	300	300	300	290
C	200	200	100	120
D	200	100	0	0
E	100	0	0	0

Notes:
1. From the Total line, the project is behind schedule and overspent. The causes can be determined by examining the individual work packages (WP).
2. WP A is completed, but overspent by $50.
3. WP B is completed and is underspent by $10.
4. WP C is one-half completed and is overspent by $20.
5. WP D should have been started and be half completed. It has not started yet.
6. WP E is not scheduled to start yet.
7. The SPI is 0.71 (500/700). The project is forecasted to take 40% longer than scheduled (1/.71 = 1.41).
8. The CPI is 0.89 (500/560). The project is forecasted to cost 12% more that budgeted (1/0.89 = 1.12).
9. The EAC is $1008 (900 x 1.12).

TABLE XV.3
Analysis of Variances

exercise close scrutiny and, therefore, proactive management, of their performance. Thus, the measures of most concern are the performance of WBS elements to schedule and budget.

In organizations performing several to many projects at a time, earned value is an excellent way of presenting the status of all projects to executive management in a simple, standard format they can quickly comprehend. Thus, there can be no question of the worth of earned value. However, careful analysis of the processes involved in preparing these reports, as compared to the physical performance of the project, is revealing. There is an inevitable delay between the reporting of status and the generation and distribution of the earned value reports. Depending on the philosophy of use of the system, there may be further delays in capturing the status of individual activities. Thus, to a large extent, per the OC, the horse is already out the barn door. Only through more proactive management can the actual performance on the project be managed. Many of the approaches to this are suggested in the previous discussion in this chapter. A more explicit discussion can be found in Chapter XVIII, Reporting and Control. One approach, commitment cost control, is sufficiently significant to discuss as an integral part of this discussion of earned value.

Commitment Cost Control

A technique that is widely used in industry is commitment cost control. Many industries have formal commitment cost control systems. The OC has observed the concept in use in other organizations where there is no formal commitment cost control system. One department head had his secretary keep a record of all purchase order requests, work orders, and other commitments against a project to ensure that he did not authorize expenditures that would exceed the budget for the project. The OC used a simple technique as a member of a Board of Education. Each month he reviewed a computer listing of all checks written. No more than fifteen minutes a month were required for the scanning. Questionable items were reviewed with the financial manager and resolved. On only a few occasions was mention made of an item in a public meeting. The important point is that all employees soon realized that the check register was being scanned and knew that they had better not charge anything to the school system that was not appropriate. On a project, you want to review the general ledger of all charges to your project. This is also important to prevent accounting charging the project for something you have not agreed to.

The importance of such a system is clear by understanding the relationship between decision-making and cost reporting for projects in many organizations. Consider any significant piece of equipment to be installed as a part of the product of the project. Suppose it is built to order with a lead-time of six months. The purchase order for this item is placed for $100,000 with payment of $50,000 upon delivery and the balance as soon as it is installed and has passed acceptance tests. The delivery is on schedule and the invoice is prepared. The invoice arrives on the 25th of the month, is approved on the 30th, and arrives in accounting on the 2nd. The next check processing cycle is on the 15th. Thus, the $50,000 payment is recognized in the budget report prepared on the 5th of the following month, 40 days after the invoice. Similarly, following completion of the installation and testing of the equipment, the check for the final payment of $50,000 is prepared on the 15th, three months later. For seven months, the project cost reports show that this activity, and therefore the project, are underspent by at least $100,000. Feeling quite confident, the project manager authorizes some unplanned overtime on another activity. Suddenly, the first $50,000 is recognized and the amount available to spend goes down. Three months later, the other $50,000 is recognized and now the project is overspent. The budget reports have been very misleading.

On a more personal basis, this mechanism can be understood by thinking about your credit card use. The OC's Visa statement is prepared on the 6th of each month. Suppose the spouse purchases a major item on the 7th and says nothing about it. The next statement will be received in the mail about the 12th of the following month. That amount, along with any other charges, is payable within about fifteen days or high interest charges are incurred. That could be a major shock to the checking account.

Perhaps your accounting system does not work that way. The last budget reports received by the OC before retiring were certainly consistent with this scenario. If you are not sure, take time to understand before your project comes in over budget. If necessary, keep your own records.

Alternatively, you may decide to install an earned value system. While it can be of considerable value, there are a lot of details required to have a successful implementation. You are advised to study Fleming's writings carefully and also *Project Management: The Common Sense Approach* (Lambert and Lambert 2000). It focuses on implementation and is an especially frank discussion of choosing to use modern project management. Installing earned value requires the understanding of what is required by both the top executives and the accounting personnel. This is particularly important in an organization that is not primarily project oriented. Even in a totally project-oriented organization, the OC was once told by the accounting manager that he intended to open no more than ten work orders to collect costs on a multimillion dollar contract.

If the organization does not commit to the changes necessary to support earned value, it is questionable how accurate the data contained in conventional earned value reports will be. In that case, it is probably advisable to implement a modified version for which the data can be collected and entered by the project office. This can be done by extracting data from the labor reporting system, invoice approvals, and other documents of this sort. With some creativity, it is possible to implement a very useful approach to earned value. The greatest difficulty will be in reconciling these records with conventional accounting reports.

COST SYSTEMS

There are many project management software systems available to perform earned value analysis. If your project is one for which the client requires earned value, it is probably advantageous to select one that has been included in a cost management system that has been certified under the specifications of the Cost/Schedule Control Systems Criteria or its successor. It is not likely to include a good commitment control capability; therefore, it should be modifiable so that this capability can be added.

SUMMARY

There are a lot of cost drivers in a project. The project manager needs to recognize all of them and ensure that someone is managing each one. Failure to do so will inevitably result in surprises, some of which may be very unpleasant.

Project cost management is most effective when it is ensuring that today's work is done effectively and efficiently, and that tomorrow's work is well planned. The project manager cannot personally supervise all the activities that are in process each day. The responsibility and authority must be delegated to ensure that such supervision is exercised daily, and that activities are coordinated to prevent problems such as the errors discussed under rework. However, you can review all charges to your project.

The primary lesson to be learned from this is that project cost management must be a proactive process to ensure that unintended costs are not incurred. By so doing, there will be less rework and less agonizing over "What do we do now?"

> Sam decided to simply use the measure of labor hours used versus estimated to measure progress and predict the total labor hours at completion. All this information was readily available. The only delay in getting the data was the time for a runner or himself to go to the forest and collect it from the parties.
>
> Sam examined the activities to see exactly what the planned work content was. These results are as follows:

```
Design
   DC                 6   ×  3   =  18
   DDD               12   ×  3   =  36          54
Gather Materials
   GML               33   ×  6   =  198
   GMH           (45 x 4) + 36   =  216
   GMV               12   ×  5   =  60         474
Prepare Materials
   MPL               36   ×  4   =  144
   MPH               18   ×  1   =  18
   MPV                6   ×  5   =  30         192
Assemble
   AD                19   ×  4   =  76
   AM                 2   ×  2   =  4           80
Test
   TD                 2   ×  17  =  34
   TM                 1   ×  18  =  18
   TFT                1   ×  16  =  16          68      868
```

> Sam considered the value of each of these elements of the project and decided to identify Design, Prepare Materials, Assemble, and Test as separate work packages. Because of their magnitudes, Sam went a level lower in Gather Materials and identified GML, GMH, and GMV as separate work packages. This resulted in the largest work package amounting to 216 labor days and the smallest 54 labor days.

APPENDIX XV.A
MARS PATHFINDER PROJECT

MARS PATHFINDER PROJECT BUDGET

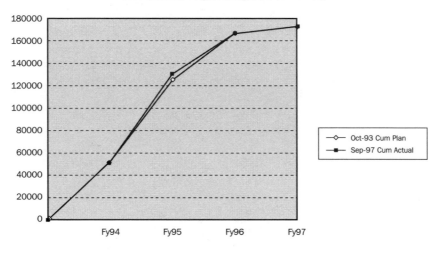

Mars Pathfinder Project Budget (FY 93 – FY 97)

Legend:
- Oct-93 Cum Plan
- Sep-97 Cum Actual

(in 000's)	Fy94	Fy95	Fy96	Fy97
Oct-93 Plan	52,004	74,569	38,047	6,380
Sep-97 Actual	52,374	78,285	34,454	5,606
Oct-93 Cum Plan	52,004	126,573	164,620	171,000
Sep-97 Cum Actual	52,374	130,659	165,113	170,719

214

Chapter XVI

Quality in Projects

Sam was concerned about the nature of the trees that would be cut down to form the floor of the raft. The members of the family were sufficiently agile to walk on a deck that was not perfectly flat. However, some of the animals did not seem to be that agile on rough terrain. Likewise, Sam wanted to be sure that the vines and thongs were strong enough to do their job well, especially if the rains started to swell the river before the transfer to the other side was completed. Sam lost some sleep over these issues and wondered what could be done to ensure the quality of the materials and success of the project.

Quality has evolved over the past fifty years, starting with the efforts of W. Edwards Deming, J. M. Juran, and others in Japan just after World War II. Largely as a result of these efforts, Japan changed its image of producing cheap, low quality goods to being the pacesetter in achieving customer satisfaction by producing high quality goods. The movement was so successful that the Japanese created the prestigious Deming Award for companies that achieved outstanding quality. It took nearly three decades for the concepts developed there to be adopted by other countries. These concepts became _the_ management concept of the 1980s, as industry elsewhere scurried to catch up to the Japanese. The notable characteristic of the Japanese concepts was that they moved the meaning of quality from an amorphous term to one that was highly measurable and that separated the concept of quality from the concept of customer satisfaction. Then, in the 1990s, it would seem to the OC, that much of the progress that was achieved in converting "quality" into a highly quantitative concept was negated by defining something called "total quality," recombining quality and customer satisfaction.

The old concept of quality was "meeting the customer's needs." There were many deficiencies in this concept that have been discussed at length in many sources. Deming argued that it was not sufficiently quantitative to really measure and, therefore, could not be controlled. The most meaningful discussion of the old concept of quality was in Crosby's *Quality is Free* (Crosby 1979). In this example, a quality manager and a production manager are inspecting a production lot and determining for each part if it is "good enough" to meet customer needs. They each have different perceptions of the customer's needs. Eventually they realize that they have not quantified customer needs, so there is no precision in the process, let alone accuracy.

The new concept defined quality as "conformance to specifications." By explicitly stating the specifications in quantitative terms, and stipulating that each specification was either met or not met, statistical concepts became far more useful in analyzing and correcting quality problems. As a result, the objective of "zero defects" was restated into achievable, though demanding, terms such as "6 sigma." This is a measure on the normal curve of probability that implies a defect rate in the order of one out of a million parts produced. Many other concepts were introduced to further define this new quality.

One might gather from the above that the OC believes that total quality was a step backward. That would be an appropriate observation. It seems to the OC that keeping quality and customer (or client) satisfaction as two separate concepts has significant operational benefits. The discussion that follows in this chapter is based on that notion. It is both operationally and pedagogically useful. The reader is free to use these concepts however they are convenient. The distinction will aid in analyzing problems in your implementation of quality, however defined.

FOUR ASPECTS OF QUALITY

There are four major aspects of achieving quality on projects—customer satisfaction, accurate and current specifications, quality of the product of the project, and quality of the project.

Client Satisfaction

It should be a primary objective of any reputable organization to satisfy its clients. It is well proven that it is far less expensive to keep a good client than it is to win a new one. Furthermore, satisfied clients share their experiences with others who may well become your clients. Gaining clients through referrals is the least expensive way to get a new client. Unfortunately, an unsatisfied client also shares experiences with others, and probably with more others than the satisfied client. Furthermore, an unsatisfied client is likely to make incessant demands for correction of problems, real or imagined, or file a claim which may be settled by an award from a jury sympathetic to the client. Thus, anyway you look at it, it pays to satisfy your clients.

Sometimes this seems impossible. Conversations with building contractors suggest that homebuyers are the most difficult to satisfy. The reader is free to speculate about the reason for this. Some contractors feel so strongly about this that they opt out of that market. There are bad apples wherever you go and whatever you do. If a potential client has a reputation for being such a client, you are better off not bidding on that client's project. If you do bid, do everything possible to ensure satisfaction, for a recommendation from such a client may be very meaningful to other potential clients.

Satisfying the client means delivering the product that the client wants and performing the project in an "appropriate" manner. Each organization will tailor its concept of these requirements to their own liking. It does not mean giving the client everything they ask for, regardless of cost. An appropriate manner implies developing a working relationship that allows frank and honest exchange of requirements and negotiation to achieve win-win outcomes. Partnering is an excellent approach that leads to customer satisfaction on each project and a continuing business relationship, i.e., more business. Fluor-Daniel Corporation, a major design-build firm, has practiced this with great success for both them and the client. The best evidence that you are seeking to act in this manner is to approach opportunities to deliver a better product with greater value to the client. When this is done in a pleasant manner, the client is more likely to deal fairly with you.

To deliver a better product with greater value, it is necessary to understand thoroughly the client's needs, not just the specifications provided to you. This requires sincere and probing questioning of the client to avoid making assumptions that are unfounded. The alternative assumptions that could be made, when the factual requirements are not available, make clear the need to obtain explicit direction. This is generally best achieved by providing the client with the alternatives and offering to aid in making the decision. All such decisions should be incorporated into the specifications as a basis for ensuring they are properly incorporated in the product of the project.

Accurate and Current Specifications

It is not sufficient to deliver the product in conformance to the originally stated specifications. There must be a continuing effort to recognize any changes in requirements of the client *and* to suggest changes that lead to a better product with greater value. This may mean extra cost to the client, but it may also mean a reduction in the work content of the project and, thus, less total revenue from performing the project. Fluor-Daniel has discussed openly the efforts that they expend attempting to reduce costs to the client. Often these are identified through the use of value engineering, i.e., a formal approach to changing the product or the process of producing it to reduce costs. Sometimes these are generated from innovative ideas. Often the latter are induced as a direct result of creating an environment for motivation through direct or indirect recognition or rewards. For example, goals are set for achieving savings and, when they are achieved, there is a celebration that includes client personnel. For more on this, read the fictionalized report of a project that was selected project of the year by Fluor-Daniel in *The World's Greatest Project* (Darnall 1996).

In addition, the client has expectations that go beyond the specifications. Perhaps the client wants you to perform the project in a manner that will preserve, and perhaps enhance, community relations. If the product of the project is a structure, the client will be living with that community for some time. It should be a peaceful existence. Perhaps the client expects a complete user's manual tailored to this product, not one that is so generalized as to be useless to the operator. Attempt to determine these expectations in the process of developing the project scope, but be alert to recognize new ones during the project. If they can be met, do so. If not, be sure the client understands why not.

A satisfied client is not suddenly created at the end of the project. Rather, creating a satisfied client is a continuing process of communicating with the client in a positive and constructive manner. A project consists of many deliverables. Each one is an opportunity to share experience with the client *and* to remind the client of the agreed to requirements and expectations. Reinforcing these along the way minimizes misperceptions of what has been agreed to when the project is finally completed. The closing of a well-managed project should be free of surprises and acceptance should simply formalize what the client has accepted along the way.

Quality of the Product of the Project

The client is primarily concerned with the quality of the product of the project. Exactly how the product was produced is of secondary concern, as discussed in the next section.

Surprises are nice when opening presents, such as on your birthday. Very few clients welcome surprises. They are paying you to produce a product that will provide certain benefits to them. The amount they are paying is not trivial, certainly when compared to their financial resources. Often, the product is for, or for the use of, other people. If the other people are not satisfied, they will seldom hesitate to voice their dissatisfaction. The consequences can range from discomfort, to extremes, such as the loss of a job or even a spouse. With such potential consequences, there should be no question as to why the client desires to determine the characteristics of the product that will be delivered. Those characteristics are defined in the specifications. If the product of the project conforms to those specifications, it is a quality product.

Product Characteristics

Quality is often confused with other terms such as "gold plating," aesthetics, luxury, and excellence, as well as functionality.

We mention gold plating because it has been used as a derisive term implying "totally excessive and uncalled for." It is a "put down" that certainly does not relate to quality, but may be used to belittle arguments for other product characteristics. Exercise care in referring to quality issues to avoid such belittling comments. Characteristics such as excellence, luxury, and aesthetics often come under attack in this manner. However, many are willing to pay for those characteristics to some degree. Several government units have decreed that a percentage of the project budget for public buildings be allotted for aesthetic features. Some features may add to the life of the product or reduce operating costs.

Products that are considered *luxurious* often come under attack, especially when paid for by public or stockholder funds. Often, luxurious refers to products that exceed the expectations of the person making the judgment. It is generally attributed to features that are available to the wealthy. They should not be precluded from consideration in the specification of a product if the client can afford the features and is willing to take the flak that may come.

Products that are noted for excellence may or may not be high in quality. They may still be highly desirable. The oft-quoted example of excellence is the Rolls Royce automobile. There is no question of the excellence of the Rolls Royce. Many people aspire to own one. It may seem strange to consider that, in a specific sense, a Rolls Royce may be of a lesser quality than some very inexpensive automobiles. It is inherent in the process of producing a Rolls Royce that there is some variability from one unit to the next, both having the same physical specifications. Production of the Rolls involves considerable handwork. Handwork is inherently variable. Thus, the product may vary from specifications. The less expensive auto is produced primarily by automated processes for which variability is minimal. If the processes are in control, every unit should conform closely to the specifications. In this sense, the less expensive car is of higher quality.

Functionality is probably the primary criterion for most clients. It characterizes a product design movement of the twentieth century that resulted in plain-faced skyscrapers, totally devoid of ornate artwork. It was executed by Japanese automobile manufacturers later in the twentieth century, who incorporated features in their products that catered to the passenger's convenience needs, such as built-in drink holders and more comfortable seats. Computers have made the term popular as a description of the range of capabilities available in an application. Care should be exercised in introducing functionality since, especially in computer applications, additional functionality can lead to complexity, as well as maintenance and other problems. Functionality in itself is not quality, but a feature. Functionality that performs the specified task in a user-friendly manner would be characteristic of a quality product.

Functionality may imply additional cost. Project costs are the most obvious. Creating the ideal product of the project may stretch the financial capabilities of the client. Once the product is available for use, operating costs may dominate. However, some clients may be persuaded to consider the total life-cycle costs of the product including project, operating, maintenance, and disposal costs.

Functionality, in itself, may or may not be a benefit to the client. If it increases the complexity beyond the ability of the user to use it, it certainly would not be a benefit. If the capability provided were not relevant to the user, it would not be a benefit. To be a benefit to the client, it must provide some utility that is relevant, usable, and affordable.

Perhaps the more important criterion for selecting between two products is value. Value is important in achieving customer satisfaction. For projects, value is simply the ratio of benefits divided by costs. If you can provide the same benefits to the client for less cost, it is of increased value. If you can provide more desired benefits for the same cost, it is of increased value. You may be able to provide the client with a product of sufficiently greater benefit as to warrant an increase in cost. Quality enters the equation in determining if the benefit is real, i.e., conforms to the specifications claimed for it.

Note that benefits are perceived differently by different people. An important factor in this is affordability. A benefit that is not affordable offers no benefit to the client. Thus, a feature that offers comfort, prestige, and a statement of success or "keeping up with the Joneses" may have little or no value for the client that cannot afford it. On the other hand, different people have different priorities for a specific benefit. Therefore, it is necessary to understand the client well to understand their perception of various benefits.

Communicating with the client to define the specifications of the product of the project is not a trivial matter. When the product of the project is one to be sold to multiple clients, such as the design of a mass-market product, it becomes even more difficult. Efforts to broaden the market for the product may create conflicts between features. A feature that is essential to one market segment may be too complex, or even "gold plated," for another. A benefit for one may be a detriment to another. If these conflicts are not resolved in the specifications of the product, they will be resolved by lower-level project team members. This can lead to an Edsel or the proverbial camel—a horse designed by a committee.

Measures of the Client's Requirements/Expectations

Client requirements and expectations are often in conflict. This is particularly true when affordability is a limiting factor. Some clients may be, or seem, totally unrealistic in resolving the conflicts. Most will respond positively when asked to rank them as to how important they really are.

In Chapter VII in *PM 101*, in the discussion of product scope management, we discussed the product breakdown structure (PBS) as a tool for clearly defining the physical requirements. In addition, product design characteristics were discussed as a means for expressing other criteria that might be incorporated in the product of the project. Often, the first pass in developing both of these might be called "wish lists." Generally, these must be pared down to meet the affordability constraints.

Paring down a wish list can be achieved by ranking each item as to its importance. Some useful categories are:

❏ Essential—must be present in product
❏ Desirable—would add utility, but could be sacrificed
❏ Nice to have—would add some utility, but not willing to pay much for it
❏ Of no interest—offers no utility.

Most projects involve multiple clients or, at least, multiple representatives. It would be highly unusual for several people to have the same wish list, let alone the same priorities for all the items on a combined wish list. It may be practicable to have each relevant person rank the combined wish list. The conflicts revealed may be resolved between the parties themselves or may require the intercession of a higher authority. Failure to identify and resolve these conflicts in formulating the project will surely result in dissatisfaction when the product is delivered. Some may never be resolved completely and some may not be identified in spite of vigorous efforts. People who have hidden agendas may well avoid revealing their true priorities and certainly the true reasons for them. Nevertheless, seeking to identify and resolve such conflicts early in the project will surely lead to greater client satisfaction.

Measuring Quality

Some people who operate in the project mode have a simple attitude that can be likened to the proverbial used car salesman. "Trust me! Would I sell you a lemon?" The fact is, examples of "lemons" produced by projects appear in the news media all too often. Some unscrupulous operators seem to go beyond "bid low and make it up on changes." Their approach is more like "bid low and then ignore the specifications." Even scrupulous individuals, when faced with dilemmas, may opt for solutions that are not necessarily in the best interests of the client. Sometimes they succumb to peer or organizational pressures. Thus, it is important to have an independent, unbiased measurement of quality, i.e., conformance to specifications.

This is perhaps the best justification for defining quality as conformance to specifications. Without an unequivocal statement of requirements for the product, decisions on whether the product meets the client's requirements will be judgments. Keeping such judgments free of bias and influence is very difficult. The production person would like all units produced to be accepted. The marketing person may only be satisfied with the "most nearly perfect" units.

To measure quality accurately and precisely, specifications must be stated in unambiguous terms. Many would argue that there are characteristics of a product that cannot be stated unambiguously. The best counter to that argument is an example from a furniture factory. It was noticed that there was considerable variation in the judgment of the quality of a specific wood component for a desk. One inspector was accepting some parts that the other inspector would reject. It was determined that both inspectors were very conscientious and knew the product well. Why was there so much difference in their results? Analyses lead to the conclusion that the difference was in the grain of the wood. When cut a certain way, the wood grain forms a pattern of "v-shaped" crowns. Both inspectors were observing the crowns, but one would accept more crowns than the other. After a conference, all parties, including management, agreed on how many crowns were acceptable. Thus, a characteristic of the part that had been deemed strictly aesthetic was quantified and the accept/reject decisions became consistent.

It has been argued that the degree of education achieved cannot be quantified. The OC, while teaching Modern Quality Management, developed a very quantitative methodology for measuring the degree of education attained in several courses. One of the unexpected benefits was the near elimination of students asking questions such as, "Now, what do you really want us to know?" Other benefits included more specificity in designing the course, preparing classroom activities, and writing examination questions.

Thus, the number of areas for which specifications cannot be made explicit is probably far fewer than conventional wisdom might indicate. Therefore, it is quite practical to measure quality in terms of conformance to specifications.

Similarly, measuring quality does not have to wait until the product is delivered. Design reviews, component testing, and system integration planning are only a few of the techniques available to aid in assuring the quality of the final product. An excellent source for understanding the concepts and techniques of quality management (QM) is Juran and Gryna (2000).

Quality of the Project

To this point we have focused attention on the quality of the product of the project. Quality concepts are also applicable to the project itself. A project that "produces the desired product to the satisfaction of the client in the optimum time, considering total applicable costs to the client" could certainly be called a quality project. This assertion requires examination to appreciate what it implies.

The concept of "desired product," discussed previously, is defined by the specifications. These are not just the specifications as originally presented to the project team. They should include all agreed to changes generated by both the client and the project team. These changes should increase the value of the product of the project to the client at a fair return to the project provider.

The satisfaction of the client should be the primary aim of every project. Satisfaction is largely a function of the value of the product of the project to the client. It is enhanced, or diminished, by the manner in which the project is executed.

The optimum time may be the most ethereal concept. If all applicable costs to the client are considered, there is a duration for the project that leads to the highest client satisfaction. To the extent that the duration is either longer or shorter, the total costs increase and satisfaction decreases. The objective for the project manager should be to achieve that optimum cost to the client. Ideally, the contractual relationship between the client and the provider is constructed to make the motivations of both parties consistent. To the extent that they are not consistent, it can be expected that the project cost will exceed the minimum for the client and satisfaction will be diminished. This is evident when considering the motivations of the client and the contractor in building a house. The contractor, in minimizing the costs of the project, may take longer to complete a house than the client expects. Client satisfaction starts diminishing as soon as the delay becomes evident.

Total applicable costs to the client include much more than just direct project costs. Interest on funds employed is certainly applicable. Costs of alternative services, e.g., rent on a dwelling until a house is ready to move into, are relevant. Opportunity costs, such as loss of revenue from the use of the product of the project, as well as loss of future business, are relevant. Even the costs of employee or personal time in resolving conflicts and problems generated by the project are relevant.

Thus, how the project is performed is clearly relevant. The client will sense when a project is not going well. This can be concealed for some amount of time, but it will eventually be discovered. In general, the greater the deviation from the plan when it is discovered, the greater the unpleasant consequences, including claims, cancellation of the contract, and possibly legal action.

There are benefits from running a project that satisfies project team members. For one thing, the key members of the team will be anxious to join you on a future project, thus enhancing your ability to run good projects. Subcontractors will be more willing to bid on your projects, as they know they will be treated fairly and not have to endure the frustrations of changes. This will likely lead to lower bid prices and a willingness to cooperate in many ways.

Two comments help to understand this. One subcontractor on the OC's house, on which the OC served in many roles, including project manager, volunteered that he "enjoyed working on this project more than any he had done." Indications were that other subcontractors shared this reaction. This was not coincidental as one of the goals of this project was to "conduct it in such a way that it left only pleasant memories." Did the house cost more as a result? By one measure, cost per square foot, it came in substantially less than normal for comparable homes. Admittedly, there were several contributors to this including owner-performed work. However, morale of the crews, productivity, and absence of rework all supported a lower project cost.

This becomes a two-way street. A more recent comment by the OC was insightful of client reaction. The prompt, friendly manner in which a local service provider performed led to the remark, "I'll call him again. I like the way he worked with me." These suggest some of the elements of running a quality project beyond simply delivering a product that conforms to specifications.

Strategies for Design

There are many strategic decisions that must be made for a project. Not the least of these is the design strategy. Four specific design strategies have been observed by the OC, each of which has certain inherent benefits, costs, and risks. All the examples discussed are based on automotive companies. (Note: These design strategies may or may not be in practice at these companies today. The strategies for the automotive companies were verified in a conversation with a vice president of research for one of the companies about 1985.)

Chrysler generally overdesigned a new product. This permitted the design to be accomplished by fewer people and, perhaps, in a shorter time. The original Plymouth Valiant was an excellent example, being designed by a small team in about twelve months. At the time, the usual design process required some thirty-six months. Over the production life of the vehicle, specific components were redesigned to reduce weight, costs to produce, and/or improve performance. Perhaps this contributed to Chrysler's reputation for design excellence.

Ford generally underdesigned the new product and conducted extensive endurance tests. Any part that failed or underperformed was then redesigned, i.e., strengthened, to remove the cause of failure. Thus, minimum design life was an important criterion. This strategy required a somewhat longer project duration, but gave a high assurance of a minimum designed cost. This was consistent with Ford's early strategy of producing a low cost vehicle that was affordable by the masses.

General Motors (GM) tended to a strategy of starting two or more versions of a product into the design process. Thus, there was a sense of competition between design teams. At some point, one of the designs was accepted and completed. The cost of designing was

227

greater, but the completed design was probably closer to optimum for the specified criteria.

It is noteworthy that, at the time of observing these differences in design strategy, it was accepted as fact that for every engineer that Chrysler had, Ford had two, and GM had four, and all were producing comparable varieties of products. The downsizing and reengineering efforts of the recent past may have changed both the design strategies and the number of engineers.

During the same time period, John Deere was using an even different design strategy—multiphase design. To design a new tractor, they would first design a prototype. It would be studied for opportunities to improve the design, reduce costs of producing the tractor, reduce costs of new facilities to produce it, reduce costs of operating and maintaining the tractor, and increase the design life of the tractor. They would cycle through this process two or three times before committing to produce a specific model. The duration and cost of the project were greater, but it resulted in a product that was less costly to produce, required lower capital facilities, cost the farmer less to purchase, operate, and maintain, and had a longer life. The latter were advantageous in the marketplace, because the farmer tended to be a discriminating buyer of a true capital good.

Software system development has produced similar strategies. Prototyping and structured programming, although not necessarily alternative strategies, are among the strategic design alternatives that must be considered.

Plan Validation

A project must have a plan, whether formal or informal. Informal plans are difficult to communicate. Thus, to ensure client satisfaction, a formal plan is desirable. For the client to feel confident that the project will be successful, the plan must have a reasonable chance of producing a product consistent with requirements. In addition, for the sake of the project manager and members of the project team, it is important that the project plan will lead to success. The best way to ensure this is to validate the plan.

The process is similar to a design review. Persons with knowledge and experience relevant to the project at hand review the project plan with the specific purpose of identifying any opportunities for improvement and potential pitfalls, as well as adequacy of the plan to produce the desired product. Ideally, this is a meeting in which the project manager presents the plan. It could be based on reading the plan's documents. The reviewers must recognize that this is a stressful process for the project manager and behave in a manner to elicit frank and honest discussion. Otherwise, the project manager may be tempted to minimize the pain by avoiding controversial areas, even though the consequences in the future may be more serious.

The review panel may be senior members of the organization performing the project. Another approach is to recruit people from the broader organization, or from outside the organization, with more specific knowledge and experience in a narrower range of projects. Many governmental projects rely on permanent or temporary advisory panels to assess the product of the project. Similar panels might be called upon to review the project plan.

Two especially pertinent outputs of the review are the overall design strategy by which the product will be designed and validation of key processes on which there may be some questions of adequacy.

Process Validation

A project is a temporary endeavor undertaken to create a unique product or service. It can be viewed as a set of processes that can be expected to produce the desired product or service. Being temporary and unique, it may be composed of processes that are unusual for the performing organization. Even the usual processes may be modified or combined in an unusual manner. Thus, there is a need for process validation, both for the individual process and for the whole. In developing a new chemical compound, it is common to verify the process in the laboratory, and then in a pilot plant, before committing to a full-scale production facility. The results of each step are reviewed to validate the plans for the next step. It makes sense to exercise the same precautions for the project plan.

While not knowing the specific steps taken, it is interesting to consider the process validation efforts that were undertaken for the Northumberland Bridge construction project. The idea of constructing these very large concrete sections of bridge spans in progressive line mode was no less daunting than moving them from the fabricating yard to their final installation site and setting them in place with a barge floating in the open sea. The cost of an error associated with this project plan would have been disastrous. Any project involving unique processes or unique relationships between processes deserves validation of the processes where there is any reasonable doubt. One of the consequences of inadequate or ineffective processes is rework.

Rework

In a series of articles published in 1993, Cooper (1993a; 1993b; 1993c; 1993d) asserts that "rework can account for the *majority* of work content (and cost) on complex development projects!" His work is based on simulation studies similar to one he conducted on the building of two new types of fighting ships for the United States (US) Navy by Ingalls Shipbuilding (Cooper 1980). There were significant delays and cost overruns on these firm-fixed-price contracts (1980). Ingalls was convinced that "a major contributing factor to anticipated overruns of $500 million was the disruption that had been evident in every phase of both projects. The complicating aspect of this was the interaction between projects as changes in one caused labor shortages that affected the other" (1980). Computer simulations corroborated this and resulted in the Navy agreeing "out of court to pay $447 million of the claim" (1980). The abstract of this article states:

> Use of the model (which was the basis for at least $200–300 million of the settlement) broke new legal ground, providing the defense and legal communities with a means by which adversary relationships can be avoided and equitable settlements of contract disputes achieved. (Cooper 1980)

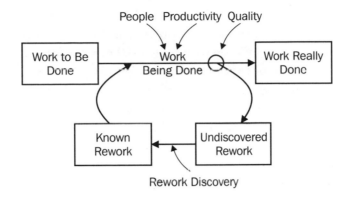

FIGURE XVI.1

The Rework Cycle

In the subsequent articles, based on the application of this modeling technique to a large number of projects, a graphic model of the Rework Cycle (Figure XVI.1) proposes one measure of quality on a project. Quality is "the fraction of work being executed that will not require subsequent rework" (Cooper 1993c). The lower the quality of the work performed, the greater the number of rework cycles and amount of rework. Based on empirical data from a large number of projects, Cooper makes the following observations.

❑ "The lower the quality and the longer the rework discovery times:
  ◆ The larger the gap between real progress and that which is perceived, and
  ◆ The longer-lasting the gap" (Cooper 1980).
❑ "The later in the project/stage that a significant gap persists:
  ◆ The greater and longer-lasting the uncertainty in the size of the gap; and
  ◆ The later the point of maximum uncertainty about real progress" (Cooper 1980).

He offers insight into, and a very rational explanation of, the "90 percent syndrome," commonly expressed as "it takes 90 percent of the planned project duration to complete 90 percent of the work and another 90 percent of the project duration to complete the remaining 10 percent of the project." Every project manager should thoroughly understand this phenomenon and Cooper's recommendations of what to do to minimize its impact on your project.

ACHIEVING QUALITY

There are several concepts of Modern Quality Management that are applicable to achieving quality, regardless of whether it is of the project or the product of the project. They include: do the right thing right the first time (DTRTRTFT), the customer is the next person/operation in the process, and, ultimately, statistical process control.

Do the Right Thing Right the First Time (DTRTRTFT)

"Measure twice; cut once!" is an old adage that relates to this. Another is, "If you don't have time to do it right, when are you going to find time to do it over?" Management has a heavy responsibility in this. Often, the pressures to deliver the product leads to pressure on project team members to "get it out the door." Inherent in this is the risk of product failure after delivery, or at least failure to perform to expectations. The cost of not pursuing DTRTRTFT is not just the immediate rework necessary to make the product work right. It potentially includes rework of every subsequent activity that is performed relying on that work product until the error is corrected. Then there are delays while all that rework is performed. Thus, the cost can increase rapidly and the delays in the project may lead to the consequences of the domino effect.

The Customer is the Next Person/Operation in the Process

One of the often-practiced rules of behavior in an organization has been, "go along and get along." Thus, it has been considered inappropriate to complain about the work product coming to you. As a part of the revolution in quality in Japanese manufacturing, this concept was reversed by defining the customer as the next person or operation in the process. Thus, if the work product of the preceding operation was not adequate, it did not continue through the process and result in greater investment in a bad product. Instead, the process was halted until a good product was received and the previous operation adjusted.

In the 1960s, the OC was designing a project management system for new car development. A major problem was determining precisely who would be responsible for expressing the logical relationships in the project network diagram (PND). We spent considerable time examining the consequences of alternative approaches. It became clear that the person responsible for an activity could not be held responsible for knowing all the other activities that would use the work product of that activity. On the other hand, it did seem feasible for the person responsible for an activity to know what work product was necessary before that activity could be started. Thus, it was necessary for that person to accept the work product coming in and to report regularly on the status of the preceding work product. This concept was not implemented at that time, as it was before the acceptance of the precepts of Modern Quality Management and, thus, considered too risky in terms of labor acceptance. This concept is discussed further in Chapter XVIII, Reporting and Control.

Statistical Process Control

W. Edwards Deming was a statistician who became interested in quality control. Thus, he was very aware of the conditions under which a process could be subjected to statistical process analysis and control. One of the famous stories of the success of his approach was at Nashua Corporation. Their process for applying chemicals to paper to make carbonless paper was not producing a uniform product. Deming was brought in before a major expenditure was made to replace the process equipment. The first thing he did was to insist that the process be operated for twenty-four hours without changing the control settings. The result of this experiment was to demonstrate that the process was actually fairly stable. The search for causes of variation from specifications for the product revealed that the three operators responsible for the process each had different ways of operating the equipment. When each operator came on duty, he immediately adjusted the controls. After each adjustment there was a period of instability before the process reached equilibrium. Having discovered the cause, the operators were trained to operate the process in the same manner. The process immediately stabilized. The net result of this experiment was that the major capital expenditure was canceled, the process control set points were narrowed *and* lowered, the product was improved, and the amount of chemicals applied was reduced, providing substantial savings in operating costs.

This experience has been replicated throughout industries with comparable results. Statistical analysis and process control has been proven as a viable approach to eliminating defects, or reducing the number of defects produced, while generating substantial savings.

Two things are necessary to permit the application of the same techniques to processes in projects. First, we need to recognize that a substantial amount of the work on projects is repetitive in nature, or can be modified to be repetitive. Analyzing these processes, modifying the methods used, and providing appropriate test equipment can make them amenable to statistical methodology. Second, we need to train project personnel in how to achieve quality on their work so they can recognize additional opportunities to modify their work methods.

There is much more to modern quality than can be discussed in a short chapter. The important message is that there are more opportunities for QM than are often recognized.

WHO BENEFITS FROM QM?

The popular conception is that improving quality is primarily a benefit to the customer or client. That is only the beginning.

The QM process starts with an intimate knowledge of the client's needs and expectations. Those needs and expectations are carefully managed to ensure ultimate client satisfaction with both the product of the project and with the project itself. Satisfied clients return to the provider for future project work. They also inform others of their satisfaction, leading to more work. Thus, the provider of the successful project prospers. As the provider of the project prospers, so do its suppliers. The employees of both the provider and the suppliers benefit through job security and earnings.

Probably the one single person who benefits the most is the project manager. The fastest way for aspiring project managers to advance their careers is to complete projects that provide satisfaction to, not only the client, but all members of the project team. The client wants that project manager on future projects. The project manager's employer recognizes his value to the organization. The best project team members want to be associated with the successful project manager on future projects. Thus, success indeed breeds success.

A seldom-recognized benefit was well expressed by the project manager of the Toroidial Fusion Project, the development of a laboratory machine for testing fusion energy generation. The OC was visiting this state of the art project. While discussing the project in the project manager's office, with the quality manager at the table, the OC inquired about the relationship between the two. The OC expected at least some negative reaction based on the general attitude that quality personnel are the ones who "harass" production personnel. The project manager quickly volunteered that he considered his quality manager his best friend and protector. "What would happen to me if we spend all this money and the thing doesn't work?" he said. He went on to explain that the quality manager helped his peace of mind so he could sleep well at night knowing that he had a friend helping to ensure project success. In short, all stakeholders benefit from excellent QM on projects.

Sam recognized that those who would be going out to cut and return the trees might have motivations that could lead to getting trees that were not the most suitable, i.e., they might not conform to specifications. Sam wondered how those motivations could be countered. Sam talked to one of the elders who had been one of the best woodcutters around until he became crippled. They discussed the possibility that the elder could go along on the hunt for the trees if he did not have to do any of the work. It was agreed. The elder would accompany the group going after the trees and approve every tree before it was cut down.

Similarly, another elder would go with the vine crew and one of the women elders would accompany the hunting crew. The latter was important because it was expected that the meat from the animal would be brought back for the family to eat. She was also skilled at tanning hides and would be able to ensure that the hides were suitable before they were brought back.

In addition, Sam decided it would be wise to call a meeting of the elders in the cave where the project plans were on the wall. Sam would review both the design of the raft and the plans for the project. Not only would this ensure that the design was adequate and that the project plan was good, but also gain the elder's buy-in to the project. This could be invaluable when the matriarch started raising questions about either the design or the project plan.

They held the meeting and it proved really worthwhile. One of the elders raised a question about how the movement system could not be assembled until the raft was assembled. Thus, a flaw in the plan was identified and corrected. Sam recognized that this was an appropriate change and added another activity, attach movement to deck (AMD), which followed AM and AD and preceded TM. It would require one day at the most. Sam did some quick calculations and determined that this would not affect the schedule.

APPENDIX XVI.A
MARS PATHFINDER PROJECT

PROJECT QUALITY MANAGEMENT

The Mars Pathfinder approach to quality management had one overriding theme: instill a sense of personal responsibility for and commitment to quality on the part of each team member. If people are given the responsibility and authority to do the job, they feel a sense of ownership, and therefore personally responsible for its success. There was also a commitment to employing "common sense" approaches rather than rigid, traditional approaches. By streamlining traditional processes, exhibiting flexibility and taking a measured degree of risk, Pathfinder achieved mission success without sacrificing quality.

For example, the Pathfinder mission assurance program was the first truly "tailored" mission assurance approach at JPL. It featured flexibility, common sense, concurrent engineering and lower cost. Documentation was cut significantly, team members were empowered to make decisions, selective redundancy was employed. Q.A. was based on processes (not historical points). The electronic parts program was a combination of Cassini project common buys and military grades. The mission assurance cost was less than one third of the tradition, and the number of Problem/Failure reports was less than one-quarter of normal (and only one-third the normal closure cost each). There were no significant deviations from the plan created during the three years leading up to the launch.

Chapter XVII

Uncertainty and Risk Management[1]

Sam worried a lot. This was not a bad trait, as it had resulted in all of Sam's earlier efforts going well because, when trouble occurred, Sam was ready for it. Since this was the most ambitious effort to date, Sam was worried that there was too much to worry about. Is there a more systematic way to worry without losing so much sleep? Sam discovered that one of the elders had been there, done that, and still seemed to sleep well. Incidentally, Sam noticed that this elder was the only one of that age who still had jet-black hair. Sam set about thinking of what risks were inherent in this project and what could be done about them.

In addition, Sam was concerned about the chances that the project would be completed by the scheduled finish date. How could Sam be comfortable about the schedule when there clearly were some activities for which there was considerable uncertainty? Sam started looking for answers to these questions.

---

[1] Throughout this chapter I refer to decision theory. I focus on its usefulness on projects, not on its actual application. This is done purposely because the proper development of decision theory would require too much space for the purposes of the current work, and an excellent treatment of the subject is available in *Decision Analysis in Projects* by John R. Schuyler (see Appendix XVII.C).

It is the rare project that does not involve some uncertainty and risk. Indeed, projects that involve pushing the state-of-the-art would probably take much longer and cost much more if all risks were avoided. Some, such as manned space flight would be impossible. Innovation, and its concomitant uncertainty and risk, has been a key element in the success of many projects.

If the project manager is too risk aversive, subordinates will withhold knowledge of the risks that exist. Without knowledge there is no opportunity to manage the risks. Even worse, without coordination of risk analysis it is likely that the approaches to risk will be inconsistent if not opposing. That is, two people may be affected by the same risk event. One may assume that it will occur, the other that it will not. Thus, regardless of the outcome of the risk event, one is bound to lose, causing the project to be delayed. At minimum, both should bet the same way. This requires knowledge and coordination of assumptions about risk events and actions to mitigate them.

Management must be alerted to the conscious acceptance of such risks and the related potential cost overruns. This not only is a responsibility, but also a necessity for the career of the project manager. Your management and other key stakeholders must be apprised of the identified risk events and their consequences. They may be opposed to taking a specific risk. If so, you may need to do some replanning. If the risk is accepted, their assessment of the actual outcome, whether favorable or unfavorable, will be more rational.

By implication then, the project manager must be informed of any such risks undertaken by any part of the project team. Risk analysis is maturing rapidly with several software packages now available to aid in evaluating and managing risks. The concept of risk management is certainly an integral part of project management today.

As the project manager you can influence some risks, while you must simply react to others. You can also influence project team members in a manner that can have a direct impact on the time required to perform the activities in a project, as well as how they deal with other aspects of uncertainty and risk.

	Outcomes	Probability	
Certainty	Known	Known	0 or 1
Risk	Known	Known	$0 < \mathrm{Pr} < 1$
Uncertainty	Known	Unknown	$\mathrm{Pr} = ?$
Ignorance	Unknown	Unknown	$\mathrm{Pr} = ?$

TABLE XVII.1
States of Knowledge of an Event

UNDERSTANDING UNCERTAINTY AND RISK

To understand uncertainty and risk management it is first necessary to understand some basic concepts. For example, what conditions define uncertainty versus risk? What can we say about some future event, one that has consequences that are either favorable or unfavorable, or both? What is probability and what are some of the properties of probability with which we should be concerned? Table XVII.1 characterizes the difference between certainty, risk, uncertainty, and ignorance. The implications of this table are discussed in the following.

In most things we do in life we behave as if we are certain about the outcome. When we turn the key in the ignition of our car we assume that it will start. Actually, it is a risk situation. There are two possible outcomes: it will start or it will not start. On most days, under most conditions, the probability that it will not start is so low that, for all practical purposes, it is zero. On some days, in some places, we recognize that it is not zero. For example, in midwinter in Fairbanks, Alaska the probability that it will not start, all other things being equal, is so close to one that, for practical purposes, it is one. Without planned action to counteract the ambient condition, we might as well stay in bed. Planned action in this case includes having an electrical heater to keep the engine, and especially the engine oil, warm. Diesel trucks in these conditions are started at the beginning of winter and run continuously until spring. In a more moderate climate, we can get a new battery, have the engine tuned, or get a new car. Our employer and others expect that we will manage this situation to reduce the probability to very nearly zero that the car will not start. Alternatively, we can use another form of transportation.

In a risk situation we know all the possible outcomes and the probability that each will occur. The probabilities are between zero and one, and the sum of all probabilities is one.

Sometimes we know all the possible outcomes but do not know their probabilities. This is a case of uncertainty. It is not hopeless, as we can often assign a probability based on judgment. We often do this in assessing the weather. We look out the window and decide that, while it is not raining now, it looks threatening. We conclude that the probability of rain is sufficient to warrant carrying an umbrella. Thus, while we do not have knowledge of the true probabilities we have sufficient *subjective* knowledge of the probabilities to make an intelligent decision. It has been demonstrated that by making the best estimate of subjective probabilities and using probability theory rigorously, one can make better decisions than making a WAG. Often, it is sufficient to estimate maximum or minimum values of such probabilities.

It is not unusual to find ourselves in a state of ignorance. We may know that the situation is not certain and know one or more possible outcomes. We realize that there are other outcomes but really do not know what they are. Therefore, we cannot know the probabilities of the outcomes. As with uncertainty, we can make subjective estimates and proceed to apply them in a rigorous manner.

Thus, we have established the notion that ordinary events generally are not certain. We can and do manage such events in a manner that modifies the probabilities or the consequences. Therefore, risk management is a concept with which we are all familiar.

Events

In probability, *events* are relatively simple, such as attempting to start the car. The *possible outcomes* are the car starts or the car does not start. In reality, events are more complex.

Consider the probability that it will rain. The television weather forecast says that there is an 80 percent chance of rain. What does this really mean? Does it mean that there is an 80 percent chance that it will rain over the entire area of the forecast (as opposed to a 20 percent chance that it will not rain over the entire area)? Maybe. Does it mean that it is certain that it will rain over 80 percent of the area that is within the broadcast area of the television station? If so, what 80 percent? Does it mean that, during the next twenty-four hours, there is an 80 percent chance that it will be raining somewhere in the area? That makes sense. Does it mean that there is an 80 percent chance that it will rain wherever you are? Not likely. The television weather forecast is not very precise, perhaps due to lack of precise knowledge, difficulties with conveying that knowledge, or as a means to avoid being accused of not knowing. Regardless, what we hear often affects how we dress and behave in other ways. The moral to this is that it is necessary to be very precise in defining the events and the outcomes to speak meaningfully about the probabilities.

In business, and especially for projects that are performed outdoors, we need more precise information about weather. Commercial forecasters specialize in forecasting the probability that it will rain on a very small geographical area. If you plan to pour concrete tomorrow, such a forecast can provide very specific information. Not only that, such a forecast can provide information on several facets of such an event. For example, what time is this likely to occur? How long will it last? How much precipitation will fall? Thus, there is a concept of *precision of information*.

Forecasts of this type cost more than turning the television on. Thus, there is a *cost of information* that must be considered in deciding how to manage a risk event. The cost of getting the television version weather forecast is quite low. The cost of getting a more specific forecast is more.

For each outcome there is a *value of the outcome*. It may be either favorable or unfavorable. The cost of a light rain on freshly poured concrete is often very small. The cost of a heavy rain may be more. However, either of these costs can be modified by taking mitigating action such as laying plastic over the freshly poured concrete. However, if the rain comes before the final troweling is completed, there still may be additional costs.

Sometimes we have to accept a risk as it is. Often we can change the consequences of the risk by modifying the possible outcomes, the value of those outcomes, or the probability of the outcomes.

Outcomes

The sun comes up each morning. This is a certain event. It has a probability of one. There is another outcome—the sun does not come up. It has a probability of zero. Thus we know the two possible outcomes and the probability for each.

In betting on a horse race we might consider there are two outcomes: our horse wins or it does not win. This might lead us to say that it is a 50-50 proposition. Few of us really approach it that way. Similarly, if there are ten horses in the race we might say there are ten possible outcomes—one for each horse winning the race. From that we might conclude that the probability of our horse winning is one-tenth or 10 percent. That would be rather naive, as we are provided information on each of the horses and know that some have won more often than others. Horse A may have run against each of the other horses at one time or another and always beat them, whether horse A won the specific race or not. From this we might conclude that the probability of horse A winning is substantially greater than any other. Should we place our bet on horse A?

Suppose we read further and find that horse A has never won a race if the track is muddy. It is raining and the track is getting muddy. Should we place our bet on horse A?

This example could be continued ad nauseam. It has established the notion that there are alternative outcomes and there is a probability associated with each outcome. While necessary, that information is not sufficient to make a rational decision. We need to know the values of the outcomes and the probability each will occur.

Value of Outcomes

The values of the outcomes of a horse race are expressed as "odds." Thus, if the odds are 10 to 1, we can expect to get back $10 for every dollar we bet—if our horse wins. Note that the odds associated with a horse winning seem to be an expression of the probability. This is partially correct but not wholly. The odds are, in part, an expression of the consensus of all bettors' opinions about the probability as represented by the sum of all bets placed on that horse—including the naive bettors who behave as if the probability is 50-50. Thus, it would be an error to use that information as probabilities of the outcomes. Rather, the odds are numbers that enable the bookie to hedge all the bets and increase the probability that he wins regardless of which horse wins. They are the payoffs that balance something called expected values for the bookie. For us as bettors, however, they are the values of the outcomes. Thus, horse A may be shown as 2 to 1, meaning if we bet one dollar on horse A and horse A wins, we get two dollars back. Naturally, we would like to bet on a horse with odds of 100 to 1 and have that horse win. However, the expectation of that horse winning, as expressed by the betting actions of all bettors, is rather low.

Similarly, in testing a module of software, we may conclude that there are two outcomes—it works and it doesn't work. We may be willing to make the naive assumption that these two outcomes are equally likely. (That would certainly be ignoring Murphy and all his laws governing such events.) However, the costs of these two outcomes are likely quite different. For example, if it works we get to spend the weekend enjoying our favorite pleasure. If it doesn't work, we get to spend the weekend looking for the bug and fixing it. The reader is left to imagine other outcomes and the value of each for an event of their choice.

Probability and Its Properties

There are some properties of probability with which the risk manager must be familiar. For example, probabilities always have values equal to either zero or one or something in between. They are never greater than one nor less than zero.

The sum of the probabilities of all possible outcomes must equal one. That means that it is certain that one of the outcomes will occur. Sometimes we cannot, practically, identify all possible outcomes and must resort to grouping all other outcomes into a single class—other. Nevertheless, the sum of the probabilities of all outcomes must equal one. For example, the horse race could be a fiasco, with all horses being disqualified. That might have a probability of 0.0001.

In testing the computer program module, one of the outcomes might be that the computer is not working. It might have a probability of 0.001, for example. (Note that some corollary to Murphy's Law would argue that the more onerous the value of that outcome, the higher the probability of it occurring. However, in the interests of proper theory of probability we will ignore Murphy. However, the OC's personal experience would argue that Murphy resides on the shoulder of every project manager.) Actually, the probability of 0.001 that the computer will not be working may be quite realistic if we restate it as follows: it is likely that of 1,000 attempts to use the computer on Saturday morning, on one of those mornings it will not be working.

How do we get the probabilities for the outcomes? The best source is empirical data. The tout sheet at the racecourse provides a lot of empirical data. Computer centers keep extensive records of downtime, whether for routine maintenance, crashes, or whatever. Personnel probably has good empirical data on absence and tardiness experience for each individual. Thus, there are often excellent sources for empirical data. Sometimes special efforts are required to obtain them, which can be time consuming, costly, and/or may not be completed in time to make the decision. Often, on projects, the decisions that have to be made relate to unique events for which there is no empirical data.

Note that in using empirical data we are assuming that the future will be just like the past. To overcome this, we might adjust the empirical probabilities to what we believe are more realistic values for the current situation. This must be done with caution to avoid adjusting the probabilities simply to prove our personal opinions or to justify the decision we want to make. There are techniques for avoiding bias in such estimates.

If empirical data is not available, or we are convinced the circumstances are different, we might resort to subjective probabilities. We all do this. We observe the television weather forecast and then observe the actual weather. Sometimes they are consistent. Sometimes they are not. It is doubtful that we make formal observations and keep records. Thus, we make a judgment that the weather forecaster is correct only 60 percent of the time when predicting rain. From this we might multiply the 80 percent forecast of rain by the 60 percent probability of being correct and conclude that the probability of rain (on our parade) is only 48 percent. Note that some people might interpret that as being 50-50, while others would say that it is less than 50 percent, leading to different behaviors.

Sometimes, it is sufficient to have some knowledge of what values the probabilities are not. Thus, using whatever knowledge is available we can reverse the process and calculate the probability that would cause us to behave rationally one way or another. Suppose we would cancel a picnic if we believed the probability of rain was greater than 40 percent. That could lead us to make observations and judgments as to whether we believe there is really a 40 percent chance that it will rain. That is often easier than estimating that the probability is exactly 0.32 or 0.43.

In fact, we make decisions based on all of these approaches even though we may not be conscious that we do. This may become more evident when we think about our behavior options.

Rational Behavior

Project managers face probabilistic situations often. Duration of activities is just one example. There are several ways in which to behave rationally in such situations. Ignoring the probabilities is not very rational.

The simplest behavior is to opt for the *most likely* outcome. Implicit in this is the assumption that the values (costs or gains) of the various outcomes are essentially equal. In many instances this is a reasonable assumption. It may also be applicable if it is judged that the other outcomes are preceded by some amount of warning such as to permit some mitigating action. For example, hurricanes occur infrequently and there is generally adequate warning that one is approaching to permit boarding up windows and other such actions. The most likely duration for an activity is an excellent benchmark for scheduling time for performing the activity—so long as buffers are inserted strategically to absorb overruns if they occur.

If there are significant differences in the values of the outcomes, it is generally better to use the expected value. It has some properties that are very useful in project management. It is inherent in the project evaluation and review technique (PERT) model. Using the three time estimates and the equation for the estimated time of an activity (t_e), we can use the Central Limit Theorem to determine when the project (or any intermediate event) will be completed. Note that the probability associated with the date thus calculated is 50 percent. That is, there is a 50 percent chance that the project will be completed in less time *and* a 50 percent chance that it will require more time. Generally we are not very comfortable making a promise to deliver the product of a project if there is only a 50 percent chance of meeting that promise. Thus, we rely on another principle of the Central Limit Theorem that allows us to determine the probability distribution for the completion of the product.

Similarly, when making a decision between two options it is rational to compare the expected value of the outcomes of the two options. The expected value is simply the sums, over all outcomes, of the products of the probability of each outcome multiplied by the value of that outcome.

Thus, expected value is a valuable tool to the project manager. However, it must be used with some caution. For example, inherent in the expected value concept are three assumptions. First, it is assumed that the distributions of the individual outcomes are independent. This requires careful consideration of the definition of outcomes and the examination of this assumption for the outcomes. If there is not independence, it may require a more complex model of the decision options, perhaps using decision trees (Schuyler 1996).

The second assumption is "ceteris paribus," i.e., all other things being equal. In many physical situations this is reasonable. However, in managing a project, we should always be looking for ways to modify circumstances to our advantage. It may be appropriate to provide extra resources to an especially risky activity or to assign two teams to pursue alternative solutions to a problem, selecting the first acceptable solution. Thus, we seldom accept probabilities as fate if there is anything we can do about them. Perhaps the major benefit of taking the time to estimate the probabilities of activities durations and the outcomes of alternative decisions is in the information it provides. This helps the project manager to recognize where the opportunities exist to enhance project performance.

The third assumption of expected value is that it is the value that can be expected in many repetitions of the same process or decision. The probability that exactly the expected value will occur is near zero. We can only make propositions about the probability that the outcome will be greater than or less than the expected value. On any given trial, the value of the outcome could be very good or very bad. Therefore, any time a decision is being based on expected value, careful consideration must be given to the possibility of the very bad outcome. If that outcome is not acceptable, then that alternative should be ruled out of further consideration. For example, if the bad outcome could result in serious human injury or death, it probably should be ruled out. Similarly, it should be ruled out if it could do irreparable harm to the organization.

Finally, using probabilistic approaches to managing projects may be of considerable benefit to the project manager. To the extent that it is used in a theoretically correct manner and is well documented, it is excellent evidence (whether in court or in examination of the action relevant to the project manager's career) that the project manager acted in a prudent manner given the information available at the time.

Behavior Options

Not all people behave the same given the same information. Some people are risk prone while others are risk avoiders. Most people are somewhere in between. Some people always carry an umbrella while others wear drip-dry clothes. (Some people carry an umbrella in the mistaken belief that this behavior changes the probability that it will rain. The OC does this, facetiously of course.) Generally, the apparently most risk-prone individuals go to great lengths to minimize the risk. Racecar drivers do this. Their cars are designed to protect the driver even in the worst of crashes. They wear seat belts and fire resistant clothing. The tracks are equipped with safety equipment and personnel to minimize the effects of a crash. On the other hand, some people are just foolhardy, racing poorly-equipped vehicles on narrow, winding roads with no safety equipment standing by. Project managers cannot afford to be foolhardy. Neither can they be totally risk aversive.

One possible reaction to a potential risk event is to modify the probabilities. Thus, on a construction project, test borings can provide information on underground conditions. We can change the time and date on our computer to 11:45 PM, 31 December 1999, to see what happens when it passes midnight. We can design the computer program in modules that can be tested before combining with other modules. We try new drugs on other living organisms before testing on humans.

Alternatively, we can modify the possible outcomes. Instead of a picnic, we might have a buffet dinner inside. Instead of concrete pavement, brick pavers might be considered (the effect of rain during installation might be less serious). On a product development, two teams could embark on two different approaches. This increases the probability that at least one would be successful. If both are successful, the best could be chosen. (Some advice, don't cast the other team as losers!)

We can modify the value of the outcomes. This often is done while negotiating the terms of the contract for the project. We can persuade the client to compensate us for taking risk and especially for successfully handling the risk. The picnic can be planned so it can be moved indoors if there is rain. We can pave the construction site so work can proceed in spite of rain. We can make back-up arrangements to use another computer if the primary one is not available at a specific time.

The success of these alternatives is highly dependent upon the recognition of the potential risk and the ingenuity of the project team. There are other actions that can be taken. *A Guide to the Project Management Body of Knowledge (PMBOK® Guide)* provides an excellent framework for managing risk.

PROJECT RISK MANAGEMENT

In Chapter III of *PM 101*, we discussed briefly what the *PMBOK® Guide* says about risk management. We found that "Risk management is the systematic process of identifying, analyzing, and responding to project risk. It includes maximizing the probability and consequences of positive events and minimizing the probability and consequences of adverse events to project objectives" (Project Management Institute 2000, 127). (Note: The *PMBOK® Guide* has been revised since the writing of *PM 101*. The following is based on the current version.) Here we go into somewhat greater detail.

Risk Management Planning "is the process of deciding how to approach and plan the risk management activities for a project. It is important to plan for the risk management processes that follow to ensure that the level, type, and visibility of risk management are commensurate with both the risk and the importance of the project to the organization" (Project Management Institute 2000, 129). This ensures that the risk plan is appropriate for the project and applied consistently.

Risk identification "involves determining which risks might affect the project and documenting their characteristics" (Project Management Institute 2000, 131). Two types of risks always exist—the known and the unknown. Risk identification attempts to move as many as possible from the unknown to the known. Nevertheless, it is not likely that all unknown risks will be eliminated. Therefore, the process of risk identification must be ongoing throughout the project. Neither the project manager, nor the team, can ever afford to become complacent.

Some aids in identifying risks include the work breakdown structure (WBS), the project network diagram (PND), other planning documents, historical information, and checklists. A systematic walk-through of the WBS and these documents, focusing on potential risk events, is appropriate. Repeating the process periodically for the work pending in the near term is also appropriate. The nearer we get to the work coming up the more likely we will recognize a potential risk. One checklist is provided in the next section under a discussion of A Taxonomy of Risks. Previous experience of project team members will suggest other potential risks. These should be viewed objectively to avoid being obsessive about unpleasant past experiences.

Qualitative Risk Analysis "is the process of assessing the impact and likelihood of identified risks" (Project Management Institute 2000, 133). It "prioritizes risks according to their potential effect on project objectives" for further analysis (2000, 133). It focuses attention on those risks that have the highest expected value risk scores for quantitative analysis.

Quantitative Risk Analysis is the measurement of "the probability of each risk and its consequence on project objectives, as well as the extent of overall project risk" (Project Management Institute 2000, 137). Using the tools of decision theory for quantifying risk is essential. They aid in balancing the probability of a risk event with its significance if it occurs. Expected value is the most important tool. It is simply the product of the probability of the event multiplied by the value of the outcome. Betting on the horses at a racetrack involves expected value. The astute bettor estimates the probability that a given horse will finish in the money multiplied by the payoff if it does win. Interestingly, it would seem that the lottery player ignores such calculations. However, perhaps they are behaving rationally in some other sense.

Expected value analysis should always be accompanied by an analysis of whether you can afford to play the game. Penny-ante poker may seem acceptable but if there is no limit on betting, the cost can exceed the ability to afford the risk. Thus, for every risk event consider whether you can afford to incur the adverse consequences if that outcome occurs. If not, either forego the opportunity or develop a response for the risk event that is affordable. The lottery player is considering the opposite of this, where the payoff is so large that the cost of playing is trivial in spite of a very low expected value.

Simulation, decision tables, and decision trees are just a few of the other tools available from decision theory.

The outputs from quantitative risk analysis include a "prioritized list of quantified risks" (Project Management Institute 2000, 138–39). These should be documented to ensure that the rationality of the decision is clear. Not only is this important for the project manager's future career, it provides proof of the prudent rationality of the decision in the event of legal proceedings and it provides an opportunity for upper management to review, comment, and even reverse the decision, if they see fit. Legal standards rely on the "prudence" concept. Unless the decisions are documented and prudent techniques were used in arriving at them, the project manager and others concerned may be at risk personally.

Risk response planning "is the process of developing options and determining actions to enhance opportunities and reduce threats to the project's objectives" (Project Management Institute 2000, 140). It may use avoidance, transfer, mitigation, or acceptance (2000, 140). Avoidance might consist of using proven, instead of a state-of-the-art, components. While this may reduce the risk associated with the project, it may increase the risk of obsolescence of the product of the project. Transfer might involve insurance, performance bonds, warranties, guarantees, or contract forms and provisions. Risk mitigation might consist of starting development on two or more alternatives and selecting the most suitable one after at least one is proven to be satisfactory. Acceptance might involve proceeding with construction in a flood-prone area, while taking some measures to reduce the loss if a flood does occur.

Risk monitoring and control is exercised when a risk event occurs. Efforts are exercised to energize the planned actions to deal with the event, revise the actions in view of the actual occurrence, and update the risk management plan based on lessons learned.

The greatest threat on many projects is an accident that affects human safety. Because the opportunity for such accidents is ever-present, this is a major area of continuing risk assessment and response planning. One person should be designated as safety officer, even if it is only a part-time position. That person needs training in *seeing* the potential for accidents about to happen so that corrective action can be taken to prevent the accident. That person needs the cooperation of all members of the project team. Such simple things as never entering the project site without prescribed safety equipment are essential if others on the team are to believe the policies and practice safe procedures.

Seeing the potential for accidents may seem to be a universal capability. The OC had a risk management person reporting to him for a year. After accompanying the risk team on several inspections, the OC became acutely aware that safety consciousness is not an innate characteristic, but must be learned. It could have prevented a back hoe from falling into the excavation or saved the life of an electrician who had not locked open the master circuit switch before working on the circuit. Then there was the very large police officer on the team who shook every standing object (such as file cabinets) to ensure they would not tip over on the user. Suffice it to say that the OC became much more safety conscious as a result of those tours, sometimes to the chagrin of his associates and, especially, spouse.

Next, after accident prevention, is responding to an accident. There is precious little time to discuss what to do if there is an accident. Potential accidents must be planned for and the responses practiced. One of the most vivid examples of this for the OC, although not on a project, was in a paper mill. A break in the paper web causes lost production, a lot of cleanup, and could threaten a human's well being. While touring a mill, the web broke. This is a continuous sheet of paper about twelve feet wide. It was running at a speed of about fifty miles per hour. People came on the run from many other operations, moving directly to their responsibility, and in seconds the operation was restored to normal. This could not have happened without thorough training.

Accidents such as these are easily visualized. Other risk events are often less vivid but still require preparation, training, and vigilance. Anyone who has worked with computers is acutely aware of the risk event of losing files due to power or other computer failure or getting a computer virus. Careful adherence to backup procedures can minimize the costs of file loss. Avoiding importing unauthorized programs can minimize the chances of shutting down the entire computer system, especially due to a virus.

A TAXONOMY OF RISKS

The first step in managing risks is the recognition of the possible risks on a specific project. The *PMBOK® Guide* suggests some common sources of risks, such as changes in requirements; design errors, omissions, and misunderstandings; poorly-defined or understood roles and responsibilities; poor estimates; and insufficiently skilled staff (Project Management Institute 2000). A more definitive taxonomy can reduce the probability of failing to recognize a significant risk as well as improve our understanding of what can be done to cause the consequences to be more favorable. The *PMBOK® Guide* suggests "technical, quality, or performance risks; project management risks; organization risks; and external risks" (Project Management Institute 2000, 131–32). An alternative taxonomy starts by recognizing that some risks are primarily associated with the project, while others are primarily associated with the product of the project.

Project Risks

There are many possible risks associated with the project itself. Some of them are discussed below.

Safety

This should be your first risk concern. It is applicable to members of the project team, the community, and especially to visitors. On some projects this is a major concern while on others it is almost an incidental concern. It is a major concern if the project involves height or depth, hazardous materials, mechanical equipment, electricity, pressures, temperatures, or a host of other factors. You must comply with all federal and state laws and regulations. You must take actions to minimize the risks such as requiring safety equipment, ensuring that people know how to use it, and ensuring that they comply with the rules. You and your core team must lead by example by wearing your safety equipment when appropriate. Even a project performed totally in an office environment has hazards. People have been known to stab themselves with scissors, get hands caught in office equipment, and trip over extension cords. Few of us have an "eye" for accidents waiting to happen so you should call on a safety expert to tour your facilities and bring them to your attention.

Safety consciousness goes beyond eliminating causes of accidents. It also requires contingency plans, supplies, and equipment to deal with safety problems should they arise. For example, if hazardous chemicals are required, there should be a spray facility to wash them off the body. There should be fire suppression equipment in addition to alarms and a means of alerting fire-fighting crews, whether they are a part of the project team or the local fire-fighting agency. Similarly, plans and equipment must be in place to deal with the other crises that can happen. Your organization's personnel or safety departments should be available to ensure that your project has adequate plans.

Technology

One of the most tempting ways to improve project performance is to use a new technology or method. Using the latest computer program may speed up the work, *unless*, the software is not thoroughly tested and bugs show up before the required results are obtained. There are four levels at which state-of-the-art technology must be considered. First is the science. Is it thoroughly developed and has it been tested for possible unintended consequences? Second, has it been proven in industry practice? Inventors and salespeople are always looking for the early adopter and are notorious at espousing the benefits while ignoring the risks. Third, has your organization had experience with this technology? Fourth, have you had experience with it? In the last two instances, perhaps there is someone who can supplement your experience at critical stages in decision-making and application.

Rework

The old adage, "haste makes waste," certainly applies to projects. Rework most often results from trying too hard to expedite the project. Work product that is released before being completed, inadequate checking of the work product, failure to document changes, and simply failing to communicate adequately are major causes of rework. Constant vigilance is necessary to minimize the impact of rework. An excellent discussion of this subject can be found in a series of articles published in the *PM Network*® and the *Project Management Journal*® (Cooper 1993a; 1993b; 1993c; 1993d).

Personnel

There are at least three aspects of this. Are key people going to be available when needed? This may be a key craftsman, professional, consultant, or upper management decision-maker. Are you likely to have difficulty with unions? On many major projects, special contracts have been negotiated with the relevant unions for the life of the project. By dealing with their concerns and grievance procedures up front, the projects were able to proceed without interruption. Finally, will the requisite personnel be available in the quantities needed, at the time they are needed. For example, if economic activity is especially high, either overall or in a specific area, the demand for certain categories of labor may exceed the supply, making the project vulnerable to delays, slow down, or unexpected demands. For example, there have been demands for overtime, whether the productivity warranted it or not. It was a way of increasing take-home pay for the worker in the short run. In other instances, management may authorize only a portion of the personnel you request to execute the project. In such a case, you may well want to consider formally revising the schedule, decommiting on some of the objectives, or decommiting the project altogether. Be mindful of the potential effects on future employment before opting for any of these alternatives, but also of the potential effects of failure to meet objectives.

Equipment

There are two types of equipment; that which will be a part of the product of the project and that which is necessary to execute the project. On the former, we need to be concerned with delivery and performance. Ideally, delivery will be just-in-time (JIT) to be off-loaded and installed. Any earlier than that will result in per diem costs for the personnel and transport delivering the equipment, as well as excess handling and storage. Late delivery can result in even more delays on the project and additional costs. Consideration must be given to the degree of follow-up appropriate. Some items may warrant one or more visits to the manufacturing facility of the supplier. Some may warrant setting up a system, computer or manual, to obtain progress reports at critical progress points. One of these progress points is certainly the actual shipment. The report should be designed to get specific detail such as the truck/car number and routing, not just a "check-is-in-the-mail" type response.

Equipment that is used to execute the project must be capable of meeting the needs of the task at hand, must be available when needed, and must be reliable, i.e., not breakdown at a crucial point. Mostly this is accomplished by selection of a reliable supplier and ensuring that proper preventive maintenance has been done on the equipment.

Suppliers

The suppliers must be capable of delivering the required materiel. Either they must be able to produce a quality product or have suppliers with such capability. They must have the capacity to perform in the relevant time period. They must have the financial strength to perform all necessary work without delay or requiring unacceptable financial assistance. A steel supplier that is nearing bankruptcy is a poor risk regardless of their low bid.

Materials

Factors applicable to materials include availability, suitability, and quality. Availability includes not only its existence, but also its existence in the quantity required, at the desired location, and when it is required. Suitability for the particular application is critical. While fill dirt may seem readily available, it does not always have the characteristics necessary for the particular purpose. This can result in additional costs and time to bring it to the site. Quality, as measured by conformance to specifications, is a must. Steel beams or columns that are not exactly to size will have to be modified in the field. Paper that is not of the specified quality may jam a printer. Thus, materials management must include checking for conformance to specifications before the material is to be used.

Environment

Environmental risks may be visible or hidden. Visible factors include terrain, weather, and traffic. One contractor who erects modular homes minimizes the effects of weather and terrain by having a bulldozer on site on the day of erection. He considers it a small price to pay to ensure that the crane and the trucks hauling the modules can get to the site for installation without delay. Hidden environmental risks include subsurface conditions that were not apparent before. These can be unexpected rock or archeological findings that must be treated in special ways by law. Research and borings can reduce the risk of surprises but cannot totally eliminate them.

Government

There are two major risks associated with governments—timeliness of action and changes in requirements/regulations. Timeliness of action is very difficult to deal with. Bureaucrats value their independence highly. Pushing them to hurry generally makes them less concerned with your problems. This is especially risky if there is to be an ongoing relationship such as with building inspectors. The OC has been very fortunate in having good relations with building inspectors. What seemed to work in this case was being upfront with them by reviewing plans with them early on, seeking their advice, and following their suggestions where possible. Compliance with their demands was never a question, although politely asking for the basis of the requirement and alternatives that would be acceptable to meet such demands was never ignored.

Community

Many projects have potential impacts on the community where they are located. Any project that affects traffic flows has the potential for community reaction. Affected business owners generally have the greatest political clout as well as the most significant reason to react. Failure to consider the concerns of the community can galvanize them into actions that may delay the project as well as add substantial costs. A proactive approach is often the most effective way to deal with this. Providing benefits and minimizing onerous features, when accompanied by appropriate public relations efforts, can reduce the potential for negative reactions. This is important because, once the organizational mechanisms are in place and any success is achieved, the potential for further action is increased. On the other hand, care must be exercised to avoid energizing any such organizational effort. Thus, it is important to develop a very well-thought-out plan for dealing with community concerns. There are several reports of successful efforts to deal with community concerns in showcase articles in the *PM Network®* (Mask and Kilgore 1990; Padgham 1991; McMichael 1994).

Product Risks

While often not in the purview of the project manager, risk associated with any of the following factors could impact the project due to changes in the requirements for the product or even cancellation of the project. The project manager needs to comprehend the client's concerns to appreciate pressures and priorities, to be sensitive to the client's expectations of the project, and to be alert to possible cancellation to minimize the consequences of such an action. On some projects, the scope of the project may well include specification of a consumer product, selection of manufacturing location, as well as determination of the timing. Some of the risks are discussed in the following sections.

Type of Product

The introduction of a new product is always fraught with uncertainties. One recent product development is an excellent example. Digital television had at least two major uncertainties—the format and the number of customers who will actually buy a new TV set when programs are broadcast in that mode. A manufacturer might start a project to manufacture TV sets to operate in the mode that was not adopted by the market place. If that error was discovered while the project was in process, the project could be canceled or changed drastically. Similarly, predicting the demand is difficult because opinions may well change after consumers are able to witness the differences in reception and other features. But that did not happen until the start of programs being broadcast in digital mode. This has a direct affect on pricing that relates back to the projects that are necessary to launch production. The project costs will have to be amortized over the number of units produced. The higher the project costs, the greater the margin in pricing necessary to recover the project costs.

Cultural factors may impact the product of the project. For example, the introduction of labor saving devices and foods into the American kitchen was deterred by a cultural value that this was a sign of the laziness of the homemaker. Thus, it led to uncertainty of demand.

Timing

Even the value of the best features of a new product can be negated if the project takes too long and misses the market opportunity. This was, in part, the problem with the Edsel—and many other new products. Timing in the economic cycle can be a major concern, especially if the product is dependent on discretionary income. For example, completing a "spec" building after a downturn is well underway can lead to major costs of funds employed as well as cash flow requirements for debt repayment.

Features

The project may be to develop a new feature for a computer. Often potential customers do not perceive that they need that feature. Sometimes the feature may require more effort or expertise to use than is extant in the market. Early computers suffered from this and the market was limited to "computer geeks."

Location

It is often said that the three major factors leading to retail success are "location, location, location." Location of manufacturing facilities may be equally important, but also related to a number of other factors including labor supply and skills, material supplies, market, utilities/ services, and the community milieu as applicable, especially for managers and other key personnel.

UNCERTAINTY

Uncertainty is a fact of life in projects. It is a fact of life, period. We drive to work each day. Seldom does it take exactly the same time as the day before. Traffic flows differently. One day we hit all green lights and the next all red. Sometimes there is an accident. If we were to record our time each day and analyze the data we would find a distribution of the times. It would have a mean time, the arithmetic average of all of them, and a standard deviation, a measure of the dispersion of those times about the mean. From this data we could calculate the time we should allow to ensure that we are late no more that once a year, ten times a year, or fifty times a year. We can do the same on projects.

In Table XVII.1 uncertainty was characterized by knowledge of possible outcomes without knowledge of their probabilities. This requires clarification for understanding uncertainty in this context. Note that in the discussion of risk there were two or more discrete outcomes with values and probabilities for each. For uncertainty in this section we focus on only one outcome. We really assume that it will happen with certainty but we are not really sure when (with respect to duration), how much (with respect to cost), or how well (with regard to technical performance). There is a range of values for each of these and we assume that the value actually experienced is randomly selected from that range.

Uncertainty generally has an impact on one or more of three aspects of a project—time, cost, and technical performance. In Chapter XVIII these variables are discussed in more detail as we focus on controlling them. Here we will simply discuss how we handle the uncertainties in these three areas.

The duration of an activity can be affected by many factors. That is, there can be many outcomes of related events that impact an activity's duration; including delays in receiving inputs and variabilities in the efficiency and effectiveness of the human resources involved; including errors, unexpected difficulties, and delays due to weather or other uncontrollable factors. The probability of each of these on a given activity is unknown. In fact, if pressed hard, we would have to argue that we approach a state of ignorance about the specific outcomes on a specific activity. However, people familiar with the nature of the work content of a given activity can apply judgment to estimating the effect of all such variables on the range of durations for an activity. Thus, without knowing specifically what may contribute to the variability in an activity's duration, reasonable estimates can be made that reflect the net effects. Thus, we can deal with the uncertainty of the duration for a project activity.

In a similar manner, there is uncertainty about cost and technical performance. The net effect of uncertainties in these two variables is a bit different. The objectives of a project are generally expressed in terms of time, cost, and technical performance. The relative importance of these measures varies across projects depending, for example, on the client; the potential impact of the product of the project on human life and the environment; and costs of failure. If human life is at stake, the performance requirements may be very demanding, with time and cost being somewhat less demanding. In this circumstance, if there is trouble in meeting performance requirements, cost and duration will likely absorb the uncertainties. If cost is primary, technical performance may absorb the uncertainty. Simply, on any given project, these three variables are rank ordered. The one that is in the third position will absorb most of the impact of uncertainties. However, in reality it is not that simple.

As the duration of an activity changes from some theoretical optimum duration, its costs generally increase also. The interdependence between these measures of an activity, and therefore projects, makes it very difficult to deal directly with the uncertainties of cost. Thus, in predicting future costs, we generally revert to some assumption about the relationship of cost to time. For example, for a specific work package we may assume that expenditures will continue at the same rate they have on that work package to date.

Technical performance uncertainties are generally reflected in additional time to achieve expectations and therefore, in cost also. One strategy for dealing with technical performance uncertainties, when cost and/or time are primary, is to accept a reduced performance level across all measures of performance. Perhaps a better strategy is to delete some of the functions required and maintain the level of performance on all other functions.

Time

PERT was developed to focus on the uncertainties of time. It required three values for the estimated duration of an activity. These define a distribution of the time required to perform the activity. The distribution has a mean and variance (standard deviation squared). The distribution can be, or most likely is, skewed—that is, not symmetrical. By assuming that the distributions of the activities in a project are independent, the means of the distributions can be added just as the durations were added in the example in Chapter XI. The resultant total duration of the project was assumed to be normally distributed based on the theory of the Central Limit Theorem. Similarly, the variance of that distribution was assumed to be the sum of the variances along the critical path. With these measures it is feasible to make some statements about the probability of completing the project on or before (or after) any given target date. This gives management information on where to focus their attention in order to expedite the project or to set target dates that have a high probability of being met. These calculations are presented in Appendix XVII.A.

PERT provided some significant contributions to the Polaris Missile Weapons Project, for which it was developed, as well as for many other projects. It was soon recognized that it had a major flaw, however. Since the variation of the end event was based only on the activities on the critical path, it failed to recognize the potential contribution to variation by activities not on the critical path.

The solution to this problem is to use Monte Carlo Simulation. This concept was well received in the early days of computers but it required considerable computer time for the computations. As the cost of computer calculations came down, it started to become popular for project calculations.

Monte Carlo PERT uses the same type of inputs to calculate a large number of completion dates for the project. Each calculation is exactly as discussed in Chapter XI with one exception. The duration for each activity is derived by randomly sampling from its duration distribution. Thus, the duration for a given activity is different for each iteration and the completion time is different. From the data obtained from, perhaps, 100 iterations, a distribution of completion times, with mean and variance, for the project is developed. This provides a measure of the uncertainty for completing the project from which the probability of completing on any given date can be calculated. Note that by this procedure the distribution of completion dates is affected by all activities in the project, not just the activities on the critical path.

Why is understanding uncertainty so important on projects? On the original application of PERT to the Polaris Missile Weapons Project, the system tests were of major concern. The test launching of a missile required the deployment of large numbers of ships, people, and equipment to launch, track, collect data, and recover the missile. This was very expensive and Admiral Rayborn, program manager, wanted to avoid such a deployment if all systems were not ready. Using the PERT analyses, dates were set for system tests that had a high probability of all systems being ready. Perhaps more importantly, his project team was able to pinpoint activities that threatened these target dates and to take preemptive action to expedite deliveries. Articles on the development of PERT credit its use with saving a year on the development program. While no claims were made, it is reasonable to assume it also saved considerable costs for unnecessary or premature deploying of resources before all systems were ready.

Anyone bidding on a fixed-price contract, especially with a penalty clause for late completion, should be concerned with the probability of meeting the contract date. Better yet, they should be concerned about these uncertainties while negotiating the terms of the contract.

Most projects have meetings at which the project work product to date is reviewed and key decisions are made. These are generally preceded by a large number of activities being completed just prior to the meeting. Thus, the start of the meeting is called a convergence point. The planner/scheduler for Chrysler Styling recognized that such events had a tendency to experience one or more activities being late. To compensate for this he scheduled "water" preceding the executive styling committee meetings. "Water," an activity for which there was no work content, allowed time for those few late activities to be completed.

This can be analyzed more formally today by using the uncertainty information generated by Monte Carlo PERT. Consider the likelihood of an activity being late. (Note: This analysis will ignore other alternatives for reacting to this uncertainty such as all out overtime, and so on, which is feasible for many situations.) From the accumulated uncertainty of all preceding activities the mean and standard deviation of its completion time might be 100 days and 5 days. Thus, the probability of that activity being completed in 100 days or less is 50 percent. Most people would not like to call a meeting of the top executives of an organization if there was only a 50 percent chance of being prepared for the meeting. Thus, the meeting might be scheduled for day number 105 for which the probability of being prepared would be 84 percent. We would be late 16 percent of the time. To have a 97 percent chance of being prepared we could set the meeting at day number 110. We would be late only 3 percent of the time.

Now consider that there are two activities that must be completed to be prepared for the meeting, each having the same mean and standard deviation. Using the same logic as in reliability theory, the probability that at least one of those activities will not be completed by day 105 is not 16 percent, but 29 percent. If we set the target date at day 110, the probability of at least one activity not being ready is 6 percent. If there are three activities coming into this merge point the probabilities are increased to 40 percent and 9 percent respectively. If there are 10 merging activities the probabilities become 83 and 26 percent. The probability of being ready for the meeting by day number 100 is only 0.1 percent. Thus, it can be seen that "water" can be very important for the meeting scheduler's career.

The recent development of Critical Chain concepts relies on buffers in much the same manner. It goes beyond just merge points to include buffers as a protection against overruns on activities requiring a critical resource. The concepts are essentially the same. However, they are based on gross simplifications of theory and therefore introduce considerable errors in the calculations. They should be modified to base the buffers on more accurate calculations, preferably using the three time estimates of PERT and, where appropriate, basing the calculations on the results of Monte Carlo PERT.

Clearly, major meetings are not the only causes of merge points. Integration testing of more than one subsystem, such as in computer system development, would experience this phenomenon. Erection or installation of major components on a construction project requires several activities to have been completed. The costs of holding equipment and people at the ready are not trivial. Thus, consideration of the interactions of activities at merge points is certainly not a trivial exercise. On the other hand, there are other actions that should be taken to improve performance, especially on those activities, and their predecessors for which the uncertainty is greatest, as discussed in Chapter XI. They should all be considered before setting target dates that are unacceptable. However, constantly resorting to overtime, for example, can have negative consequences for the project team and its members.

It would be a mistake to discuss merge point uncertainty without a reminder of the domino effect in scheduling. Because activities following a merge point are especially susceptible to delays that are compounded by the domino effect, all merge points should be reviewed for the build up of probability of being late. If this poses a problem with scheduling a critical resource, perhaps some "water" should be introduced.

The poignancy of buffers, especially at the end of a project is most evident on projects having a penalty clause associated with the completion date. The organization certainly does not want to commit to a completion date for which it has only a 50 percent chance of success. Monte Carlo PERT provides excellent information on which to base such commitments. Indeed, the OC anticipates that it will not be long before Monte Carlo PERT is integrated with the time-cost tradeoff capabilities of critical path planning and scheduling (CPPS) to directly address the question of how much additional to spend to increase the probability of completing the project in time and benefit from incentive payments or minimize the impact of penalty costs. This capability was first introduced in the 1960s at General Motors Reality (Bildson and Gillespie 1962). It could also be extended to analyze alternatives for accelerating a project that has gotten behind schedule or to assess potential costs of accelerating a project to meet an earlier target date, such as bringing a product to market a year early.

SUMMARY

Uncertainties and risks are a fact of life on projects. Recognizing and managing them is becoming increasingly important. There are some excellent approaches available but they require some degree of knowledge and sophistication for proper use. Some of these require minimal additional knowledge to use. Monte Carlo PERT is an example. The concepts of Critical Chain are excellent provided that they are implemented based on accepted theory of probability. Decision theory offers excellent tools to aid in making decisions that occur in managing projects but it requires somewhat more knowledge to apply properly.

It behooves the project manager to learn more about probability and decision theory so it can be used properly. It is inevitable that such tools will be used more in the future, as competitive pressures require more precision in bidding on and performing projects. Clearly, competitive pressures for reliable prediction of completion dates and faster performance of projects have created an interest in Critical Chain concepts.

It also behooves organization executives to learn more about uncertainty and risk management to enable them to behave in such a manner as to promote the acceptance of these concepts in their organizations. This is especially evident in the application of Critical Chain concepts such as expecting project activities to be performed in their most likely duration most of the time. It only takes one executive or manager in the management chain to cause persons responsible for activity estimating and performance to revert to providing duration estimates that include padding to protect them from "punishment" for exceeding estimates.

Similarly, executives must adapt to the variability associated with outcomes in order to deal with decisions based on applicable decision theory. Project managers need to take the lead in educating their superiors in this regard. Clearly, the more knowledgeable the project manager, the more likely there will be success in such educating. It is also clear that the project manager must act prudently in introducing these concepts into the organization to minimize the chance of a setback that would hinder further progress, and perhaps cause the organization to reverse progress to date.

Further Reading

Nocharli, Paul H., and Kim T. Hayes. 1991. Applied Project Risk Management. Proceedings: *Project Management Institute Seminar/Symposium*, Sept. 28–Oct. 2, Dallas, TX: 236–238.

Orr, J. Barry. 1992. The Management of Risk—A Contractor's Viewpoint. Proceedings: *Project Management Institute Seminar/Symposium*, Sept. 21–23, Pittsburgh, PA: 9–17.

Sam made a list of the things that could happen on each aspect of the project. First were concerns of physical safety. They ranged from a tree falling on a person, someone getting cut by an axe, an animal charging a hunter, and a tanner being exposed to tanning substances to a person falling off the raft prior to its completion. Plans were developed to deal with each of these. In addition, Sam vowed to talk personally to each group about the importance of safety.

Next Sam considered the risks associated with the product of the project. It seemed that the greatest risk was for the vines to break, washing the raft downstream. A plan was developed for that contingency requiring the gathering of some more vines so the raft could be tethered to the shore. This way, the raft, and any occupants, could be saved, repairs made, and the operation continued. The next greatest risk was a person, or one of the animals, falling off the raft during the transporting operation. Since all could float to some extent it was decided to use any thongs not required in constructing the raft as safety lines that would be attached to the center pole and tied to each individual or animal.

There were some other risks that were dealt with appropriately. The above represented the major risks and the plans for dealing with them.

Sam then turned attention to the risk associated with the project completion date. The first step was to examine each activity to determine the degree of its uncertainty. Sam made the following observations and estimates of the variation of durations by activity.

		Duration (Days)	Uncertainty	Cause
Concept Design	DC	6	+ - 1	testing prototype may lead to changes
Detail Design	DDD	12	+ - 1	little or no problems
Gather Materials - Logs	GML	33	+ - 10	may have to go farther to find straight trees, may not
Gather Materials - Hides	GMH	45	+ - 30	uncertainty in finding animals
Gather Materials - Vines	GMV	12	+ - 2	little or no problems
Prepare Materials - Logs	MPL	36	+ - 2	little or no problems
Prepare Materials - Hides	MPH	18	+ - 2	little or no problems
Prepare Materials - Vines	MPV	6	+ - 2	little or no problems
Assemble - Deck	AD	18	+ - 1	little or no problems
Assemble - Movement	AM	2	+ - 1	minor problems
Attach Movement to Deck	AMD	1	+ - 0	no problems anticipated
Test - Deck	TD	2	+ - 1	minor problems may require adjustments
Test - Movement	TM	1	- 0 +2	minor problems may require adjustments
Final Test	TFT	1	- 0 +2	minor problems may require adjustments

Based on these estimates, Sam made the following PERT calculations. (It was just too much work to perform the manual calculations for Monte Carlo PERT and computers were still a few centuries away.)

Activity	Predecessors	Duration	Estimated Time	Early Start	Early Finish	Late Start	Late Finish	Slack
DC	-	5-6-7	6	0	6	2.4	8.4	2.4
DDD	DC	11-12-13	12	6	18	9.4	21.4	3.4
GML	DC	23-33-43	33	6	39	8.4	41.4	2.4
GMH	DC(SS+1)	15-45-75	45	1	46	3.4	48.4	2.4
GMV	DC(FS+33)	10-12-14	12	39	51	56.4	68.4	17.4
MPL	DDD, GML(FS-20)	34-36-38	36	19	55	21.4	57.4	2.4
MPH	GMH(FF-9)	16-18-20	18	37	55	39.4	57.4	2.4
MPV	GMV	4-6-8	6	51	57	68.4	74.4	17.4
AD	MPL,MPH	17-18-19	18	55	73	57.4	75.4	2.4
AM	MPH,MPV,DDD	1-2-3	2	57	59	74.4	76.4	17.4
AMD	AD,AM	1-1-1	1	73	74	76.4	77.4	3.4
TD	AD	1-2-3	2	73	75	75.4	77.4	2.4
TM	TD,AMD	1-1-3	1.3	75	76.3	77.4	78.7	2.4
TFT	TM	1-1-3	1.3	76.3	77.6	78.7	80	2.4

Based on the expected completion time the project plan and schedule still looked feasible. However, Sam was concerned about the large uncertainty associated with the hides. Sam calculated the variances and probabilities for both critical paths.

On Path	DC-	GML-	MPL-	AD-	TD-	TM-	TFT	Total
(b - a)/6	2/6	20/6	4/6	2/6	2/6	2/6	2/6	
Variance	4/36	400/36	16/36	4/36	4/36	4/36	4/36	436/36

Standard Deviation	3.5
Probability of completing in 80 days	<75%
Probability of completing in 90 days	~100%

On Path	DC-	GMH-	MPH-	AD-	TD-	TM-	TFT	Total
(b - a)/6	2/6	60/6	4/6	2/6	2/6	2/6	2/6	
Variance	4/36	3600/36	16/36	4/36	4/36	4/36	4/36	3636/36

Standard Deviation	10.0
Probability of completing in 80 days	<65%
Probability of completing in 90 days	~90%
Probability of completing in 100 days	~99%

Sam noted two things from these calculations. First, getting the hides created a problem. There was at least a 35 percent chance of problems if the rains came early and resulted in flooding before the project was completed. There was about a 10 percent chance of experiencing the normal flooding. Second, Sam noted that the PERT calculations, without further examination, can be misleading. Maybe Monte Carlo PERT would be worthwhile on a larger project.

But what could be done to improve the chances of finishing the raft before the floods? Sam thought about it a while and decided that the hunters should leave immediately, as the animals were likely to still be near the watering hole and that might solve the problem entirely. If it did, the resources released could then be transferred to bringing the logs back sooner.

Sam was sure glad to have done all this analysis because the plan was better and even better understood.

APPENDIX XVII.A
PROGRAM EVALUATION AND REVIEW TECHNIQUE
(PERT)

In Chapter XIV we used a simple project to illustrate the time/cost tradeoff concepts. We use the same project here to illustrate the program evaluation and review technique (PERT) calculation, the Monte Carlo PERT calculations, and the type of information available from each.

In previous discussions we have considered time estimates to be certain and therefore completely defined by a single time estimate. The PERT concept permits us to convey more information about the duration by using three time estimates. Specifically, we can say something about the uncertainty associated with the duration.

This is easy to think about when we consider one of the activities in the project involving driving from New York to Los Angeles used in Chapter XI. Consider any trip involving driving over a mix of roads. For example, we drive faster on Interstates than on rural roads. We drive faster on a clear, dry day than on a wet day, and especially an icy day. We are often able to react to a route stoppage better on urban streets than on an Interstate—there are more options available in terms of opportunities to turn onto other streets. On the Interstate we are limited to where the ramps are. On some routes we might be willing to take greater risks than on others, such as exceeding the speed limit. Thus, if we were to drive the same route many times, such as going to work each day we would *not* want to start at the latest possible time if it is important to us that we arrive on time.

If we are required to be at work on time, we probably would not be satisfied with a departure time based on the average time it took us to drive that route last year. We would arrive on time or before about 50 percent of the time. We would be late 50 percent of the time. Unless our boss was rather sophisticated about probabilistic events, we might not have to make that drive any longer. To avoid that consequence, we might recall the longest time that we took last year and use that to determine our departure time. But that would mean we

272

would get to work quite early on all but one day a year. This phenomenon is well described by the Normal Distribution, one that is well-known and widely used. Using it, we could state the percentage of the time, i.e., the probability, that we would accept for being late and determine how much driving time we should allow. Thus we could be reasonably sure that we would not be late that percentage of the time and be able to get those extra minutes of sleep each day. Note that this process assumes that all other things are equal. In fact they are not equal. We get weather forecasts, reports of road repairs, and traffic reports. These allow us to modify our behavior accordingly, which we certainly do. However, we have a solid benchmark to which the additional knowledge can be applied.

This same process can be applied to projects. Using the PERT calculations, we can predict how long it will take to complete a project with a, say 90 percent, chance of success, i.e., completing it on or before the promised date. This is especially valuable where a penalty for being late is involved. It is also relevant in a competitive business where the organization that promises the earliest delivery often gets the order. They often get follow-on business if they then meet those promise dates. PERT has a very well-developed theory underlying it that has been challenged, tested, and proven sound—with one significant exception. That exception has been resolved by Monte Carlo PERT, the subject of the next appendix.

Now, consider the application of PERT to the example project shown in Figure XVII.A.1. The first difference from critical path method (CPM) is that three estimates are required to provide the additional information to describe the probability distribution. These are called the optimistic (a), most likely (m), and pessimistic (b) times. Originally, the optimistic and pessimistic times were considered once-in-a-hundred occurrences types of events (i.e., + or - 3 standard deviations). A later paper argued persuasively that they should be considered more like once in twenty (i.e., + or - 1.645 standard deviations). We will stick with the once-in-a-hundred description for this discussion. That would be similar to the two shortest and two longest times you took to drive to work during the last year.

There is a problem though. Projects are unique. We do not have the past year's experience to base our estimates on. Therefore, we use subjective estimates, much like we do when betting on a football game. The two teams have not played before and will not play again. Nevertheless, we estimate the chances that our team will win and place our bets. That is the same for a and b. The most likely is exactly that, the time we think it would most likely take to perform the activity. It is the time that it took to drive to work most of the time.

This sounds like a lot of extra work to make three time estimates when we are accustomed to making only one time estimate. Well, the OC has observed that most activities in a project have relatively little variation in duration. An estimate of plus or minus one or two days would probably be quite adequate for many activities. Then there is a group of activities that may vary from minus 10 percent of the duration to plus 30 percent. In fact, the OC has observed that it would be adequate to have five categories of variation from the most likely; this would describe the variation of at least 90 percent of the activities in a project. The uncertainties represented by these categories should be skewed to the right, i.e., the variation above the most likely is generally greater than that below. (The duration cannot be less than zero.)

The remaining 10 percent, at most, would require relatively little time to estimate more precisely. Indeed, it is appropriate to think seriously about these activities, as they are the ones most likely to cause problems on the project. Thus, the extra work in estimating the variation in the duration of activities is relatively small compared to what ought to be usual practice anyway. Indeed, the benefits from having better knowledge about the uncertainties in your project could well exceed the extra cost of estimating work on that 10 percent of the activities.

The three estimates are converted into an expected value of activity completion, t_e, a value that, according to probability theory, has certain properties that are relevant for the calculations involved in CPM and the representation of the variability of the completion time for the project. One of those properties is that there is a 50 percent chance of taking less time than t_e and a 50 percent chance of taking more time. This expected time is calculated as follows:

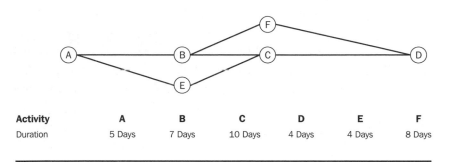

Activity	A	B	C	D	E	F
Duration	5 Days	7 Days	10 Days	4 Days	4 Days	8 Days

FIGURE XVII.A.1

Example Project for Illustrating PERT and Monte Carlo PERT

$$t_e = (a + 4m + b) / 6$$

(Note that the divisor is 3.29 for the 1 in 20 assumption.)

The sums of these t_e along any path through the network gives the time for which there is a 50 percent chance of completing the path in less time and a 50 percent chance of taking more time.

The purpose of estimating a and b is to describe the uncertainty. For calculation purposes we need a single number that represents that variation. It is called the variance (s^2). It is calculated simply as:

$$s^2 = (b - a)^2 / 36$$

(Note that the divisor is 10.8 for the 1 in 20 assumption.)

This measure also has some useful properties, mainly that the sum of the variances along any path in a project network is the variance for the completion of that path. Using the expected completion time and variance for such a path, we can say some useful things about the variability of the completion of that path. For example, the probability of completing the path in t_e or less is 50 percent. The probability of taking as much as t_e plus s, i.e., the square root of s^2, is about 84 percent. The probability of completing in t_e plus 2s is about 98 percent. With only these two values we can decide if we have "enough cushion" in the path. For most purposes it is reasonable to assume that the probability for $t_e + 0.5s$ is about 69 percent. (The error caused by assuming that the relationship between each of these pairs of points is linear is

Activity	Follower	a - m - b	t_e	Start	Finish	Start	Finish	Slack	s	s^2
A	B,E	2 - 5 - 8	5	0	5	0	5	0	6/6	36/36
B	F,C	5 - 7 - 9	7	5	12	5	12	0	4/6	16/36
E	C	3 - 4 - 5	4	5	9	8	12	3	2/6	4/36
F	D	2 - 5 - 26	8	12	20	14	22	2	24/6	576/36
C	D	8 - 10 - 12	10	12	22	12	22	0	4/6	16/36
D	-	3 - 4 - 5	4	22	26	22	26	0	2/6	4/36
								s^2	=	72/36
									=	2.00
								s	=	1.4

TABLE XVII.A.1
PERT Calculations

insignificant for most project purposes. Where it is significant, the user should have a good acquaintance with probability theory.)

Looking at the larger picture, the expected completion time for the project is the expected completion time for the critical path of the project. The expected variation in the completion time is represented by the variance for the finish of the critical path. The probabilities cited in the above paragraph are derived from the Normal Distribution tables, which can be found in a variety of sources. This information can be very useful in cases involving penalties or rewards associated with the completion of a project by a target date.

However, the last paragraph identifies the Achilles Heel of PERT. The expected completion date of the project is dependent only on the set of activities on the critical path. It may happen that another path has greater variability and therefore has a greater impact on the completion date of the project than does the critical path. The solution to this is the use of Monte Carlo PERT, as discussed in Appendix XVII.B.

To complete the discussion of PERT, it is applied to the example problem as shown in Table XVII.A.1, PERT Calculations.

From this we see that the expected completion time is 26 days. There is a 50 percent chance that the project will be completed earlier than 26 and a 50 percent chance it will be completed after day 26. The standard deviation, the square root of the variance, is 1.4 days so we can say that there is a 75 percent chance of completing it in 27 days and about a 90 percent chance it will be completed in 28 days. Thus, we might be willing to commit to delivering the product of the project in 28 days. If we are really conservative we might go for 29 or 30 days with close to 100 percent chance of on-time delivery. However we have to recognize that someone else may be willing to take more risk and get the bid on the basis of an earlier delivery date. (Note: These values are approximated.)

But notice the large variance on activity F, an activity not on the critical path but on A-B-F-D. That path requires 24 days to complete but has a standard deviation of 4.1 days ($s^2 - 632/36 - 17.6$) Based on this path we can say that there is about an 68 percent chance of the project requiring 28 days or only about 85 percent chance of completing it in 30 days. Perhaps there is a better way to determine likely finish dates. Ah ha! Monte Carlo PERT.

APPENDIX XVII.B
MONTE CARLO PERT

The following is a simplified illustration of Monte Carlo program evaluation and review technique (PERT) to facilitate demonstrating the concepts. For example, using a random number to sample the true distribution of the duration estimates is somewhat complicated to do manually—it is a snap for the computer. Thus, we will use random numbers to sample a rectangular distribution, applying some judgmental bias to get nearer to representative results. If Monte Carlo were done on a computer, we would sample from a normal (or perhaps a Beta) distribution and might do a hundred or even a thousand repetitions. We will do only ten here.

First we have to generate ten sets of duration estimates for the activities. (Note: If you are interested in doing this, use the random number function of any spread sheet, simply identify the range, i.e., 2–8 for activity A, for the random number, and recalculate the sheet. Each time you will get a number back within this range, inclusive. Repeat this ten times for each activity.) The sets of durations used in this example are

Set	Activities					
	A	B	E	F	C	D
1	4	7	3	7	10	4
2	2	6	5	15	9	5
3	6	8	5	4	9	4
4	7	7	4	9	10	4
5	8	5	3	12	9	3
6	5	7	5	7	8	3
7	7	9	5	25	8	5
8	8	6	3	12	8	5
9	2	5	4	26	8	5
10	3	7	5	2	10	4

TABLE XVII.B.1

Random Samples from the Duration Estimates

shown in Table XVII.B.1, Random Samples from the Duration Estimates. These durations were used in calculating the example project by the usual critical path method (CPM) a total of ten times.

The results of these calculations are shown in Table XVII.B.2, Results of Simplified Monte Carlo Simulation.

Using this data and a very small number of iterations, we can draw some illustrative conclusions. For example, there is an equal likelihood that activity C or F will be on the critical path. There is a 50 percent chance that the project will take 29.6 days to complete. There is about 20 percent chance that it will take thirty-six days or more. There is about 2 percent chance that it will take forty-three days or more. What a difference when we take the uncertainties of all the activities in this project into full consideration. Clearly, we exaggerated this example to make the results very obvious. Normally there would not be this great a difference in results.

Monte Carlo PERT is definitely recommended if there are many activities with a high degree of uncertainty or if there is a significant risk of penalty costs for overrunning the target date.

Iteration	Project Duration	Critical Path
1	25	A-B-C-D
2	28	A-B-F-D
3	27	A-B-C-D
4	28	A-B-C-D
5	28	A-B-F-D
6	23	A-B-C-D
7	46	A-B-F-D
8	31	A-B-F-D
9	38	A-B-F-D
10	24	A-B-C-D
Average	29.8	
Standard Deviation	6.72	

TABLE XVII.B.2
Results of Simplified Monte Carlo Simulation

SOME CAVEATS

There are several caveats that must be stated here to keep the theory in perspective as it is applied in practice.

Ceteris Paribus

The theory of both PERT and Monte Carlo PERT assumes "ceteris paribus," i.e., all other things being equal. One of the responsibilities of the project manager is to ensure that things are not equal. Every effort should be made to modify probabilities to the advantage of the project and to complete all activities in less than their expected time. However, these efforts must be genuine steps to improve performance, not simply wishful thinking that by reducing the estimate it will happen.

Faith and Trust

To get the full benefit of using Monte Carlo PERT, as well as Critical Chain concepts, it is important that management develop a sophisticated attitude toward uncertainty. With the proper attitude, project participants will develop a degree of trust in management that will enable the participants to give honest, unpadded estimates of the time required to perform their activities. This will result in shorter activity estimates and shorter projects. However, the first time that a participant gets reprimanded for taking longer than the expected time, then all estimates will likely return to being padded.

Capturing Success

Steps must also be taken to assure project participants that the fact that they beat the expected time this time will not result in a demand of doing this every time in the future. Otherwise, no activity will be reported completed before the expected time has been used up. At the same time, following the Critical Chain philosophy of "relay-race" mentality, steps must be taken to ensure that when an activity is completed early, its successors are started early. This will shorten the project duration even further.

Provide Incentives to Perform

Create an environment that values beating the odds. Celebrate successes in reducing durations, lowering costs, improving the product of the project, and so on. Use the discussion of success in *The World's Greatest Project* (Darnall 1996) to stimulate your thinking in this regard, even if it means going swimming in frigid water. Make your project fun!

APPENDIX XVII.C
DECISION THEORY

Decision theory as a specific area of knowledge is a development of the Twentieth Century. While many of the tools were developed and available before 1900, it was not until World War II that decision theory started to become recognized. One of the first studies to mark this new discipline was the examination of the optimum patterns in which to search for enemy submarines. This was undertaken by a multidiscipline team of scientists whose efforts were tagged "Operations Research." Out of this came the Operations Research Society of Americas (ORSA). Soon another similar organization was formed with the name of The Institute of Management Sciences (TIMS). Eventually, a third organization, now called simply Decision Sciences, was established with more of an academic-based membership. All of the people belonging to these three organizations combined the capabilities of computers, mathematics, probability and statistics, and knowledge of how various systems, both artificial and natural, worked to develop new ways of making decisions.

These efforts have led to a large number of techniques. Some of these are immediately applicable to managing projects, while others are more applicable to decisions about the products of projects. Among those applicable to projects are critical path method (CPM), critical path planning and scheduling (CPPS), program evaluation and review technique (PERT), and Resource Requirements analysis. These have been instrumental in the development of modern project management. In addition there are many other techniques that can aid the project manager including simulation, decision tables, and decision trees.

The OC has personally applied techniques such as linear programming, inventory management, queuing theory, simulation, and a number of other techniques to decisions involving either the project or the product of the project. For example, linear programming was used to determine the optimum operating conditions for three different melt processes for a casting plant to aid in selecting the process to be used in a major new casting plant.

The project manager of the future will employ more and more of these techniques in the process of managing a project. Therefore, the younger project manager should set learning objectives for becoming sufficiently familiar with the techniques to recognize an opportunity to improve decision-making, know whom to call for assistance, and be able to discuss the application intelligently. Notice, this did not specify knowing enough about the technique to apply it directly. This would be appropriate only if the technique had continuing applicability on a project or on successive projects.

There is a significant problem with the literature in this area at this time. Almost all the examples are drawn from volume manufacturing or similar contexts. Very few examples relate directly to problems encountered on projects. Fortunately, there is one book that is dedicated to applying decision theory on projects, *Decision Analysis in Projects* (Schuyler 1996). It should be the first source for all aspiring project managers. After that there are many books that might be perused. As authors begin to understand the project environment, and the need for better decision-making tools on projects, more sources will be published that are based on project-type problems.

APPENDIX XVII.D
MARS PATHFINDER PROJECT

PROJECT RISK MANAGEMENT

There were many technical and financial risks encountered by the Mars Pathfinder project during its development and mission operations phase.

There are few endeavors with more inherent technical risk than landing on the surface of another planet from space. The complexities of required hardware and software, combined with uncertainties about the planet's environment (atmosphere, landing site conditions) makes a mission such as Mars Pathfinder an extreme technical challenge. In addition, returning to the surface of Mars for less than 10% of the cost (in real year dollars) of the Viking missions presented the project with increased financial risk.

One of the keys to mitigating risk on Pathfinder was understanding what the risks were very early in the project. For example, the Pathfinder management team decided early on that volume, cost and schedule constraints would require a largely single string design, which in itself is higher risk. By knowing this up front, the Pathfinder team was able to select a high percentage of more reliable Class S parts from the Cassini project stores to help mitigate the risk associated with single string design. One factor in Pathfinder's favor was the relatively short seven month cruise period and low radiation environment on Mars. Management planned on getting 1,000–2,000 hours of operating time on the electronics before flight, and this goal was exceeded, with most hardware getting 2,600 hours of test time prior to launch. By doing this, the project substantially reduced their risk of an electronic parts failure during the mission.

Risk was also reduced in the early stages of the project by accomplishing system, inter-subsystem and subsystem failure modes, effects and criticality analysis (FMECA) between Preliminary Design Review and Critical Design Review. Management made a commitment to devote resources to building hardware and software flight test beds for development and troubleshooting early on in the project. Due to this foresight, the Pathfinder team had integrated 80% of all spacecraft electrical subsystems (including all science) into the Flight System Test Bed before assembly and test even began. Having the test bed in place was one of the cornerstones in a key Pathfinder strategy of reducing risk by conducting a vigorous test program. Part of the test program included a functional demonstration of each element of the Entry, Descent, Landing System in the most realistic environment possible within the constraints of budget, schedule and Earth's environment. This included functional testing of the airbags, parachute, bridle and rockets assisted decelerators. In addition to the physical tests, Pathfinder engineers performed literally thousands of Monte Carlo simulations of entry, descent, landing scenarios. Another important factor in the success of Pathfinder was starting the Assembly, Test and Launch Operations phase 18 months prior to launch. This allowed for plenty of time to work out issues related to mechanical integration and environmental test, while getting over 2,600 hours on most electronic parts.

Financial risk was managed by starting with adequate project reserves, and metering out the reserves rationally throughout the life of the project. One of the secrets to Pathfinder was not over committing reserves up front, so that potential cost growth during ATLO could be accommodated. Another important strategy for managing financial risk was developing a set of de-scope options which could be implemented if necessary. In Pathfinder's case, the planned reserves covered all of the cost growth and there was no need to implement de-scope options.

Schedule reserve was budgeted for each phase of the project based upon the degree of perceived schedule risk. For the 37 month development schedule, approximately 20 weeks of schedule margin was planned. This time phased schedule margin proved to be adequate for delivering and launching on time.

Chapter XVIII

Reporting & Control

COMMIT ONLY TO THOSE THINGS YOU CAN DO; DO WELL
THOSE THINGS TO WHICH YOU COMMIT.

Sam had determined earlier that an important aspect of managing the project was to monitor the labor days used versus the plan. In addition, Sam wanted some measure of actual progress on a day-by-day basis. Sam recognized that people were reluctant to report bad news and to indicate that work on an activity was completed until all the labor days had been used up. What to do?

Reporting and control are inextricably connected. You cannot control that of which you are not aware. On the other hand, having people report things that are not going to be controlled is more than a waste. It irritates those who have to report, tempts them to be blasé about reporting, and often leads to poor morale.

If you attempt to control things that can be delegated you will certainly slow a project and may bring it to a halt. Those whom you most need on your team, the talented and capable individuals, will avoid your projects or seek the first opportunity to move on. And yet, failing to control those things essential to the success of the project will have at least as devastating effects.

Striking the right balance in reporting and control is probably *the* critical art of management. Therefore, we need to examine the two together to understand what we can control, what we should control, and how we can structure our systems to minimize the amount of control that needs to be exercised.

Finally, while I use the word control in this chapter, it should be clear that without recourse to severe punishment, one can seldom control human activity. Thus, keep in mind that whenever the word control is used I am really implying "manage" in the sense of modifying behavior toward achieving objectives as planned.

WHO CAN YOU REALLY MANAGE?

Critical path techniques aid us in measuring the time dimension and predicting project completion time (see Chapter XI). Earned value techniques aid us in measuring what we have accomplished relative to the money expended and how much we are likely to spend by project completion (see Chapter XV). Product inspection and testing help to ensure that the product of the project performs according to specifications (see Chapter XVI). Are these really the techniques we need to control the project or do they really just tell us whether we have achieved our objectives to date?

These techniques are somewhat like driving a car by looking into the rear view mirror. As long as the road is straight, it may be possible. However, if there are any curves in the road it is more difficult. You are likely to veer off the road at each curve until you see in the mirror that you are off the road. There are lags in the reporting of time, cost, and technical performance. By the time these reports are available, your project may already have veered off the road. It is the view of the OC that these variables and techniques are invaluable in conveying, in a concise manner, the overall status of the project, but that they do not provide the tools for control. Rather they identify the results, and the need for control, of other aspects of the project.

The typical measures of project success are *time, cost, and technical performance*. We discussed that in Chapter X. We saw there that cost is really an outcome variable. Technical performance is really a function of project scope and the project plan. The time required to perform an activity is a function of the activity performance requirements and the application of resources. Thus, the variables of a project that are really controllable are *scope, work package/activity definition, time and budget allocations, resource motivation, and some elements of the project itself; such as negotiating tradeoffs on technical requirements as the work progresses.*

This notion has been made very clear in one of the "new" organizational concepts associated with project management, the matrix approach to management. It is really very similar to the typical bureaucratic model, as a matter of fact. Experience in large bureaucracies indicates that everyone has a functional home, often represented by a corporate staff. If you ever expect to rise in the organization you must have the support of that corporate staff. They prescribe *how*, and often when, you perform tasks related to that staff's authority. If it is not done to their satisfaction they will let you know. Matrix management is simply an extension of that concept. Those who perform the work of the project belong to a functional department. That department generally exercises control over who performs the work, how it is done, and when it has been completed satisfactorily. That leaves you as the project manager to manage what is to be done, when it should be done, and how much should be spent doing it.

MANAGING THE MANAGEABLE

You as project manager are ultimately responsible for all aspects of the performance of a project. Many of these responsibilities have been discussed in the preceding chapters. Here we want to emphasize some of the most important aspects and some approaches to each.

Managing Scope

Project control starts at the inception of the project. Setting realistic objectives is the first step. It is the rare project that has no limits on either time or cost. Great mansions are examples of such rarities. The Hearst Castle must have been one. Bill Gates' house sounds like one. The new Getty Museum would surely appear to be one.

It is nearly as rare for the client to have limited expectations for the features, functions, and characteristics. There is an inherent motivation to get the very most for the money expended. Thus, conflict is inevitable between minimizing cost and time and maximizing features, functions, and characteristics. In Chapter VII, Scope Management, in *PM 101*, we saw how every feature, function, and characteristic implies a minimum work content. The more features, functions, and characteristics that are expected, the greater the work content and, therefore, the greater the time and cost.

It is helpful to view defining scope and establishing objectives as an iterative process. Using the ranking of feature, function, and characteristics, plus some hard questioning and examination of the client's perceptions of these, you need to analyze what are the important performance areas to the client. Associated with this, identify the areas of greatest risk in achieving the required performance. These become the basis for understanding the critical areas in which you need to establish realistic objectives and establish a means of measuring achievement of those objectives. This ensures an orderly and consistent allocation of objectives down through the work breakdown structure (WBS).

A complicating factor in managing the feature/function/characteristics versus cost conflict is rapidly changing technology. This is especially evident in defense systems acquisition. The lead-time in developing and deploying, plus the operational life of, modern defense systems places a premium on using the latest technology to avoid premature technological obsolescence of the product of the project. This pressure leads to adopting state-of-the-art technology, often with considerable risk. Sometimes the outcomes of these risks are unsuccessful.

The media generally treats such instances as disasters and they get lots of attention. The instances where such risk taking is successful seldom get similar attention.

All of these considerations are captured in the scope of the project. The scope of the project defines what is to be delivered, when it is to be delivered, and how much it should cost. It further amplifies on the nature of the product in terms of features, functions, and characteristics. It may also amplify on how the project is to be carried out. Thus, to a very large extent the work that must be performed, and therefore its cost, is determined by the scope of the project. It becomes the basis for the contractual relationship between the project and the client.

Client Expectations

The overriding purpose of any project is to achieve client satisfaction. This means understanding what the client expects, by when, and for how much. If the expectations are unrealistic you must help the client understand what is feasible. This may be through raising questions and providing answers, submitting alternative proposals, or in negotiations to arrive at a feasible balance of objectives.

This must be a continuing effort, as rarely are client expectations static. Anyone familiar with building a custom house is aware of the tendency for the client to request changes during the project. It is the rare change that does not take extra work and time. Often the costs go beyond the immediate change, as unanticipated effects of the change are manifested later in the project, including the domino effect of delays. Thus, change management must be thought of in two dimensions—managing the client's expectations and managing approved changes.

Managing the client's expectations requires frequent contact with the client not only to reinforce the advantages of having limited changes, but also to identify the need for changes as early as possible to minimize their negative impacts on project progress. If a change is called for, it must be recognized formally, analyzed carefully, and incorporated into the project scope, plan, schedule, and cost.

Commitments

Managing commitments is done at two levels. First, commitments are made to the client. Second, the commitments are made in performing the project. A useful guide is, "Commit only to those things you can do; Do well those things to which you commit."

Managing commitments to the client is covered previously. Commitments in performing the contract are just as important. Generally this is thought of as contracts management. It focuses on ensuring that your project team delivers everything called for in the contract with the client, as well as ensuring that your subcontractors deliver on their contracts.

The Vision

The starting point for controlling the project must be the vision of the product of the project and of the project itself. It may not be clear that these are two different visions. What is the difference between the project and the product of the project? Simply, a dinner is the product of the project; the project is the process of preparing the dinner. It is easy to imagine a vision of the dinner. It might be as simple as frozen dinners served on the packaging trays. Or, the vision might be of an elegant dinner of several courses, fine wines, background music, and special guests. The vision of the projects to create these two products would be quite different. The first may involve only a few activities. The second involves many activities that must be properly meshed to meet the high expectations implied by the vision of the product. The "project team" would receive considerable guidance and direction in performing their tasks from these alternative visions.

Given the overall specifications of what the client expects, you can focus on conveying a clear vision of the project to the team, design your management system to ensure that people are doing the right things, identify the critical decisions in which you must be involved, and practice the "art of the gentle nudge." Through this process you can empower your team members, encourage them to behave as you would like, and concentrate on maintaining the momentum of the project. It takes discipline and perseverance. It takes discipline to take the time at the beginning of the project to develop the shared vision

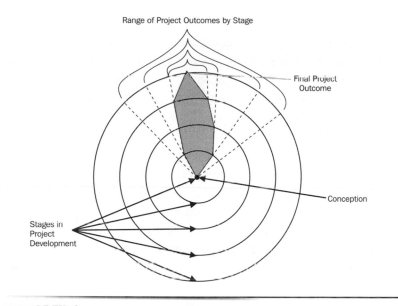

FIGURE XVIII.1
The Progressive Elaboration of a Project

with as many of the team members as possible. It takes perseverance to continue this process as both the project and the product of the project evolve through progressive elaboration.

The diagram in Figure XVIII.1, The Progressive Elaboration of a Project, will clarify the management of the visions over time. Suppose we divide the life of a project into five equal segments. Now consider the inner circle as representing all the possible perceptions of the product of the project. The shaded area represents the collective perceptions of all the team members. One member might see it as an easy ride to retirement. Another may see it as an opportunity to apply some new technology. Another sees it as an opportunity to justify new equipment. Another sees it as an opportunity to build an edifice, and so on, and so on. You as project manager must bring these disparate perceptions to a focus so that all members agree on a common vision, as represented by the darker area. It is unlikely that it can be brought into complete focus in the first period, i.e., a single point, as that would imply that there were no unanswered questions on the project.

In the next period, as elaboration progresses, the collective vision can spread as shown in the shaded area of the second circle. As project manager, you must ferret out these divergent tendencies and refocus a common vision. This process continues in each period until, at project completion, it is represented as a point on the outer circle.

Now, with this concept established, we can ignore the finite periods and see this as a continuous process of moving from the kernel of an idea about the product of the project, through its progressive elaboration, to its final delivery. With this conceptual view of the process of elaboration of the project, we can now turn to more specifics of the process of controlling the project.

The strategy by which the project will be executed is critical. For example, most buildings are constructed from the first floor up to the top floor. Some buildings have been constructed from the top floor down to the first floor. (Actually, all floors were poured at first floor level and jacked up into place.) Similarly, some houses are stick built and others are manufactured. Computer software might be coded in a compiler language or it could be developed in a database language. These are different strategies. There are other elements of the strategy of dealing with different facets of the project. This is primarily the responsibility of you as project manager.

This selected strategy is then interpreted into the WBS. It is at this stage that you determine for what you will be directly responsible, especially in terms of managing the interfaces between elements of the WBS and project team members. This is where you have the greatest impact in decision-making throughout the life of the project. The work content of the project becomes further defined. It is then converted into the project plan as interpreted in a project network diagram (PND). You, as the project manager, are directly responsible for the top level PND but can exercise influence upon the further detail as developed by members of the project team.

One of the arts of management is to identify the critical decisions in which you must be involved. It is easy to be involved in too many decisions. This leads to you being the bottleneck on the project as well as to your team members not contributing their best on the project. Probably the best way to ensure you are involved in the right decisions is to discuss with the key project team member(s) the criteria by which the decision will be made. If agreement can be reached on this prior to the decision being made, you are probably safe in delegating the decision-making. If agreement is not achieved, then you should probably be in the meeting. Otherwise, be prepared to support a decision that may not be the best or provide very convincing reasons why you should not accept it. This process is especially applicable to the progressive elaboration of the technical characteristics of the product of the project.

Specifications

The objective of the design stage of a project is to establish specifications for the product of the project as well as for the processes by which these specifications will be determined. You have an excellent opportunity to influence these decisions. There will be many tradeoffs involving technical requirements, costs, and risks. Some of the specifications may be dictated by the client, but more likely by the performing organization. Where they are not dictated by the client or by regulations and standards, you have an opportunity to determine exactly how the project will be carried out.

Work Package/Activity Performance Requirements

Ideally, the documentation of activities should provide all information necessary to define the work content and work product of each activity. Often, organizations will have written standards that provide guidance. It is important to consider those circumstances where the information is incomplete or inadequate.

What can the person responsible for a work package/activity reasonably be expected to know? It seems unreasonable for a person to know all of the uses of the work product of their activity. It does seem reasonable that they should know what work products and information they require to successfully perform their activity. Thus, with a little help, they should be capable of checking with those people performing activities upstream from theirs to ensure that their work product will be adequate.

Some work packages/activities will require critical technical decisions from time to time. You must ensure that you either participate in the meeting or are briefed on the issue, alternatives considered, the decision, and its rationale. Such decisions generally have an impact on cost and/or schedule.

It seems almost hypocritical to consider producing a product that is anything less than the best of our ability. However, aspiration levels that are too high can lead to excessive efforts and the use of the entire estimated duration, and sometimes more. Even if the objectives of an activity are met in less than the estimated duration, work will continue. While it is well to aim high, trying to achieve more than is really required can increase the duration, as well as the costs of the project. You must monitor the activities that are in process, especially those on the critical path or involving a critical resource, to ensure that they are moving along well, are reported completed as soon as the work is finished, and that the next activity starts promptly.

Changes

It is easy to believe that the ideal project is one that is executed according to plan with no changes. That is not a realistic expectation. It implies perfect knowledge of the future and all conditions affecting the project. It denies the learning that is inevitable in performing a project. It ignores the opportunity to save time and/or money through innovations, whether through inspiration or deliberate problem solving, such as value engineering. It denies that the client's needs may change due to market shifts and competitor's actions. It implies ignoring technological advances that could result in greater satisfaction to the client. Remember that the overriding purpose of performing the project is client satisfaction.

Change may be applicable to the product of the project, the project, or, more likely, to both. Some changes may be initiated by the client. Others may be initiated by the project team. Every change must be recognized formally, analyzed carefully for obscure impacts, documented, and incorporated into the project scope, plan, and schedule—including implications on resources. Often this requires checking with suppliers and subcontractors to verify impacts and gain commitment to the change. The changes must be communicated to all affected parties. Failure to do so will inevitably lead to rework or other *unintended consequences*.

You should monitor all such changes to ensure that they are carefully considered, that they are incorporated into the project scope, that all appropriate actions are taken to accomplish the change, and that the changes are accurately communicated to all concerned.

Documents

Closely associated with change control is document control. The nature of the progressive elaboration process implies that occasionally some implications of a design or decision may not be fully recognized when made. A document may be released that later has to be modified. The modification must be communicated to those who are relying on the original document. Thus, an accurate record is necessary to know who received what documents, what versions were received, and that new versions are received in a timely manner. It may be desirable to precede the actual issuing of the revised document with an alert that a change is coming and the general nature of the change. When the change is issued, it should make explicit the nature of the change to ensure that the recipient recognizes the precise nature of the change. In some environments, it may be appropriate to require acknowledgement of receipt of the revised document and action taken.

Managing Work Package/Activity Performance

The work of the project actually gets done through the work packages and activities identified in the WBS. If this is where the action is, then this is where the managing opportunities are. This process starts with authorizing the work to start and proceeds through reviewing costs and ensuring that advantage is taken of opportunities that arise during the process of performing the work.

Work Authorization

The actual work of the work package should not proceed until you authorize and assign budget for it. If there are any questions as to what will be charged to the budget account they should be resolved at this point. The accounting system should provide for all charges to the account to be approved by you or your designee. Monitoring of progress allows the account to be closed as soon as the work is completed. This is important to prevent extraneous charges to be applied to the account to use up any remaining budget.

Activity Duration

In Chapter XIII we saw that as time varies from some theoretical optimum for each activity, the cost increases. Thus, if there is pressure to complete the project by a specific date, earlier than is indicated by the critical path, the cost will go up. Thus, to control costs we must control the duration of the activities. There was a day when this was accomplished by the "Bull of the Woods" through threats and intimidations. These may work in isolated instances today but not for long. People have too many options today to endure such treatment. Project managers today must be far more adroit in persuasion and guidance to achieve good results in the long run.

The most common method of measuring progress on activities is to ask the responsible person to report the percent completion. It is the OC's firm opinion that this measure is about as close as you can get to useless. We even joke about it via the proposition that, "It takes 90 percent of the duration to complete the first 90 percent of the work; it takes another 90 percent of the duration to complete the last 10 percent of the work." Is this a fact or fancy?

Some project managers have overcome this by dictating that no progress can be reported on an activity until it is completed. This may lead to subdividing activities to the point of identifying too many activities. Other project managers behave as though the duration of an activity is a known quantity. This leads to two problems. There may be a tendency to report activities completed only after the estimated duration has been expended and the time used on other activities that are causing difficulties. This will negate any opportunities to gain time on the project as a whole. There will also be a tendency to pad estimates of the activity duration to provide a cushion. In the long run, it is advantageous to accept that some activities will require longer than the estimated duration. This will enhance the probability that activities that are completed early will be reported as such. This probability can be further enhanced by specifically recognizing those who report their activity completed early.

Critical chain advocates recommend not displaying the estimated project duration on reports to the person responsible for performing the activity. Rather, they recommend creating a practice of reporting an activity completed as soon as the work is finished. Activity progress is monitored based on changes to the buffer at the end of a critical chain. This approach requires the existence of trust in two respects. First, the performer must trust management to accept variability of durations as they manage the project and behave accordingly. This is necessary for the performer to provide an unpadded estimate. Second, management must trust the performer to report the activity completed as soon as the work is finished. If such trust does not already exist, it may be difficult to develop. The adequacy of this approach depends on the degree to which the attitudes in the organization conform to those specified by critical chain proponents. An intermediate step might be to monitor activity completion against the "expected" time required. Alternatively, it seems that it would be just as acceptable, and more logical, to use the most likely duration as provided by the three time estimates of the program evaluation and review technique (PERT). The implication of this is that the duration of an activity, as represented by three time estimates, is skewed to the right. Thus, the expected time is greater than the most likely time. If the most likely time is what the name implies, it seems reasonable that most of the time the activity should be completed in that time. Buffers should still be based on the expected values.

An approach to managing activity durations and schedule that worked exceedingly well on a major construction project will be described later under the heading System Design.

Schedule

Managing schedule requires that people behave in a constructive manner and provide you with the information on which you might be able to take action. Members of the project team make commitments to complete specific activities by a certain date. Others depend on receiving the results of these activities to start their activities. If the predecessor activity is late, it may delay the successor activity, and on, and on. You must ensure that all participants understand the importance of performing to, or ahead of, schedule and that they behave consistent with that.

Activity Start and Completion

It is tempting to focus our interest on when an activity is completed. That is too late to take corrective action without incurring delays in the project. Ideally, you want to be informed of potential delays while you still have an opportunity to modify the outcome. This seems to be counter to human nature. Most people are reluctant to suggest that they need help until they can no longer deny the facts. Thus, it is important to design the forms for reporting progress, and for you to behave in such a way as, to encourage honest reporting.

Project team members must understand that the first step in completing an activity on or before schedule is starting it on schedule. They must also accept responsibility for solving problems that might prevent them from starting on time. If they cannot find a solution they must be willing to seek your assistance early enough that you can get involved.

The best way to encourage a person to plan ahead is to provide information on all predecessors to their activity. This information should include whether the predecessor will be finished on schedule, the name of the responsible person, and their phone number/email address. Direct contact should be encouraged, preferably face-to-face. If a predecessor is going to be late, the two persons should be encouraged to seek a solution that would permit the activity to be started, perhaps with partial information, or at least with knowledge of what is open to change. If the predecessors will be finished early, plans can be made to start the next activity earlier than planned.

Details on how this can be done are discussed later under the heading System Design.

Slack

Slack should always be considered a valuable resource. The most valuable use of slack is in absorbing perturbations to the schedule due to uncontrollable delays on activities. Slack is to project schedule what a contingency fund is to budget. You need to clearly establish the notion that you are the only one with authority to allocate slack. This requires that you have a feasible project schedule and that you monitor activity starts as well as finishes.

Slack provides a flexibility that you need in scheduling. It allows you to solve scheduling conflicts at essentially no cost. Once the slack on a path is used up however, it is no longer available to solve other scheduling conflicts.

Maintaining a Sense of Urgency

The longer the duration of a project is, the more likely it is that the sense of urgency will wane. A project that will not be completed for three years often leads people to feel that they have plenty of time to perform their activity. Using Critical Path Techniques helps to overcome that on activities that are on the critical path. Others wax and wane as the person responsible is faced with other requests, both on the job and at home. You must design things into your project plan that will aid in retaining that sense of urgency over all activities. Scheduled progress reports, technical reviews, project plan reviews, and such, can accomplish this. Another approach is to set intermediate objectives and target dates and celebrate the success of achieving them. One project manager swam across a pond in January because certain objectives were met.

It is this sense of urgency that will help team members to decide that working on your project is more important than a myriad of other uses of their time.

Relay-Race Mentality

The "relay-race" mentality is a relevant concept. In many organizations the typical mentality is to report activities completed only after their scheduled completion date. It is justified by:

❑ "I can make it better with a little more time."
❑ "I can use the extra time to make up for problems on other activities."
❑ "If I report it completed in less than the estimated duration, I'll be expected to do it in the shorter time in the future."
❑ "I can start another activity and avoid being late on it. This is important because if I am late on an activity, I get 'chewed out'."

The typical organizational climate makes these behaviors perfectly logical. The proponents of Critical Chain Project Management (CCPM) argue for a more enlightened management that supports the relay-race mentality. That seems like a worthwhile objective for every project manager. It is not an easy transition but it appears to be worth the effort in order to capitalize on those instances in which the activity is completed in less than the estimated duration. Without this mentality, or very close monitoring of progress on individual activities, the following activity will not be started until the date shown in the Critical Path Method (CPM) schedule. To overcome this, CCPM proposes not publishing schedule dates on critical chain activities. Instead, it requires the person responsible for an activity to be aware of progress on the preceding activity(s) and be prepared to start their activity as soon as all preceding work is accomplished. This permits preserving the time saved on one activity by starting the following activities in the chain earlier. It also encourages the performance of all activities in less time than is typical with conventional CPM schedule reports.

Technical Objective Achievement

Probably the best way to monitor technical objective achievement is to "manage by walking around." When supported by reports that identify these objectives and the results of tests for these objectives, talking to people who conducted the tests can reveal information that never gets in the reports. Care must be exercised to use such information as the basis for hypotheses to be verified, rather than the basis for immediate action. It is interesting to observe the differences in behavior in an organization as people recognize that you will be asking questions based on direct observation rather than just the written reports.

Where there is a deliverable that is a system composed of several individual components, it is probably useful to design a report that shows the current degree of objective attainment for the system based on related measures of component performance. Such a capability was reported in the early 1960s under the title of *Reliability Maturity Index* (Malcolm 1963). It was based on information derived from component tests to date and tracked progress toward system objectives over time.

It provided an early warning if the index was lagging expectations. The OC is aware of nothing of a similar nature having been reported on in project management literature since.

Cost Control

Managing cost requires managing the decisions that will eventually affect costs while they are still manageable. This was discussed in part in Chapter XIV under the heading Commitment Cost Control. Many organizations have their own in-house systems for commitment cost control but it is noticeably absent in project management software with which the OC is familiar. If your organization has such a system, use it. If not, be sure you set up your own system and require members of your core project team do likewise within their realm of responsibility.

The essential notion is that costs are generated one day at a time. If cost performance is adverse today, it will likely continue to be adverse tomorrow, unless some action is taken to change it. This requires that knowledge of daily productivity and costs be available before the next day starts if any change is to be made. Care must be exercised in using such data because performance cannot be expected to be constant day after day. There are good days and bad days. If you react to every adverse perturbation to performance, expect to receive reports that show no variation, regardless of the facts.

This may seem hypercritical of your associates but you must review every charge to your budget accounts. If it appears easy to do so, some people will charge things to any open account if it makes their performance appear better. This is especially true if their account is in trouble. Of course, neither you nor I would ever engage in such practices, at least intentionally.

Less cynically, accounting has to make assumptions about certain indirect costs, or even direct costs where there is some ambiguity. These assumptions may be inconsistent with your perceptions of how they ought to be treated. These need to be caught as early as possible to be corrected and, even more importantly, to prevent such charges in the future.

Carpe Diem

Finally, you must be prepared to seize the opportunity of the moment. While we often do this in our personal lives, it is seldom that a project management system provides information specifically to facilitate this. For example, on a construction project the schedule may call for pouring concrete on Friday. Weather reports suggest that it is likely to rain Friday. This could lead to postponing the pour to Monday, not only resulting in delays to other activities but also in idle time for many of those persons scheduled to help on the pour. It should be feasible to quickly analyze the possibilities of pouring early, on Wednesday or Thursday, and mustering the resources necessary to do so if warranted. Do not assume that delaying the activity is the only option!

Similarly, on most any type of project a critical resource may be available earlier than expected, and not when scheduled. Your system should facilitate revision of schedules to seize this opportunity. Such opportunities permit accelerating the project rather than accepting delays as inevitable.

Managing Resource Application

In Chapter XII we discussed the management of the range of resources available to you as project manager. In Chapter XIII we discussed the scheduling of resources. Here we want to focus on the role of resource application on the duration and cost of an activity and, therefore, on the project.

If resources have been scheduled properly and they are assigned to the activity as planned, presumably their application to the activity should generate the least cost necessary to complete the work. Clearly, this is an assumption that should be challenged whenever there is a doubt.

Given the scheduled application of resources, you must be aware of the actual application and ensure that it is consistent with the schedule. Timely arrival of physical resources is the first requisite. Late arrivals will surely result in late start and, almost as assuredly, in late finish of the activity. If the project is being run in just-in-time mode, you need to provide for expediting to ensure that the scheduled items are going to be shipped on schedule and arrive on schedule. Information must be sought that cannot be faked. "The check is in the mail" is not an adequate response!

Unless there is a convincing explanation, inadequate human resources applied to an activity will likely result in a longer duration and often increased costs. Using the wrong resources may also increase costs. For example, using a skilled tradesperson to perform work that can be done adequately by unskilled labor causes that task to cost more. Having a professional person perform an unfamiliar task will probably take longer and may result in less than best performance of the task.

These are a few of the things of which you must be aware about resource application. It provides a framework for preparing to manage by walking around. You should always be aware of critical events and be present if at all possible. Often you will host key stakeholders at such events. Examples of these critical events include installation of a major component in a structure, test of a prototype, and start up of a system or facility.

On a regular basis, you need to review what should be happening today. Ideally, a report should be generated that lists those things. It may be organized by relative importance of the item to the project, by a measure of its urgency, or by area to be visited. It should provide the name of the responsible person, names of key performers if applicable, the number of individuals scheduled to be working, and the critical physical resources due to be available.

These should never be used to micromanage the activities. Rather, they should be used to reinforce the perception that you know what should be happening, who is doing it, and what conditions are necessary for success. You should always check in with the responsible person wherever you go. It is a courtesy that will be appreciated. That person may wish to escort you in their area. Sometimes that may be appropriate, but, at least some of the time, you may want to discourage it, both to avoid taking them away from more urgent tasks and to permit you more freedom in wandering around. Knowing the names of key performers permits you to greet them on a personal basis. Knowing how many people are scheduled to be working permits counting of noses and asking questions if relevant. Knowing the critical physical resources that are due to arrive can also lead to relevant questions. This display of knowledge about the day-to-day work on the project will make clear that you are aware of what has to be accomplished, that you comprehend the issues and want to learn more, and that you care about the people and their inputs. At first it may seem that this requires a lot of your time. After only a few such walks around the project, it will be well known that you may be back at any time, asking pertinent questions. After that they can be less frequent and require less time. We will return to this later in the discussion of management style.

There are different things you need to be concerned about depending upon the type of resource. For human resources you need to ensure that:

❑ They are available, in the market or within the organization.
❑ They are capable of performing the required tasks. If not, what training do they require?
❑ Will they be assigned full time to your activity until it is completed? Remember that if they are multitasked, not only will the duration of the activity be longer but the productivity will also be less and the work product may be less than desired.
❑ Will they be utilized productively? Will all the materials, equipment, and information be available when required?
❑ Will they be motivated to do their best on your project? This will be affected by the organization climate you create and the rewards you use to recognize achievement.

For equipment you need to ensure that:

❑ It is capable of performing as required.
❑ It will be available when needed.
❑ It is scheduled in a manner that will not cause unnecessary delays.
❑ It will be utilized to the fullest extent possible while available and then released from the project.

For materials and supplies you need to ensure that:

❑ They will be available when required. This requires an appropriate logistic system to order, receive, and process them so they will be ready to use.

❑ They conform to specifications.
❑ They are placed where they will require minimal handling and minimal effort by the skilled people who use them. This may mean that the logistics system repackage and deliver them to the place of usage consistent with actual usage plans. Construction projects often have marshaling yards to accomplish this.
❑ They are in a secure environment where waste, scrap, and pilferage are managed. This will promote the objectives of cost control. You also need to create an attitude of not being wasteful with materials and supplies. Your behavior when walking around will enhance cost consciousness in this regard.

Managing the Project Itself

There are some other aspects of managing the project that will enhance your ability to bring it in on time, within budget, and satisfy your client. These include providing visibility, maintaining a sense of urgency, managing interfaces, reviewing overall cost performance, ensuring that your management systems are working properly, and directing replanning when appropriate.

Visibility

You need visibility for your project. Sometimes you may wish for less visibility. In general you need to seek it. This is important to ensure that your project team is fully aware of project status and outlook and to maintain a sense of urgency for your project. It is also necessary to keep your management informed of and supporting the project.

Before resource leveling was really useful, the OC was known to display a time-phased PND showing all activities at their earliest start and finish dates. This was to avoid having any team member look at their activity (that had positive slack) and believe that it should be performed later. That was for team members' use. If an executive or client were visiting the chart room the early plot would be replaced with one that showed only the latest start and finish dates. This was to avoid questions as to why an activity was not finished yet even though it had considerable slack. (Executives have a tendency to want to "help" in such situations.) This approach is really not recommended.

Visibility is important to maintain support of your client and other stakeholders in your project. It should stress the benefits that will be derived from completing the project as well as its status and outlook. A time-phased connected, summary Gantt chart will show progress and what will be happening in the near future. Consider constructing it with the starting activities at the bottom and the finishing activities at the top. Then add planned and actual "S" cost curves. Show pictures or work product of recent progress and similar displays of immediate future activities and of the final product of the project.

Visibility is also relevant to maintaining the cooperation of functional managers who generally control the human resources you require on your project. When it becomes apparent that the activities of a certain functional manager are lagging behind schedule, their cooperation tends to increase. It is generally enough to show them as late in red. It may be desirable to "train" your sponsor to ask questions about such activities and raise appropriate questions in executive meetings.

Maintaining a Sense of Urgency

Earlier we discussed urgency as it affects the members of the project team in performing the activities. Here we discuss the sense of urgency that is perceived for the project as a whole and the priorities that are given to the project within different functional areas.

Unless a functional manager perceives the project as being significant to the organization and to the function, it is likely to get low priorities. You must do things that will reinforce this importance to get the priorities you want for your project. This is also true for the very existence of your project. Provide reminders of what the project will do for the organization and especially for the support function.

Given that this is accomplished, then a report that clearly shows what activities are the responsibility of that function—showing the functional head as the responsible person—can enhance performance on the activities of your project. For example, in building a new casting plant, there were many activities that were the responsibility of the corporate purchasing function. All of these activities were included on an

Activity Status Report (which will be described later). The Director of Purchasing was very anxious to avoid having any activities show up on his report indicating that they were late in starting, and especially in finishing. That simple system resulted in the best performance of purchasing on a project that the OC has ever witnessed.

Thus, how you design your status reporting system can aid greatly in maintaining a sense of urgency on your project.

Interfaces

One of the most likely sources of conflict is at the interfaces in the project. There are several types of interfaces. One is where two elements in the WBS merge into a higher-level element. Misunderstandings are most likely here. At the minimum these are places for interpersonal conflicts.

Another type is organization interfaces. The higher in the organization these interfaces are, the more likely the misunderstandings. These involve the merging of two or more WBS elements or simply the completion of one organization's efforts and the beginning of another's.

Another is where the use of space is concerned such as the plumbers, electricians, and HVAC trades on a building. If they all plan to use the same space for routing their lines, there will be problems.

Another interface might be termed technical. They occur when two or more components of a system are merged. Any misunderstandings of specifications criteria can result in a failure in the merging. Inevitably, it is the other guy's fault.

All of these can be managed before they become serious if they are anticipated and reviewed before hand. The criteria for a technical interface should be reviewed. The planned and scheduled use of space should be coordinated. Most people are very cooperative if problems and solutions are identified before the fact and there are no significant time or cost implications to them.

Overall Cost Performance

You will be expected to be knowledgeable and answer questions at this level. Therefore, it is wise to use and thoroughly understand the earned value reports. While cost control is really achieved day by day, it is easy to become mesmerized by the details and not see the big picture. Furthermore, despite its deficiencies in terms of timeliness in many organizations, it is still one of the most useful tools for subcontract management. If the necessary provisions are included in the subcontract, you will be better prepared to verify the progress reported and the justification for progress payments. The earned value reports also give an excellent basis for selecting areas for project review and deciding when it may be appropriate to replan the remainder of the project.

Systems Performance

We have discussed many responsibilities you have as project manager. Many of these can be delegated and/or imbedded in the systems by which you will manage the project. Each of these is subject to slippage, i.e., variation from the performance you intended and expect from them. You must ensure that they are working as planned. Test them occasionally by selecting an aspect of a report to look at in depth. Use the Reagan principle, "Trust, but verify." This is your quality control action to ensure that the systems and delegations are performing as intended. It also aids you in ferreting out possible errors and unintended consequences in design of the systems.

Replanning

There will be times when schedule performance deviates from plan, scope changes accumulate, opportunities are recognized, or other factors will make it desirable to replan the project. You must be aware of such needs, make the decision, and participate in the replanning effort. Sometimes this will affect the entire project, other times it will affect only a portion of the plan. Do not let an outmoded plan be used too long, but do not keep changing the music and priorities too often.

Some Other Issues

Managing Risk

Risks are inherent in projects. Your active management of risk should focus on identification of potential risks, deciding whether any action should be taken, ensuring that plans exist to deal with all pertinent risks, and coordinating the decision criteria where they are related across risks. Software now exists to aid in these tasks.

Contract Terms

Many of the management tasks mentioned above will require the cooperation of subcontractors and suppliers. To ensure this cooperation, you must exert some control of the contract terms. In exercising some of your responsibilities, you will be perceived as butting into their prerogatives. If you have a proven partnering relationship with a given subcontractor or supplier, you may be able to work under a general agreement on these issues. Without such experience, you may need specific contract language to ensure compliance. Note that the precise nature of this language varies with the type of contract. For example, do not expect to have the same degree of cooperation on a fixed-price contract as you may receive on a cost-plus contract. The contract terms provide you with the leverage that may be necessary if you begin to question whether the contract is being performed as intended.

Managing Configuration

On many projects it is desirable, if not necessary, to maintain accurate and detailed records of the specific components installed in the product of the project. This is especially relevant for space and software systems projects. It is very evident when we consider what is involved in making in-flight corrections to computer programs on a space mission. Such efforts are preceded by extensive testing of the "fix" on identical hardware and software on the ground and then, when proven to work, sent to the errant vehicle. In more mundane projects it is also worth knowing the precise nature of a piece of equipment operating in a remote location so the correct replacement part can be dispatched when necessary.

Managing Records

Ideally, the project will go from start to finish without a hitch. Practically, there is always a probability that there will be conflict that will end up headed for court. When such conflicts arise, it will be necessary for you to defend your actions and decisions. The relevant criteria will be "prudence given the information available at the time." This will be judged based on contemporaneous records, i.e., records produced at the time, not based on recall from memory after the fact. It is necessary to ensure that all actions and decisions be documented, collected, and filed to ensure their availability if and when needed.

In addition, it is important to maintain records associated with the work product of the project. For construction projects this includes all technical and user's manuals and as built drawings. For software projects, every module must be carefully documented so they can be modified later, whether to correct an error or to add a new feature.

Both creating such records and collecting and filing *all* of them are chores that are considered onerous and not directly related to delivering the product of the project. You will have to be diligent, and sometimes stern, in requiring all team members to complete these tasks in a timely manner.

SYSTEM DESIGN

There are so many details to deal with in the typical project that systems are required to capture, process, and make them available. How the system is designed can affect the accuracy of information contained in it, how it is used, and how people behave relative to it. In the following we discuss some system design criteria and give some examples of approaches that have worked well.

Criteria

It seems to be the objective of many systems designers to design a system that will provide the top executive of the organization with whatever information may be required to exercise control and make decisions. This often results in information overload and a decision bottleneck. Another objective seems more desirable. If the system is designed to *elicit the desired behavior* at each level of the organization, the executive requires much less information. Second to that should be to promote *honest reporting of plans, progress, and problems*. One way to do this is to limit the response alternatives, for example to yes and no. Another is to enter key elements of responses into the system so they can be compared over time. The reports should be designed in a *hierarchical* manner so that each member of the project team can take corrective action at their level without broadcasting through the system every little variation from schedule, especially if it is something that can be handled "locally." Similarly, there should be *firewalls* that prevent unnecessary perturbations to the schedule downstream and across organizational interfaces. Buffers can be very effective in this regard.

Schedule Performance

It is to your advantage as project manager to minimize the amount of control that you need to exercise personally. This is best accomplished by designing your management system to ensure that people are doing the right things, at the right times, and providing reliable information on plans and progress. For schedule control this can be achieved by two simple report formats. These reports are provided to each person responsible for one or more activities in the near future.

Activity Status Report

The OC has used this approach with even greater success than was anticipated. It requires a minimum amount of time to provide feedback on activities and, best of all, it encourages each responsible person to behave in the desired manner. Each reporting cycle a report is provided to each responsible person showing only those activities for which progress is expected before the end of the reporting cycle. There are only two permissible responses—Y or N—for "Yes" or "No." There is no room for "weasel words" in the reporting space and none are accepted. The question is one of the following three depending on the state of progress on the activity:

❑ For activities not under way, "Will this activity start on schedule?"
❑ For those activities in process, "Will this activity be completed on schedule?"
❑ For activities due to be completed, "Was this activity completed on schedule?"

It only requires the briefest instruction to understand these questions.

It may take a little longer for responsible persons to learn the significance of reporting honestly. On the one hand, it should become quite clear as soon as the first person reports Y for several cycles and then reports N when the activity is scheduled to be completed. The appropriate question for you at this point is, "What did you discover today that you did not anticipate before?" Then, it should be carefully explained that you are paying them to anticipate problems and solve them before they delay their activity. The other side of the coin is that anyone who reports an N will be offered "assistance" if necessary, but it will not likely be additional resources or extra time.

If the answer to the question is N, then further elaboration is required. You want to know if anything can be done about the situation. Therefore, the report format provides space for an explanation.

Often not starting or completing an activity on time is beyond the control of the responsible person. It may be helpful to have a general indication of the nature of the problem. Thus, it might be useful to provide space in which to check whether it was due to problems with:
❑ Staffing
❑ Materials and Supplies
❑ Equipment
❑ Technology
❑ Decision.

Beware, though, sometimes there may really be a problem for which you have some responsibility. But that is really to the good, because some people may be reluctant to provide you with that information unless you really ask for it. Also, there may be additional, or other, categories that are relevant on your project.

In addition, the activities were coded as to their degree of urgency. (At the time this was done manually, but can be easily incorporated into a computer system today.) The most urgent was an activity that should be completed but has not been reported as started. It was given a code of "1." People abhorred having any code 1s on their reports. The next most urgent was an activity that should have been completed but is not. It was given a code of "2." An activity that had been started but is expected to be completed late was given a "3." An activity that was not started and was expected to be started late was given a "4."

The reports used in the project team meetings to review progress were sorted by degree of urgency, i.e., 1–4. The 1s were discussed first. If a satisfactory solution to the problem was reported, we moved on to the next activity. If it was not satisfactory, the responsible person and relevant others were tasked to find a solution and report back at the next meeting. After only a couple of reporting cycles, the project team's progress meetings were reduced from about four hours every Thursday to about two hours every other Thursday.

This reduction in meeting time is significant for at least three reasons. The most obvious is the cost of the meetings. They involved some fifteen key people. Thus, each four-hour meeting required sixty person hours per week. Reducing the time to two hours every other week required only thirty person hours every other week, a four fold reduction in time and cost. Second, progress on the project improved due to the people in the meeting having more time to provide guidance and direction back at their workplaces. Third, and more subtly but perhaps more important, was the motivation provided to all participants on the project to avoid having one of their activities on the coded list. Indeed, the OC became concerned that the project team was driving themselves too hard to the detriment of their health and personal lives.

Activity Planning Report

This report was designed to encourage persons responsible for activities scheduled to start in the next reporting cycle to plan ahead. It was specifically for use in new model development at Chrysler but was never implemented. At the time there was a unionization movement afoot and perturbations to the status quo were not welcome. Real-time, networked computer capabilities were still rather limited compared to current capabilities. Also, it was before the "quality movement" that introduced a new concept into organizational behavior, i.e., "the customer is the next person in the process." With that concept in place now, this report is quite feasible.

The objective was to encourage every person responsible for an activity that was due to start in the near future to check on the status of that activity's predecessors. If all the predecessors were indicated to be on schedule, then that activity could be started on time. If any predecessor was indicated to be late in finishing, then the activity might not be able to start on time. This checking was made easy because the initials and phone number of the person responsible for that predecessor were also provided. Today, their email address is relevant but direct communication should be encouraged, preferably face-to-face. These two people were encouraged to discuss the situation to determine if there was anything that could be done to enable the activity to start on schedule. If they could, there was the opportunity to make up some of the time lost or at least to reschedule other work that could be interrupted when the activity could proceed. Thus, both people were encouraged to think in terms of completing the project on schedule and within budget as opposed to focusing only on their activity. Furthermore, the information available made it easy to consider rescheduling follower activities to take advantage of earlier than expected completion of predecessors.

These two reports are examples of designing reports to encourage the types of behaviors we would like on our projects. They take away excuses for not knowing and they make providing feedback simple and easy. They also provide you with the information you need to determine where your help is most needed to enable your project to keep moving ahead. To get the most from them, you need a management style that is consistent with them and reinforces the desired behaviors.

With the advent of CCPM, these reports could be modified slightly to identify activities on a critical chain and encourage the responsible people to give those activities priority in rescheduling.

Associated with these two reports was a concomitant definition of responsibility. It became clear that on a very large project it is time consuming and difficult to define all of the logic of the PND. To overcome this we determined that we could not expect the person responsible for performing an activity to know what activities required this activity's work product. This person could be held responsible for knowing what work products were required to perform the activity. Thus, this person was responsible for ensuring that all predecessor activities of the activity were identified in the PND.

This fit well with Modern Quality Management concepts that the customer is the next person/operation in the process. Thus it was relevant for that person to "accept" or "reject" the work product coming in. To respond accurately to the question, "Will this activity start on time?" required some knowledge of the status of the preceding work product.

The concepts suggested previously should be used in designing other systems. By so doing, you will be able to keep your workload down to a manageable level.

MANAGEMENT STYLE

Management style is often a pattern of behavior we adopt without conscious consideration of its consequences. Two incidents have impressed the OC as being a management style to emulate.

The first involved a new plant manager of a volume job shop. When he arrived he noticed two things quickly. Morale was low and the shop was messy, with standard containers sitting most anywhere they could be set down quickly. Perhaps these problems were related. He scheduled an overtime day to clean up the plant. Among other things, containers were rearranged in an orderly manner and lines were painted on the floor to identify aisles. He thought he had made it clear that no containers were to be placed in the aisles. The next week he took a walk through the plant. In one department, he found a container astraddle the aisle line. His comment to the foreman of that department was simply, "Did we get that line in the wrong place? If we did we can move it!" The container was moved forthwith, the story spread around the plant, and there were no further problems with containers, or anything else that did not belong in the aisles.

The other instance occurred on the project where the Activity Progress Report described previously was first used. It was the first project team meeting at which the report was used. The meeting started and the first item of discussion involved the number two person on the project team. He did not know the answer to a question that it was reasonable to expect him to know. He spent about ten minutes on the phone getting the answer while the rest of the team engaged in idle conversation. When he returned, the project manager stated simply, "Gentlemen, these meetings are a time to report on your homework, not to do it." That was all—short, succinct, and unambiguous. There is no doubt that this brief message was understood and was a major contributor to the reduction in the time required to conduct progress meetings.

It should be noted that in both cases the individuals were plant managers, positions of considerable authority. They enjoyed both conferred and earned respect. Thus, such forthright statements were fully accepted. On your first project, you may not have either the authority or earned respect for these statements to work as well. Carefully consider your status and choose your message accordingly. Regardless, as project manager, neither a tyrant nor a Milquetoast be.

There are some guidelines of behavior that have been proven in practice. Perhaps more important, their converse behaviors have been observed in practice and proven inappropriate in the long run. Consider the following in developing your management style.

What is Your Plan?

Except in extremely urgent situations, do not tell people what to do; tell them what the problem is, what results are desired, and what the essential criteria for success are. Then ask them to tell you what they intend to do. If I tell you what to do, I have no idea what you heard. If you tell me what you are going to do, I have a good idea what you have in mind. If what I hear does not sound satisfactory, I can ask questions, suggest alternatives, discuss pros and cons, and negotiate with you for a better plan of action. In the process, I will strive to gain your commitment to whatever we agree on. I will have shared with you some of my experience and thus modified your behavior in the future. In the process I will have more faith in your capabilities to perform well in the future. Take note of two key words in this discussion—commitment and faith—two of the most important words in management.

Never Kill the Messenger!

Your most valuable resource in managing a project is factual, honest information. People dislike delivering bad news. Even more, they dislike admitting to anyone that they cannot do those things expected of them. You can raise that from "dislike" to "abhorring" by how you receive the information. If you make it more painful, they will go to great lengths to avoid the pain. Thus, if you want open sharing of both bad, as well as good, news, accept the news and move on to correcting the situation if possible. If they do not share the news with you in a timely manner, chastise them for telling you late and severely for not telling you at all. Expect mistakes; don't accept excuses. Make them learning situations.

Practice the "Art of the Gentle Nudge"

People resent being told. They like to believe they have something to contribute to solutions of problems and plans for the future, and that they are valuable to the team. Use the famous friends of journalists: who, what, when, where, why, and how? The OC favors an analogy to illustrate this "art." The question is, "How do you change the direction of travel of an elephant in a slippery mire?" The answer is, "You watch for them to pick up a foot and then you push hard on that foot in the direction you want it to go." This admonition is at least as applicable to groups as to individuals.

You may not be sure you can prevail on a crucial issue in a meeting. If it is that important, take the time to discuss the issue individually with appropriate attendees before the meeting, or preferably before you put it on the agenda. In this way you are moving the elephant one foot at a time.

Be Compassionate About Individual Needs but Expect Performance to Plan

Your team is made up of individuals. Each one has problems, needs, and hopes. You have the opportunity to ease their problems, help them achieve their needs, and keep their hopes alive. Never get directly involved in solving their personal problems. Avoid showing favoritism in trying to solve their on-the-job problems. Rather, guide them into solving their problems themselves. Use caution in making promises and ensure that any action you take on their behalf is, if possible, consistent with their needs and hopes. Do not become a nursemaid or confidant, but be willing to listen to concerns if they are relevant to the project or the person's career.

Be the Project Manager!

That is what you were chosen to be. Take the initiative to give direction to the project and do not hesitate to make tough decisions when necessary. Be sure you know what the deadline is for making a decision. When it is really important to do so, violate the rules so long as it is not illegal, immoral, or unethical. Just ask yourself, "If I were a team member, is that what I would want of my project manager?"

There are many other good admonitions. These are the ones deemed most relevant to the OC. You must make your own decisions on your management style. Just be sure to consider the consequences of your decisions carefully.

MANAGING YOUR MANAGEMENT

As discussed in Chapter XII, you should consider the executives of your organization as resources available to you if appropriate. They must be used sparingly, only on things where they can make a unique contribution. There are three aspects of this. First, they can be excellent public relations representatives if they are adequately informed. Second, they can give support to your project, internal to your parent organization in executive meetings and even on the golf course. In addition, they can affect the priorities assigned to your project by their subordinates. For each of these, they need briefing. The significance of your project to the organization will dictate the level in the organization at which such briefings should be coordinated. Certainly your project sponsor should be involved in such decisions. Regardless of the level, the principles are the same; only the titles of those involved will be different. The following assumes a project that is vital to the organization. Scale it down to meet the needs of your project.

Keeping Them Informed

The first step in keeping them informed is to brief them on the nature of the project, the benefits to the organization as a whole, and the benefits to the client. This should be in the form of an oral presentation accompanied by a portfolio of relevant information organized in a manner that permits easy access. A form of loose-leaf binder might be very appropriate. Ideally, it is a portfolio that could be carried to a public meeting. This immediately puts a limit on its contents and therefore a confidential supplement might be provided. The portfolio itself should contain the answers to anticipated Frequently Asked Questions and the like, in addition to all the appropriate background information.

The supplement should contain information that would be inappropriate to fall into public hands and should be clearly identified as such. For example, on a highly visible project, there may be aspects of the project that should be handled by only one assigned executive. For example, where there are, or may be, negotiations involved, it is important that the negotiating position be maintained. Such areas should be clearly identified. There may be sensitive areas for which it is important that all executives hew to a "company line." These should be discussed in this supplement. There may be other areas in which it is relevant to forewarn the executives of the tender spots. There have been instances in which, either lacking or ignoring such warnings, executives have inadvertently said things that later caused problems for the project.

The contents of the portfolio should be clearly identified as to date of publication or version to permit quick and easy updating. Updates should be transmitted in a manner that enables the recipient to quickly review the new or revised information and so a secretary can ensure that the latest versions are included and old versions are removed.

In addition to background information, it may be relevant to keep top-level management informed of progress on the project. On some projects, your management starts with the Board of Directors. Determine what your CEO wants in the way of reports to the board. Then provide the CEO with that information, backed up with the next level of detail necessary to answer questions that may come up at that level.

Members of the Project Executive Committee, probably a subset of the organization's executive committee, should be provided with reports a level below the CEO's, plus a summary of the operating level detail of those activities for which their area is responsible. Thus, we now have need for three levels of detail, the board, the CEO, and the Project Executive Committee members. Provisions for these reports should be built into the project WBS and network from the beginning. On most projects, it should be possible to report against these events for the entirety of the project. It is below this level that most changes will occur. Similarly, reports should be provided at intermediate levels in the organization to minimize the chances of misinformation.

At all levels, the invitation should be extended to ask for a personal briefing if desired. By providing information in this manner, you can build and maintain favorable attitudes toward your project throughout its life. Then, if and when it becomes appropriate to ask for help, you should have a receptive audience.

A final caveat in this area: Never expect that all executives will be in favor of your project. Determine who the naysayers might be, with the help of your sponsor, and develop specific plans for at least neutralizing their negative opinions and ensure that all reports on the project avoid exacerbating the issue with such executives.

SUMMARY

In summary, being a project manager is not a job for the faint hearted or someone looking for an easy life. Giving appropriate consideration to the previous information can lead to a very successful project and a very rewarding experience. Just be sure to tailor your systems and expectations to the size, complexity, and importance of your project to you and your organization.

> To keep current on progress on each of these, Sam decided to manage by walking around. While the three work packages involving gathering material would take place out in the fields, it would be easy for Sam, an avid jogger, to get to any one of them and back in a day. In addition to keeping current on progress, Sam could spend some time boosting morale where necessary and review their plans in the process.
>
> Between trips to the field, a runner could be sent out to check on progress. The runner should get reasonably accurate reports, as the teams would be conscious that Sam would be coming soon.

APPENDIX XVIII.A
MARS PATHFINDER PROJECT

REPORTING AND CONTROL

During the Mars Pathfinder project, status information was maintained via a report called the Mars Pathfinder Procurement Planning Summary. This report was issued by the Hardware Acquisition Team Manager on a weekly basis to the project staff and all participants. In addition, a color coded chart for major acquisitions called "Hardware Acquisition—Major Procurements" was initiated and presented monthly at the project Monthly Management Reviews to show schedule status on major procurements from requisition through delivery. Informally called the "Red, Yellow, Green chart," this report was very helpful to project management, NASA and our industry contractors in flagging which contracts and other procurements were on schedule for delivery (green), starting to slip (yellow), or seriously behind schedule (red). Since all major procurements were summarized on one page, it proved to be a good tool in motivating a contractor to remain on schedule so as not to reflect poorly when compared to the other contractors.

APPENDIX XVIII.B
MARS PATHFINDER PROJECT

PROJECT POLICIES AND REQUIREMENTS

3.1 Project Policies

3.1.1   Capability vs. Requirement Driven Design
The mission, flight and ground system designs shall be strongly driven by existing hardware and system capability in order to achieve cost and schedule constraints. The selection of off-the-shelf capabilities and components and those inherited from other projects should be given high priority in the design process. Cross-system capability conflicts shall be resolved through the Project Engineering Team. Re-negotiation of high level requirements in order to stay within capabilities is allowed.

3.1.2   Mission Success Criteria
Pathfinder mission success shall be evaluated using the following set of weighted criteria:
1. Successful landing and return of entry, descent, and landing engineering telemetry—70%
2. Acquisition and transmission of a single partial panoramic image—10%
3. Successful rover deployment and operation—10%
4. Complete 30 sol (Martian day) primary lander mission; complete all additional engineering, science, and technology objectives—10%

3.1.3   Implementation Strategy

3.1.3.1   Incremental Development
The Pathfinder implementation strategy shall be to develop all project systems incrementally. This strategy involves implementing, integrating, and demonstrating capabilities of each contributing project system using phased deliveries leading up to a final launch delivery. The capabilities demonstrated at

each phase should be additive to the capabilities accumulated and demonstrated in previous phases. The phased deliveries should be scheduled approximately 6 months apart.

3.1.3.2 Demonstrations

The culmination of each development phase shall be an end-to-end demonstration of the integrated Pathfinder system. Specific emphasis shall be placed on the end-to-end operation of those project elements implemented during that phase. Each demonstration shall be in lieu of a delivery review. Limited documentation shall be provided, including a description of the new capabilities (changes from previous phase), operations scenarios, procedure, user guides, and test results.

3.1.4 Operations Philosophy

The guiding operations philosophy for Pathfinder shall be to conduct the mission such that information on the state of the flight system is obtained after all key mission events. In this way, any mission failures can be associated with particular activities, thereby increasing the chances that failure mechanisms can be identified. Key mission events are defined as follows:

1. Launch
2. Initial attitude acquisition
3. Propulsive maneuvers
4. Entry attitude turn
5. Cruise stage separation
6. Parachute deploy
7. Aeroshell separation
8. Backshell/lander release
9. Radar altimeter operation
10. RAD rocket firing
11. Airbag inflation
12. Lander petal deployment
13. Transmission of EDL telemetry
14. HGA Earth acquisition
15. IMP mast deployment
16. Rover deployment
17. Rover traverses

3.1.5   Concurrent Engineering

Pathfinder shall be developed in an integrated, concurrent manner. Concurrent engineering means that the development of flight hardware and software, MOS hardware and software, and test hardware and software will proceed in parallel rather than in the traditional series arrangement. The concurrent engineering approach is facilitated by:

1. Technical team collocation.
2. Early Flight System Testbed availability for flight/ground system integration.
3. Use of modern computer technology, including advanced flight computer architectures, programming languages, and development tools/environments.
4. Focused mission design and science/technology objectives.
5. Early availability of rover component and system test articles, including flight and ground elements.
6. Early operational scenario development and analysis leading to operable spacecraft and rover designs.

Chapter XIX

An Epilogue

Sam completed the project and the entire family was transported across the river before the floods started. The project went well. The hunting team was lucky, finding a herd of elk at the watering hole, and was able to bag five animals in just a few days. Some of the resources were shifted over to other activities to speed them along. The project was completed in 65 days and with only 783 labor days versus 869 planned. Thus, the project was 16 percent ahead of schedule and 10 percent under budget. After the move was completed, the Matriarch ordered a feast to celebrate. Sam was awarded a new elk-skin wrap in honor of the successful effort.

Sam spoke briefly, thanking all who had contributed to its success, and especially the elders who had shared their knowledge with the project team and reduced the errors in executing the project to almost nil.

With that, Sam ran and jumped in the river according to the promise made to the family if the project was a success!

The OC has enjoyed sharing knowledge and experience with you. Sam and I hope you gained form the experience.

If you were a real beginner at what some have called this "unintentioned profession," you have perhaps been exposed to more than you really wanted to know about it. Hopefully, in the process, it has piqued your interest in the field. Project management certainly is not a boring profession.

If you are a seasoned veteran, perhaps this has shaken your roots a little and resurrected ideas and concepts you have used and forgotten.

If you are a senior manager interested in how project management works, perhaps you have gained insights into how you can make it more effective and how the concepts can be extended further into your organization.

The order of presentation of the subject does not imply the sequence in which the ideas and concepts should be used. It was chosen more for pedagogical reasons. In fact, exactly how you proceed to apply the tools and concepts is very much a function of the many characteristics of a project and its objectives. The fact is that every project is a learning experience, largely because your success on a small one leads to assignment on a larger one, often faster than you might desire at times.

Equally important is the adaptation of the concepts to the characteristics of the project at hand.

References

Bildson, R. A., and J. R. Gillespie. 1962. Critical Path Planning—PERT Integration. *The Journal of The Operations Research Society of America*, vol. 10 (November–December): 909–911.

Cooper, Kenneth G. 1980. Naval Ship Production: A Claim Settled and a Framework Built, Interfaces. *The Institute of Management Sciences* (December): 20–36.

———. 1993a. The Rework Cycle: Why Projects are Mismanaged. *PM Network* (February): 5–7.

———. 1993b. The Rework Cycle: How it *Really* Works ... and Reworks .... *PM Network* (February): 25–28.

———. 1993c. The Rework Cycle: Benchmarks for the Project Manager. *Project Management Journal* (March): 17–21.

———. 1993d. The $2000 Hour: How Managers Influence Project Performance through the Rework Cycle. *Project Management Journal* (June): 11–24.

Crosby, Philip B. 1979. *Quality is Free.* New York: Mentor.

Darnall, Russell W. 1996. *The World's Greatest Project*. Upper Darby, PA: Project Management Institute.

Davis, Edward W., and James H. Patterson. 1975. Resource-Based Project Scheduling: Which Rules Perform Best? *Project Management Quarterly* 6 (4) (December): 25–31.

Fleming, Quentin W. 1992. *Cost Schedule Control Systems Criteria: The Management Guide to C/SCS.* Revised Ed. Chicago, IL: Probus Publishing Company.

———. 1996. *Earned Value Project Management*. Upper Darby, PA: Project Management Institute.

Flones, Peter F. 1987. Endicott Oil Field. *Project Management Journal* 18 (5) (December): 42–50.

Hobson, William K., ed. 1992. *Maynard's Industrial Engineering Handbook*. 4th Ed. New York: McGraw-Hill.

Juran, J. M., and Frank M. Gryna. 2000. *Quality Planning and Analysis: From Product Development through Use by Quality Planning and Analysis*. New York: McGraw-Hill.

Kelley, James E., Jr., and Morgan R. Walker. 1959. Critical-Path Planning and Scheduling. *Proceedings of the Eastern Joint Computer Conference*, Boston, Dec. 1–3: 160–173.

———. 1989. The Origins of CPM: A Personal History. *PM Network* 3 (2): 7–22.

Lambert, Lee R., and Erin Lambert. 2000. *Project Management: The Common Sense Approach*. Columbus, OH: LCG Publishing.

Leach, Lawrence P. 2001. *Critical Chain Project Management*. Newtown Square, PA: Project Management Institute.

Malcolm, Donald G. 1963. Reliability Maturity Index—An Extension of PERT into Reliability Management. *The Journal of Industrial Engineering* (January–February): 3–12.

Mask, Karen J., and Judith S. Kilgore. 1990. The Westlake Story: The Need for Coordination, Cooperation and Communication. *PM Network* 4 (5) (July): 13–18.

McMichael, John R. 1994. Boeing Spares Distribution Center: A World-Class Facility Achieved through Partnering. *PM Network* 8 (9) (September): 9–19.

Moder, Edward W. J., C. R. Phillips, and E. W. Davis. 1983. *Project Management with CPM, PERT and Precedence Diagramming*. New York: Van Nostrand Reinhold.

Moshman, Jack, Jacob Johnson, and Madalyn Larsen. 1963. RAMPS—A Technique for Resource Allocation and Multi-Project Scheduling. Proceedings: *Spring Joint Computer Conference*.

Padgham, Henry F. 1991. The Milwaukee Water Pollution Abatement Program: Its Stakeholder Management. *PM Network* 5 (3) (April): 6–18.

Project Management Institute Standards Committee. 1994. *A Guide to the Project Management Body of Knowledge (PMBOK® Guide)*. Upper Darby, PA: Project Management Institute.

Project Management Institute. 2000. *A Guide to the Project Management Body of Knowledge (PMBOK® Guide) – 2000 Edition*. Newtown Square, PA: Project Management Institute.

Schuyler, John R. 1996. *Decision Analysis in Projects*. Upper Darby, PA: Project Management Institute.

Snyder, John, and Bill Caligan. 1990. Bad Creek Pumped-Storage Hydro Station: Success by Any Measure. *PM Network* 4 (6) (August): 11–29.

Webster, Francis M., Jr. 1979. Micro Characteristics of an Activity and Its Performance. *Proceedings of the Project Management Institute*: 359–71.

———. 1981. Ways to Improve Performance on Projects. *Project Management Quarterly* 12 (3) (September): 21–26.

———. 2001. The Pros and Cons of Critical Chain. Unpublished Working Paper. Available on request from fmwebster@aol.com.

Index

A

ABC categories   84

accept/reject   224

account   82, 98–9, 133, 211, 230, 295–96, 301

accountants   17, 204

accounting   20, 77, 100, 202–3, 210–12, 295, 301

accurate and current specifications 217–18

activity
  characteristics of   5, 121
  conceptual model   10–11, 21
  critical   41, 189
  dimensions   121
  duration   See duration, activity
  noncritical   41
  objectives   10, 19
  performance   293, 295
  planning report   313
  progress report   315
  status report   307

activity-on-arrow (AOA)   27, 34

activity-on-node (AON)   27, 34

actual   10, 12, 16–20
  cost of work performed (ACWP)   205
  duration   See duration, actual
  value   See value, actual
  work content   16, 20

ACWP   See actual cost of work performed

adaptive scheduling   See scheduling, adaptive

affordability   222

algorithms   141

allocating   120

alternative resources   See resources, alternative

ambient conditions   51, 58, 94

analogous   3, 115

analytical   141, 145

AOA   See activity-on-arrow

AON   See activity-on-node

appropriate resources   54, 70, 72, 126

as built   221, 310

assessment   84, 155, 240, 253

assign   18, 29–30, 32, 72, 97, 113, 169, 189, 192, 242, 248, 295

assigning appropriate resources   54, 70, 126

assignment   13, 16–17, 99, 128, 183, 189, 326

attitude   61, 63, 65, 74, 89, 172, 188, 190, 223, 235, 280, 305, 323

authority   61, 69, 87, 119, 212, 223, 237, 287, 299, 310

authorization   78, 87

availability   9, 16, 18, 54–55, 70, 78, 80, 92, 103, 107, 121–22, 128, 143–44, 151, 180, 198, 258, 310, 324

available and ready to use   72, 127

B

BCWP   See budgeted cost of work performed (BCWP)

BCWS   See budgeted cost of work scheduled (BCWS)

behavior   14, 61, 75, 119, 131, 154, 173, 232, 249, 273, 286, 300, 305, 310, 313, 315–16
  options   247

bottleneck   118, 190–91, 292, 310

break-even   197

budget   16–17, 20, 53, 96, 98–99, 105, 107, 130, 170, 180, 202, 205, 209–11, 284, 287, 295–96, 298, 301, 305, 314, 325

budgeted cost of work performed (BCWP)
205–07

budgeted cost of work scheduled (BCWS)
205–06

buffer(s)   4, 5, 87, 117–18, 133, 181,
247, 266–67, 297, 311

burst node   121

C

C/SCSC   See Cost Schedule Control
Systems Criteria (C/SCSC)

calculations
tabular   29
on the PND   27, 29

capabilities   3, 13, 15, 43, 47, 53–54, 73,
77, 79, 114, 128, 131, 133, 139,
159–60, 221, 267, 281, 313, 316,
322–23

carpe diem   105, 107, 129, 302

CCPM   See critical chain project
management

CEIR   129

celebrations   15, 60

change control   295

chart of accounts   3, 16–17

client
expectations   289
satisfaction   223, 225–26, 228, 235,
289, 294

climate   14–15, 50, 55, 119, 241, 300,
304

codes   67, 92

commitment   3, 62, 64, 80, 106, 119,
134, 172–73, 212, 237, 283, 294,
316
cost control   210, 301

commodity   56–57, 91

community   59, 75, 219, 255, 259,
260–61

conceptual model   10, 21

configuration   107, 309

conflict   76, 182, 222, 288, 307, 309

constraints   3, 13, 49, 53–54, 66, 75–76,
78, 106, 130–32, 199, 222, 283–84,
322
physical   54, 70, 131
physiological   54, 70, 131

consultants   68, 91

content   8–9, 12–13, 20, 41, 77, 122–23,
135, 185, 194–95, 204, 213, 218,
230, 262, 265, 288, 292–93

contiguous   27, 34, 83, 86

contingency   3, 39, 76, 133, 193–94,
255, 269, 298

contract   21, 43, 53, 68, 75, 79, 101,
132, 155, 174, 183, 186, 212, 226,
230, 250, 253, 265, 290
terms   181–82, 309

contribution margin   161, 163

control   42, 44, 55, 57, 59, 65, 68,
78–79, 82, 181, 194, 199, 221,
233–34, 253, 285–88, 295–96, 306,
308–12
change cost   See change cost control
commitment cost   See commitment
cost control
cost   See cost control
design cost   See design cost control
statistical process   See statistical
process control

corporate staffs   See staff, corporate

cost
performance index (CPI)   207, 209
Cost Schedule Control Systems Criteria
(C/SCSC)   202–03
theoretical minimum   78, 90
total project   16, 20, 151
control   210, 301, 305, 307
volume   196

CPI   See cost performance index

CPM   See critical path method (CPM)

CPPS   See critical path planning and
scheduling (CPPS)

CPT   See critical path technique(s) (CPT)

craftspeople   53, 69, 74, 88, 123

crash(ing)   153, 162–69, 175–76, 249

criteria   10, 22, 76, 122, 202–03, 212,
222, 228, 293, 307, 309–10, 316,
322

critical   52, 62, 68, 80–81, 93, 106–07,
126–27, 132, 136–37, 151, 155, 175,
186, 194, 256–58, 283, 288, 290,
292–93, 303–04
activity   See activity, critical

assumption   117
chain   4–5, 153, 266, 268, 280, 297
  project management (CCPM)
    115–19, 125, 133–34, 300,
    314
  scheduling   108
path   26, 34, 38, 44, 46–47, 108,
  120, 137, 142, 149, 167–69, 200,
  264–65, 267, 271, 276–77, 294,
  296, 299
  method (CPM)   27, 115, 117–19,
    159–61, 174–75, 273–74,
    278, 281, 300
  technique (CPT)   26–27, 39, 41,
    45, 47, 65, 90, 159–60, 286,
    299
  planning and scheduling (CPPS)
    159–62, 174, 267, 281
  resource   72, 118, 142, 153–54,
    266–67, 294, 302
criticality   41, 122, 283
cultural   54, 70, 75, 131, 261
culture(s)   75, 131
customer satisfaction   215–17, 221. See
  also client satisfaction

D

decision theory   239, 252, 268, 281–82
defect   216
definitive   2, 255
Deming   215–16, 233
Department of Defense (DoD)   202–03,
  208
design
  cost control   180
  strategy(ies)   227–29
deviation   29, 60, 87, 226, 237
diagram   29–30. See also project network
  diagram
direct   20, 40, 61, 63, 73, 160–61, 208,
  218, 226, 240, 260, 298, 300–01,
  314
do the right thing right the first time
  (DTRTRTFT)   232
documents   53, 92–93, 212, 229, 251,
  295
DoD   See Department of Defense (DoD)

domino effect   90–91, 181, 193, 200,
  208, 232, 267, 289
DTRTRTFT   See do the right thing right the
  first time (DTRTRTFT)
DuPont   159–61, 170
duration
  activity   2–3, 5, 9, 106, 116, 120,
    133, 137, 296–97
  actual   19–20, 174
  estimated   4, 116–19, 264, 294, 296,
    299–300
  optimum   78, 171–72, 263
  planned   16–17, 19–20
  project   19, 42, 130, 160, 163–64,
    167–69, 175, 199, 227, 232, 280,
    297

E

EAC   See estimated cost at completion
  (EAC)
earned value   77, 178, 202–03, 205,
  208–12, 286, 307–08
envelope   See upper envelope and lower
  envelope
environment   4–5, 84, 86–88, 101, 104,
  115, 172, 180, 184, 186–87, 189,
  194, 218, 255, 263, 280, 282 84,
  305
equipment   14, 18, 42, 50, 52, 55–57,
  80–85, 91, 93, 127, 133, 171,
  184–86, 190–92, 194, 196–99,
  233–34, 255, 257 58, 312
  cost management   196
  safety   253
ergonomics   73
estimate(ing)   1–6, 9–10, 12, 16, 21, 98,
  116–17, 128, 169, 174, 178–79, 200,
  204–05, 242, 247–48, 262, 268,
  274–75, 279, 297
estimated
  cost at completion (EAC)   207, 209
  duration   See duration, estimated
event   29–31, 105, 126, 241, 243–45,
  248, 252–53, 264
executive(s)   50–52, 59, 61–64, 66–67,
  82, 106, 132, 134–35, 209, 211,
  265–66, 268, 305–06, 310, 318–20
expectation   79, 116, 186, 245, 294

expected
> time   *See* time, expected
> value   *See* value, expected

expediting   40, 72, 302
> resource availability   54, 70

F
feasibility   2, 106, 134, 151, 170

feature   50, 65, 180, 221–22, 261, 288, 310

financial   13, 50, 89, 99, 100, 102, 210, 221, 258, 283–84
> resource   *See* resource, financial

flexibility   23, 27, 97, 105–06, 121, 142, 145, 154, 237, 299

Fluor-Daniel   218–19

function   6, 9, 53, 64–65, 105, 162, 174, 176, 184, 225, 277, 287–88, 306, 326

functionality   220–21

G
general considerations   54

gentle nudge   290, 317

gold plating   220

A Guide to the Project Management Body of Knowledge (PMBOK® Guide)   xiv, 2, 105, 250–51, 254–55

H
history   1

holiday   132

human   51, 112, 128, 137, 197, 249, 253, 254, 263, 286, 298
> resource   *See* resource, human
> engineering   73, 131

I
incentive   182, 267

Ingalls   230

inherent   43–44, 62, 120, 180, 186, 220, 227, 232, 239, 248, 283, 288, 308

information system   96

insight   2, 138, 142, 153, 182, 232

inspecting   216

intangibles   58

interfaces   292, 305, 307, 311

J
JIC   *See* just-in case (JIT)

JIT   *See* just-in-time (JIT)

John Deere   228

just-in-case (JIC)   84, 86–89

just-in-time (JIT)   84, 86–88, 90, 183, 257, 302

K
Kanban   87

L
labor
> hours   8, 12, 177, 213
> productivity   189

leadership   14–15, 53, 183, 189–90

lead-time   44, 81, 85, 87, 183–84, 210, 288

legal   7, 53, 57, 66–67, 75, 132, 226, 230, 252
> staff   *See* staff, legal

leveled   114

leveling   108, 115, 305

location   92–93, 187–88, 194, 258, 260–61, 309

lower envelope   138, 145, 148–49, 151, 153

luxurious   220

M
maintaining a sense of urgency   305, 307

make-ready   8, 104, 124–25, 171, 192

make ready   124

manage by walking around   130, 300, 303, 321

managerial resource   *See* resource, managerial

managing materials   84, 184

management style   74, 304, 314–16, 318

Maslow   74

material   14, 18, 50, 52, 55, 57, 67, 84–90, 127, 178, 183–84, 187–88, 190–92, 198, 213, 215, 255, 258, 304–05, 312 requirements planning (MRP)   85

max-min   84

merge node   135–36

methodologies and technologies   12, 153

methods   2–3, 40, 54, 57, 70–71, 107, 122–23, 128, 160–61, 178, 181, 183, 185, 191, 194–96, 234, 256

milestones   34, 105–06, 120, 132, 135, 155

modern project management (MPM)   46, 107, 119, 160, 181, 211, 281

Monte Carlo program evaluation and review technique (PERT)   5, 134, 136, 264, 266–68, 270–73, 276–80

Monte Carlo PERT   See Monte Carlo program evaluation and review technique (PERT)

motivational   137

MPM   See modern project management (MPM)

MRP   See material requirements planning (MRP)

multitasked   304

multitasking   5, 118, 125, 128

O

objective   11, 54, 78, 106, 108, 125, 134, 162, 216–17, 225, 293, 300, 310, 314

operation(al)   6, 20, 44, 64, 88, 120, 127, 130, 191, 203–04, 216, 232–33, 254, 269, 288, 315, 322, 323–24

operations research/management science (OR/MS)   128

opportunity cost   161

optimum   9–10, 83, 128, 160, 169, 174, 195, 225, 228, 281, 296

   duration   See duration, optimum

OR/MS   See operations research/management science (OR/MS)

order-of-magnitude   2

other staffs   See staff, other

outcomes   6–7, 58, 94, 217, 241–50, 262, 268, 288

overdesigned   227

overruns   201–02, 208, 230, 240, 247, 266

overscheduling   60

overtime   9, 18, 39, 58, 72–73, 75, 107, 131–32, 149, 153, 163–64, 168, 172–73, 175, 192, 200, 211, 257, 266–67, 315

P

padded   117, 280

padding   117, 268

part of the project   50, 58, 80–81, 95, 183, 240, 256

partition   85

partnering   217, 309

performance objectives   6, 21, 126

person/operation   232, 315

PERT   See program evaluation and review technique (PERT). See also PERT/Cost

PERT/cost   See program evaluation and review technique (PERT), PERT/cost

philosophy   87, 90, 99, 209, 280, 323

physical   13, 18, 50–51, 53, 63, 73–74, 112, 131, 186, 196, 209, 220, 222, 248, 269, 284

   constraints   See constraints, physical

   resources   See resource, physical

physiological constraints   See constraints, physiological

planned

   cost   16–17

   duration   See duration, planned

   resource usage   16

   work content   20, 213

PMBOK® Guide   See A Guide to the Project Management Body of Knowledge (PMBOK® Guide)

PMI®   See Project Management Institute (PMI®)

PMT   See project management team

PND   See project network diagram

policies   52, 64, 92, 253, 322

practical work content   13

preliminary   2, 283

process(es)

   project   2, 112, 185, 202, 209, 221, 229–30, 234, 293

   risk management   251

scheduling 141

validation 229, 230

product

of the project 50, 55–57, 59, 80, 86, 89, 95, 210, 257

characteristics 220

productivity 14–16, 18, 21, 54, 72, 172–73, 187–89, 226, 257, 301, 304

program evaluation and review technique (PERT) 5, 134, 136, 174, 202, 248, 264–68, 270–73, 276–81, 297

PERT/cost 202–03

programming 13, 82, 123, 161, 195, 228, 281, 324

progressively 8

project

characteristics 5

duration See duration, project

management team (PMT) 60–61, 63, 73

network diagram (PND) 26–27, 29–30, 34, 36, 456, 104–07, 115, 121, 128, 132, 135, 141–43, 151, 161, 165, 167–68, 233, 251, 292, 305, 314–15

sponsor 51–52, 318

team 43–44, 50–52, 60–61, 64–66, 76, 107, 137, 173, 183–84, 208, 250, 267, 290, 292–94, 301, 305–06, 311, 313, 315–16, 325

member 15, 53, 66, 119, 226, 232, 235, 240, 251, 298

Project Management Institute (PMI®) 2, 75, 105–06, 251–53, 255, 269

prototype/prototyping 22, 196, 228, 270, 303

provisioning 149, 191

prudence 67, 252, 310

purchase(ing) 52, 64–68, 82, 85–86, 92, 154, 178, 181, 184, 210, 228, 306–07

costs 184

put-away 8, 104, 124–25, 192

put away 124

Q

QM See quality management (QM)

quality 6–7, 19, 41, 43, 45, 57, 64, 74, 79, 91, 96, 131, 185, 188, 193–94, 202, 215–16, 220–21, 223–24, 227, 231, 255, 258, 308, 313

achieving 217, 232

aspects of 217

benefits 234

measuring quality 225

of the product of the project 123, 217, 219, 225

management (QM) 225, 232–35, 237, 315

of the project 217

quantified 216, 224, 252

R

RAMPS See Resource Allocation and Multi-Project Scheduling (RAMPS)

rank(ing) 121, 151, 175, 222–23, 263, 288

activity 142

backward 142

forward 142

reallocate 19, 41

reassign 41

reject 134, 224, 315

Reliability Maturity Index 300

replanning 240, 305, 308

required dates 132

requirements 15–16, 18–19, 42, 78, 83, 148–49, 180, 184–85, 202, 217–19, 224, 228, 254, 259, 260–61, 263, 281, 287, 293, 322

client 19, 57, 222

communication 187

legal 66, 75

resource See resource requirement(s)

security 194

resource 6, 8–10, 12, 16–19, 38, 51–52, 54, 58–59, 69, 70–72, 74, 90, 92, 94–96, 99, 103, 105–09, 114–15, 118, 121–22, 126

Resource Allocation and Multi-Project Scheduling (RAMPS) 129, 272

alternative 10, 13, 18, 128, 129

application rates 17

appropriate 54, 70, 72, 126

assigning appropriate   54, 70, 126
assignment   13
capabilities   3
financial   54, 77, 79, 219
human   16, 50, 53, 54, 63, 66, 68,
    69, 70, 73, 74, 75, 76, 91, 97,
    127, 130, 133, 262, 303, 304,
    306
management   18, 86, 98
managerial   50
physical   50, 55–56, 80, 302–04
productivity   13
rates   3
requirement(s)   3, 16–18, 106,
    108–09, 112, 114, 142, 145, 149,
    151
resource-constrained scheduling   108,
    115
taxonomy of   50
responsibility   xiv, 18, 40, 44, 50–51, 53,
    60, 63–65, 67, 97, 190–91, 212, 232,
    237, 240, 254, 292, 298, 301, 306,
    312, 314
return on investment (ROI)   54, 89, 132
rewards   15, 218, 276, 304
rework   6, 8–9, 14–15, 41–43, 46, 61,
    73, 76, 92, 96, 112, 137, 174, 181,
    189, 201, 213, 228, 230–32, 256,
    294
    costs   201
risk   40–42, 58, 67, 79, 81, 87, 94, 99,
    114, 133, 241–42, 245, 249–55,
    258–60, 262, 269, 277–78, 283–84,
    288–89, 308
    event   240, 243, 250, 252–54
    management   106, 133, 240, 241,
        242, 250, 251, 253, 268, 283
    product   260
    project   250–52, 255, 283
    taxonomy of   251, 254
ROI   See return on investment (ROI)

S

safety   56–57, 74, 85, 112, 180, 188,
    191, 194, 249–50, 253–56, 269
schedule   105
    performance   100, 308

Schedule Performance Index (SPI)
    206, 209
scheduling
    types of   108
    adaptive   129
scope   43, 75, 98, 100, 153, 177–80,
    186, 219, 260, 284, 287–89, 294–95,
    308
    management   7, 178, 180, 222, 288
s-curve   205
set-up   83, 100, 124
simulation   230, 252, 264, 278, 281
slack   27, 29, 33–35, 38–39, 46–47,
    59–60, 96, 112, 114, 142, 144–45,
    168, 298–99, 305–06
slope   162, 169–70
social   53, 74, 76, 131
societal   54, 70, 75
society(ies)   75, 281
space   14, 36, 43, 51, 58, 73, 81,
    86–87, 89, 93–95, 104–06, 132, 142,
    168, 172, 178–79, 239–40, 283, 307,
    309, 311–12
specification   154, 184, 193, 216, 220,
    260
SPI   See Schedule Performance Index (SPI)
sponsor   52, 61–64, 67, 306, 320
staff
    corporate   51–52, 59, 64
    legal   67
    other   67
    personnel   66, 69
    project   95, 101, 321
    purchasing   64
stakeholders   52, 59, 61, 75, 78–79, 82,
    97, 235, 240, 303, 306
standard deviation   262, 264, 266, 273,
    276–77
start   4, 10, 12, 14, 26. See also time,
    start
    early   26–27, 30, 32, 35, 38, 145
    late   26, 32, 35, 37–38, 47, 105,
        302
statistical   191, 216, 233, 234
    process control   232

status   50, 52, 62, 100–01, 119, 130, 135, 173, 191, 204, 209, 233, 286, 305–07, 313–16, 321

stock-out   84

strategic   49, 174, 181, 227, 228

strategy(ies)   42–44, 60, 86, 100, 116, 227–28, 263, 284, 292, 322

subcontract   42, 178, 308

subcontractor   71, 129, 182–83, 226, 309

supplier(s)   45, 52, 80, 82, 87–88, 92, 105, 181, 184–86, 235, 257–58, 258, 294, 309

T

tabular calculations   29

tangible   95, 161, 170

target(s)   34, 36–37, 39, 42–43, 65–66, 132–33, 138, 160, 174–75, 180–81, 202, 264–67, 276, 278, 299

task   13, 18, 25, 29, 42, 61, 104, 115, 122, 124, 127, 128, 171, 172, 173, 183, 189, 190, 192, 195, 221, 258, 303

team   101–02, 104, 112, 139, 172, 181, 192, 226–27, 235, 237, 240, 250–51, 253–56, 274, 281, 283–85, 290–92, 299, 316–18, 321–22, 324–25. See also project management team. See also project team

    member   60–61, 76, 99, 188, 190, 305, 310. See also project team member

tear down   124

technical   6–7, 19, 21, 60, 88, 98–99, 101, 126, 184–85, 255, 262–63, 283, 286–87, 293, 299, 307, 310, 324

    objective achievement   300

    performance required   184

technique(s)   85–86, 123, 128, 130, 134, 160–61, 176, 181, 183, 191, 194, 202–03, 207, 210, 225, 231, 234, 246, 252, 281–82

    critical path   See critical path technique (CPT)

technological   16, 92, 288, 294

technologies and methods   70, 128

technology(ies)   7–9, 12, 21, 41–42, 70, 83, 98, 122–23, 128–29, 171, 181, 186–87, 195, 256, 288, 291, 312, 322, 324

theoretical   8, 12, 78, 135, 263, 296

    estimated time   See time, estimated, theoretical

    start time   See time, start, theoretical

time

    estimated   3–4, 98, 117, 248

        theoretical   3–4, 98, 117, 248

    estimate(s)   5, 248, 266, 272, 274, 297

    expected   4, 297

    start   26, 29–31, 36, 145

        theoretical   26, 29–31, 36, 145

time/cost   162, 169–70

    tradeoff   132, 159–60, 170, 174–75, 272

time-constrained scheduling   108

time-cost   181, 267

timing   80–81, 185, 260–61

total quality management (TQM)   7

TQM   See total quality management (TQM)

tradeoff   10, 42, 176, 179, 181, 267

transportation   87, 184, 186–87, 193, 241

trust   44, 62, 117, 119, 223, 280, 297, 308

U

uncertainties   85, 90, 123, 154, 176, 260, 262–65, 268, 274, 278, 283

uncertainty   5, 79, 84–85, 87, 90, 112–13, 122, 133, 138, 154, 174–75, 183, 231, 239–42, 261–63, 265–72, 275, 278, 280

unique   3, 5, 10, 50–51, 53–54, 56–57, 69, 70, 75, 91, 98, 127–28, 131, 137, 176, 188, 194, 229–30, 246, 274, 318

unproductive   72, 76–77, 105, 107, 173, 199, 200

upper envelope   145, 148, 151

urgency   1, 40, 73, 299, 303, 305–06, 312–13

usage   19–20, 41, 53, 83–85, 88, 100,
    131, 184, 190, 194, 305
user-friendly   221
utilization   18, 76

V

value   52, 78, 84, 142, 159, 169, 174,
    204–08, 218, 221–22, 225, 235,
    245–46, 248–50, 259, 261–62, 274,
    294
    actual   10
    earned   See earned value
    engineering   185
    expected   4, 116
    of the outcome   243–50, 252
variability   4–5, 116, 118, 133, 196, 204,
    220–21, 263, 268, 274–76, 297
variables   1–2, 6, 10, 262–63, 286–87
variance   64, 203–07, 264–65, 271,
    275–77
variation   82, 92, 115, 117, 189, 224,
    233, 264, 269, 274–76, 301, 308,
    311
visibility   64, 193, 251, 305–06
vision, the   51, 290–92
visualize   27, 56, 168

W

water   56–57, 88, 94, 104, 133, 135–37,
    181, 265–67, 280
WBS   See work breakdown structure (WBS)
weather   18, 38, 57–59, 76–77, 81, 90,
    92, 94, 105, 122–23, 129–30, 156,
    194, 242–43, 246, 258, 262, 273,
    302
work
    authorization   99, 295
    breakdown structure (WBS)   3, 10, 16,
        21, 49, 60, 98, 99, 205, 251, 288,
        292, 295, 307, 320
    content   8–9, 12, 41, 77, 122–23,
        135, 185, 194–95, 204, 218, 230,
        262, 265, 288, 292–93
    package/activity   287, 293
workarounds   123

Upgrade Your Project Management Knowledge

with First-Class Publications from PMI

A Guide to the Project Management Body of Knowledge (PMBOK® Guide) – 2000 Edition

PMI's *PMBOK® Guide* has become *the* essential sourcebook for the project management profession and its de facto global standard, with over 900,000 copies in circulation worldwide. It has been designated an American National Standard by the American National Standards Institute (ANSI) and is one of the major references used by candidates to study for the Project Management Professional (PMP®) Certification Examination. This new edition incorporates numerous recommendations and changes to the 1996 edition, including: progressive elaboration is given more emphasis; the role of the project office is acknowledged; the treatment of earned value is expanded in three chapters; the linkage between organizational strategy and project management is strengthened throughout; and the chapter on risk management has been rewritten with six processes instead of four. Newly added processes, tools, and techniques are aligned with the five project management processes and nine knowledge areas.

ISBN: 1-880410-23-0 (paperback)
ISBN: 1-880410-22-2 (hardcover)
ISBN: 1-880410-25-7 (CD-ROM)

PMI Project Management Salary Survey – 2000 Edition

This 2000 Edition updates information first published in 1996 and expands coverage to over forty industry affiliations in nearly fifty countries in seven major geographic regions around the world. Its purpose is to establish normative compensation and benefits data for the project management profession on a global basis. The study provides salary, bonus/overtime, and deferred compensation information for specific job titles/positions within the project management profession. It also contains normative data for a comprehensive list of benefits and an array of other relevant parameters. *The PMI Project Management Salary Survey – 2000 Edition* is a vital new research tool for managers and HR professionals looking to retain or recruit employees, current members of the profession or those interested in joining it, researchers, and academics.

ISBN: 1-880410-26-5 (paperback)

Project Management Research at the Turn of the Millennium: Proceedings of PMI Research Conference 2000

Project Management Institute
This state-of-the-art compilation includes the full text and graphics of the 46 papers presented at the first PMI project management research conference, held in Paris, France in June 2000. The conference's themes were professional needs assessment, the future of project management, inspiring project management research, project management information, and advancing the project management profession. Presenters included respected academics, researchers, and practitioners from around the globe. Their topics covered a span of 40 years of past, present, and future research efforts, and, by being gathered into this one volume, actually form one of the baseline documents for the modern project management profession.

ISBN: 1-880410-88-5 (paperback)

Selling Project Management to Senior Executives

Janice Thomas, Connie Delisle, and Kam Jugdev
Available in December 2002, this handbook presents new research findings about successful techniques to raise awareness of project management among senior executives. It also details ways to gain their support in implementing project management capabilities and practices throughout an organization.

ISBN: 1-880410-95-8 (paperback)

Quantifying the Value of Project Management

C. William Ibbs and Justin Reginato
Available in September 2002, this new guide covers current research documenting the financial and organizational returns that accrue to organizations that invest in focused or enterprise-wide project management capabilities.

ISBN: 1-880410-96-6 (paperback)

Best Practices of Project Management Groups in Large Functional Organizations

Frank Toney and Ray Powers
The best thinking of some of the world's leading project management practitioners is presented in this comprehensive study of current project management practice. In benchmarking project management, Toney and Powers provide specific key success factors and core best practices that practitioners can apply to their own workplace; information about the results of benchmark analysis; a detailed set of guidelines to enable others to replicate the benchmark process; and templates consisting of letters, agendas, ethical codes, and surveys for practitioners to use in the conduct of their own benchmark activities.

ISBN: 1-880410-05-2 (paperback)

The Benefits of Project Management: Financial and Organizational Rewards to Corporations

C. William Ibbs and Young-Hoon Kwak

This study documents the organizational and financial benefits that result from implementing project management tools, processes, and practices. In particular, it looks at the return on investment that organizations can realize by investing in all aspects of project management and provides tools for estimating the kind of return on investment they can expect from taking certain actions.

ISBN: 1-880410-32-X (paperback)

The PMI Project Management Fact Book, Second Edition

Project Management Institute

First published in 1999, this newly enlarged and updated "almanac" provides a single, accessible reference volume on global project management and PMI. Topics include the history, size, explosive growth, and the future of the project management profession; parameters of the typical project; a statistical profile of the individuals working in project management based on recent, global research; the organizational settings in which project management activities take place; and valuable information about the world's largest professional association serving project management, the Project Management Institute. Appendices offer an additional wealth of information: lists of universities with degree programs in project management and PMI Registered Educational Providers; PMI's Ethical Standards; professional awards; a glossary; and an extensive bibliography. This is the central reference for those working in project management and a career guide for those interested in entering the profession.

ISBN: 1-880410-73-7 (paperback)

Project Management Institute Practice Standard for Work Breakdown Structures

Project Management Institute

PMI's first practice standard to complement and elaborate on A Guide to the Project Management Body of Knowledge (PMBOK® Guide) - 2000 Edition, this new manual provides guidance and universal principles for the initial generation, subsequent development, and application of the Work Breakdown Structure (WBS). It introduces the WBS and its characteristics, discusses the benefits of using a WBS, and demonstrates how to build a WBS and determine its sufficiency for subsequent planning and control. A unique feature is the inclusion of 11 industry-specific examples that illustrate how to build a WBS, ranging from Process Improvement and Software Design to Refinery Turnaround and Service Industry Outsourcing.

ISBN 1-880410-81-8 (paperback)

People in Projects

Project Management Institute

This important new book focuses on one of the nine knowledge areas of the PMBOK® Guide and one of the most important aspects of every project—human resources management. It is a collection of the best articles relating to the people side of project management that PMI has produced in the last five years. The authors are acknowledged experts in their fields, and the wide-ranging topics include leadership, negotiation, relation-ship building, job evaluation and appraisal, worldwide teams, and managing change.

ISBN:1880410729 (paperback)

Project Management for the Technical Professional

Michael Singer Dobson

Dobson, project management expert, popular seminar leader, and personality theorist, understands "promotion grief." He counsels those who prefer logical relationships to people skills and shows technical professionals how to successfully make the transition into management. This is a witty, supportive management primer for any "techie" invited to hop on the first rung of the corporate ladder. It includes self-assessment exercises; a skillful translation of general management theory and practice into tools, techniques, and systems that technical professionals will understand and accept; helpful "how to do it" sidebars; and action plans. It's also an insightful guide for those who manage technical professionals.

"The exercises and case studies featured here, along with the hands-on advice, hammer home fundamental principles. An intriguing complement to more traditional IT management guides, this is suitable for all libraries." — Library Journal

ISBN: 1-880410-76-1 (paperback)

The Project Surgeon: A Troubleshooter's Guide to Business Crisis Management

Boris Hornjak

A veteran of business recovery, project turnarounds and crisis prevention, Hornjak shares his "lessons learned" in this best practice primer for operational managers. He writes with a dual purpose—first for the practical manager thrust into a crisis situation with a mission to turn things around, make tough decisions under fire, address problems when they occur, and prevent them from happening again. Then his emphasis turns to crisis prevention, so you can free your best and brightest to focus on opportunities, instead of on troubleshooting problems, and ultimately break the failure/recovery cycle.

ISBN: 1-880410-75-3 (paperback)

Risk and Decision Analysis in Projects
Second Edition

John R. Schuyler

Schuyler, a consultant in project risk and economic decision analysis, helps project management professionals improve their decision-making skills and integrate them into daily problem solving. In this heavily illustrated second edition, he explains and demystifies key concepts and techniques, including expected value, optimal decision policy, decision trees, the value of information, Monte Carlo simulation, probabilistic techniques, modeling techniques, judgments and biases, utility and multi-criteria decisions, and stochastic variance.

ISBN: 1-880410-28-1 (paperback)

Earned Value Project Management
Second Edition

Quentin W. Fleming and Joel M. Koppelman

Now a classic treatment of the subject, this second edition updates this straightforward presentation of earned value as a useful method to measure actual project performance against planned costs and schedules throughout a project's life cycle. The authors describe the earned value concept in a simple manner so that it can be applied to any project, of any size, and in any industry.

ISBN: 1880410-27-3 (paperback)

Project Management Experience and Knowledge Self-Assessment Manual

Based on the *Project Management Professional (PMP) Role Delineation Study*, this manual is designed to help individuals assess how proficiently they could complete a wide range of essential project management activities based on their current levels of knowledge and experience. Included are exercises and lists of suggested activities for readers to use in improving their performance in those areas they assessed as needing further training.

ISBN: 1-880410-24-9 (spiral paperback)

Project Management Professional (PMP) Role Delineation Study

In 1999, PMI® completed a role delineation study for the Project Management Professional (PMP®) Certification Examination. In addition to being used to establish the test specifications for the examination, the study describes the tasks (competencies) PMPs perform and the project management knowledge and skills PMPs use to complete each task. Each of the study's tasks is linked to a performance domain (e.g., planning the project). Each task has three components to it: what the task is, why the task is performed, and how the task is completed. The *Role Delineation Study* is an excellent resource for educators, trainers, administrators, practitioners, and individuals interested in pursuing PMP certification.

ISBN: 1-880410-29-X (spiral paperback)

PM 101 According to the Olde Curmudgeon

Francis M. Webster Jr.

Former editor-in-chief for PMI®, Francis M. Webster Jr. refers to himself as "the olde curmudgeon." The author, who has spent thirty years practicing, consulting on, writing about, and teaching project management, dispenses insider information to novice project managers with a friendly, arm-around-the-shoulder approach. He provides a history and description of all the components of modern project management; discusses the technical, administrative, and leadership skills needed by project managers; and details the basic knowledge and processes of project management, from scope management to work breakdown structure to project network diagrams. An excellent introduction for those interested in the profession themselves or in training others who are.

ISBN: 1-880410-55-9 (paperback)

The Project Sponsor Guide

Neil Love and Joan Brant-Love

This practical guide is intended for executives and middle managers who will be, or are, sponsors of a project, particularly cross-functional projects. It is also helpful reading for facilitators and project leaders.

ISBN: 1-880410-15-X (paperback)

Don't Park Your Brain Outside: A Practical Guide to Improving Shareholder Value with SMART Management

Francis T. Hartman

Hartman has assembled a cohesive and balanced approach to highly effective project management. It is deceptively simple. Called SMART™, this new approach is **S**trategically **M**anaged, **A**ligned, **R**egenerative, and **T**ransitional. It is based on research and best practices, tempered by hard-won experience. SMART has saved significant time and money on the hundreds of large and small, simple and complex projects on which it has been tested.

ISBN: 1-880410-48-6 (hardcover)

The EnterPrize Organization: Organizing Software Projects for Accountability and Success

Neal Whitten

Neal Whitten is a twenty-three-year veteran of IBM and now president of his own consulting firm. Here he provides a practical guide to addressing a serious problem that has plagued the software industry since its beginning: how to effectively organize software projects to significantly increase their success rate. He proposes the "Enterprize Organization" as a model that takes advantage of the strengths of the functional organization, projectized organization, and matrix organization, while reducing or eliminating their weaknesses. The book collects the experiences and wisdom of thousands of people and hundreds of projects, and reduces *lessons learned* to a simple format that can be applied immediately to your projects.

ISBN: 1-880410-79-6 (paperback)

Teaming for Quality

H. David Shuster

Shuster believes most attempts at corporate cultural change die because people fail to realize how addicted they are to the way things are, the root causes of their resistance to change, and the degree to which their willingness to change depends on the moral philosophy of management. His new book offers a stimulating synthesis of classical philosophy, metaphysics, behavioral science, management theory and processes, and two decades of personal teaming experience to explain how individuals can choose change for themselves. Its philosophy-to-practice approach will help people team in ways that promote exceptionally high levels of bonding, individual creative expression (innovation), and collective agreement (consensus). Shuster shows how personal work fulfillment and corporate goals *can* work in alignment.

ISBN: 1-880410-63-X (paperback)

The Juggler's Guide to Managing Multiple Projects

Michael S. Dobson

This comprehensive book introduces and explains task-oriented, independent, and interdependent levels of project portfolios. It says that you must first have a strong foundation in time management and priority setting, then introduces the concept of Portfolio Management to time-line multiple projects, determine their resource requirements, and handle emergencies.

ISBN: 1-880410-65-6 (paperback)

Recipes for Project Success

Al DeLucia and Jackie DeLucia

This book is destined to become "the" reference book for beginning project managers, particularly those who like to cook! Practical, logically developed project management concepts are offered in easily understood terms in a light-hearted manner. They are applied to the everyday task of cooking—from simple, single dishes, such as homemade tomato sauce for pasta, made from the bottom up, to increasingly complex dishes or meals for groups that in turn require an understanding of more complex project management terms and techniques. The transition between cooking and project management discussions is smooth, and tidbits of information provided with the recipes are interesting and humorous.

ISBN: 1-880410-58-3 (paperback)

Tools and Tips for Today's Project Manager

Ralph L. Kliem and Irwin S. Ludin

This guidebook is valuable for understanding project management and performing to quality standards. Includes project management concepts and terms—old and new—that are not only defined but also are explained in much greater detail than you would find in a typical glossary.

ISBN: 1-880410-61-3 (paperback)

The Future of Project Management

Developed by the 1998 PMI® Research Program Team and the futurist consultant firm of Coates and Jarratt, Inc., this guide to the future describes one hundred national and global trends and their implications for project management, both as a recognized profession and as a general management tool. It covers everything from knowbots, nanotechnology, and disintermediation to changing demography, information technology, social values, design, and markets.

ISBN: 1-880410-71-0 (paperback)

Also Available from PMI

Project Management for Managers
Mihály Görög, Nigel J. Smith
ISBN: 1-880410-54-0 (paperback)

Project Leadership: From Theory to Practice
Jeffrey K. Pinto, Peg Thoms, Jeffrey Trailer, Todd Palmer, Michele Govekar
ISBN: 1-880410-10-9 (paperback)

Annotated Bibliography of Project and Team Management
David I. Cleland, Gary Rafe, Jeffrey Mosher
ISBN: 1-880410-47-8 (paperback)
ISBN: 1-880410-57-5 (CD-ROM)

How to Turn Computer Problems into Competitive Advantage
Tom Ingram
ISBN: 1-880410-08-7 (paperback)

Achieving the Promise of Information Technology
Ralph B. Sackman
ISBN: 1-880410-03-6 (paperback)

Leadership Skills for Project Managers
Editors' Choice Series
Edited by Jeffrey K. Pinto, Jeffrey W. Trailer
ISBN: 1-880410-49-4 (paperback)

The Virtual Edge
Margery Mayer
ISBN: 1-880410-16-8 (paperback)

The ABCs of DPC
Edited by PMI's Design-Procurement-Construction Specific Interest Group
ISBN: 1-880410-07-9 (paperback)

Project Management Casebook
Edited by David I. Cleland, Karen M. Bursic, Richard Puerzer,
A. Yaroslav Vlasak
ISBN: 1-880410-45-1 (paperback)

Project Management Casebook, Instructor's Manual
Edited by David I. Cleland, Karen M. Bursic, Richard Puerzer,
A. Yaroslav Vlasak
ISBN: 1-880410-18-4 (paperback)

The PMI Book of Project Management Forms
ISBN: 1-880410-31-1 (paperback)
ISBN: 1-880410-50-8 (diskette)

Principles of Project Management
John Adams et al.
ISBN: 1-880410-30-3 (paperback)

Organizing Projects for Success
Human Aspects of Project Management
Series, Volume One
Vijay K. Verma
ISBN: 1-880410-40-0 (paperback)

Human Resource Skills for the Project Manager
Human Aspects of Project Management
Series, Volume Two
Vijay K. Verma
ISBN: 1-880410-41-9 (paperback)

Managing the Project Team
Human Aspects of Project Management
Series, Volume Three
Vijay K. Verma
ISBN: 1-880410-42-7 (paperback)

Value Management Practice
Michel Thiry
ISBN: 1-880410-14-1 (paperback)

The World's Greatest Project
Russell W. Darnall
ISBN: 1-880410-46-X (paperback)

Power & Politics in Project Management
Jeffrey K. Pinto
ISBN: 1-880410-43-5 (paperback)

Best Practices of Project Management Groups in Large Functional Organizations
Frank Toney, Ray Powers
ISBN: 1-880410-05-2 (paperback)

Project Management in Russia
Vladimir I. Voropajev
ISBN: 1-880410-02-8 (paperback)

A Framework for Project and Program Management Integration
R. Max Wideman
ISBN: 1-880410-01-X (paperback)

Quality Management for Projects & Programs
Lewis R. Ireland
ISBN: 1-880410-11-7 (paperback)

Project & Program Risk Management
Edited by R. Max Wideman
ISBN: 1-880410-06-0 (paperback)

A Framework for Project Management
ISBN: 1-880410-82-6, Facilitator's Manual Set
(3-ring binder)
ISBN: 1-880410-80-X, Participants' Manual Set, (paperback)

Project Management Software Survey
ISBN: 1-880410-52-4 (paperback)
ISBN: 1-880410-59-1 (CD-ROM)

New Resources for PMP® Candidates

The following publications are recommended resources that candidates may study to prepare for the Project Management Professional (PMP) Certification Examination.

PMP Resource Package

The Cultural Dimension of International Business, Fourth Edition
by Gary P. Ferraro

Doing Business Internationally: The Guide to Cross-Cultural Success
by Terence Brake, Danielle Walker, Thomas Walker

Earned Value Project Management, Second Edition
by Quentin W. Fleming and Joel M. Koppelman

Effective Project Management
by Robert K. Wysocki, Robert Beck Jr., David B. Crane

Focus Groups: A Step-by-Step Guide
by Gloria E. Bader and Catherine A. Rossi

Global Literacies: Lessons on Business Leadership and National Cultures
by Robert Rosen (Editor), Patricia Digh, Carl Phillips

A Guide to the Project Management Body of Knowledge (PMBOK® Guide) – 2000 Edition
by Project Management Institute

How to Lead Work Teams: Facilitation Skills, Second Edition
by Fran Rees

Human Resource Skills for the Project Manager
by Vijay K. Verma

The New Project Management
by J. Davidson Frame

Organizational Architecture: Designs for Changing Organizations
by David A. Nader, Marc S. Gerstein, Robert Shaw, and Associates

Principles of Project Management
by John Adams, et al.

Project & Program Risk Management
by R. Max Wideman, Editor

Project Management Experience and Knowledge Self-Assessment Manual
by Project Management Institute

Project Management: A Managerial Approach, Fourth Edition
by Jack R. Meredith and Samuel J. Mantel Jr.

Project Management: A Systems Approach to Planning, Scheduling, and Controlling, Seventh Edition
by Harold Kerzner

Order online at www.pmibookstore.org

Book Ordering Information:

Phone: +412.741.6206
Fax: +412.741.0609
Email: pmiorders@abdintl.com
Mail: PMI Publications Fulfillment Center
  PO Box 1020
  Sewickley, Pennsylvania 15143-1020 USA

Visit PMI's Website at *www.pmi.org*
or Shop at Our Online Bookstore at *www.pmibookstore.org*